Praise for *Kissed by God—Hol*

In telling her readers about the Holy Women, Shirley Cunningham has captured the allurement that is **Thérèse of Lisieux** in her beautiful and authentic stories. Those who have known this saint from their childhood will have meaningful memories of praying with and to her ... roses, blessings, visions, new awarenesses. Who cannot relate to living a simple spirituality based on love?
—Victoria S. Schmidt, speaker, author, and executive director of
   Theresians International, a global network of women focused
   on Theresian spirituality

Kissed by God—Holy Women Create! is a reflection on the slow work of God unfolding over time in ordinary daily life ... a worthy contribution to contemporary spirituality. Cunningham uses her own experience to introduce her readers to the insights of **St. Clare** and other Holy Women; she offers pertinent reflective questions to encourage us to nourish our own awareness and desire for God.
—Fran Marie Sulzer, Franciscan Sister of Perpetual Adoration,
   D. Min.

Among the Holy Women Kissed by God chronicled here, **St. Brigid** of Ireland stands out for me—her namesake! The art and stories about her reveal Brigid's creativity in bridging Celtic spirituality and Christianity, her concern for the downtrodden, and her great love of God. As if she knew the saint intimately, the author draws the reader into friendship with Brigid. This highly recommended, warm compilation of Holy Women will move you.
—Rev. Deacon Brigid Waszczak, women's ministry and spiritual
   director, St. Matthew's Episcopal Church, Tucson, Arizona

(more)

This book brings together a chorus of Holy Women, each with a timeless message: the **Samaritan Woman** calls out, "Let me tell you about the One who loves you as you are." Take a moment. Listen to all their voices that you might stand tall, head high, holy, and kissed by God.
—Rev. Carolyn Herold, master of theological studies, assistant
    priest, St. Laurence Anglican Church, Calgary, Alberta

My affinity to **St. Joan of Arc** has expanded through Shirley Cunningham's depth of research and personal discovery of this young saint. I realized in reading *Kissed by God–Holy Women Create!* that the stories of the Holy Women are my story, our story. I experienced the truth of our unity with them and at the same time, found inspiration to hear more clearly my own voice, know my own gifts, my very self. This book, an engaging sequel to the author's first book, *Chasing God,* launches us into new zones where only Divine Imagination can take us.
—Jeanne Colasanti, PhD, participant in Kissed by God:
    Holy Women Create! retreats

Kissed by God

Kissed by God
—Holy Women Create!

Shirley Cunningham

Amoranita Publishing Company
Heart n Soul Books
Glendale, Arizona

Grateful acknowledgment is made to Inner Traditions International and Bear & Company for permission to print the poem excerpt on page 91: *Hildegard of Bingen* by Gabriele Uhlein, ©1983. All rights reserved. http://www.innertraditions.com Reprinted with permission of publisher.
And to Christine Valters Paintner for permission to reprint her poem that appears on pages 96–97.

Design by Meadowlark Publishing Services.

Published by Amoranita Publishing Company
Heart n Soul Books
www.artfromheartnsoul.net
21681 North 61st Avenue
Glendale, AZ 85308

Manufactured in the United States of America.

ISBN 978-0-9720571-1-0

Published 2017

To the God beyond our naming
Who kisses us gently and fiercely
Each moment of our lives

Contents

Acknowledgments

My first thanks are to the God I chased—who actually caught me! I am still reeling from the surprise of that Divine Kiss, and from its energy, which spun me into the work of creativity you now hold in your hands.

My gratitude then goes to those who have had roles in this book and in my life: my parents, Ron Cunningham and Anita Eulberg Cunningham Keppler; my grandparents, Florence and Jim Cunningham and Elsie and Henry Eulberg, my first husband, Bob McCauley; my son, Kelly Benedict McCauley, and his wife, Christine McCauley; and to my second husband, Jerry Smith; and to my sister, Mary Jane Keppler Cole.

Others—friends, mentors, and colleagues—have been on the stage here also: Marilyn Nagel, Darlene Thornhill; the staff and friars of the Franciscan Renewal Center, Rev. Scott Haasarud, Fr. Ernie Larkin, O. Carm; my companions on the Holy Land Pilgrimage, Black Madonna Pilgrimage, and Goddess Gate pilgrimage, especially Cecilia Corcoran, FSPA, and Jean Kasparbauer, FSPA; my companions on the Pilgrimage to the Sacred Edge of Ireland, especially Christine Valters Paintner; my colleagues in the enterprise of forming and leading the Arizona Ecumenical Institute for Spiritual Directors, especially Elizabeth Cummins, OSF, Pat Julian, and JoAnne Rapp; and the staff of Brigid's Place in Houston, Texas, especially Teresa Maron.

My gratitude also goes to those individuals and groups from whom I have learned: the Franciscan Sisters of Perpetual Adoration, the Shalem Institute, Spiritual Directors International, Abbey of the Arts, Heard Museum library staff, Ira Progoff's Intensive Journal workshops, Julia Cameron's *The Artist's Way* workshops, Seena Frost's SoulCollage, Aviva Gold, Esalen Institute, and Michelle Cassou's Intuitive Painting workshops, Jo Toye's and Cathy Taylor's classes on water media/alcohol ink, Fort Crawford Museum and its director, Mary Antoine, Rev. Lauren Artress, Rev. Christine Bourgeault, Ilia Delio, OSF, and my counseling and spiritual direction clients, retreatants, and workshop participants.

A special thanks go to the amazing staff at my local Apple store who have pulled me out of many techy black holes during the creation of *Kissed by God: Holy Women Create!*, especially Doug Kaufman, my go-to crisis interventionist!

Last but not least, I am grateful to my editor, Sheridan McCarthy and her crew at Meadowlark Publishing Services. Their professional guidance, efficiency, and patient support were above and beyond my expectations.

Introduction

Kissed by God–Holy Women Create! is both a love story and an invitation. The God beyond our naming gently and fiercely kisses us each moment of our lives... and waits lovingly for our response. May you recognize in these pages that God has kissed not only our holy sisters and foremothers, but you!

The recognition of being a woman kissed by God has been somewhat slow in coming to me, partly because the voices of women gone before us have largely been lost. Remember Eden: in one version of that story, woman was made from man. She has held a secondary place in society and culture ever since. Then in ancient myth, we hear mention of Amazons. Later in ancient history, we hear of some indigenous matriarchies, and a few survive today. That said, for the most part, the work, stories, gifts, art, and writing of women over millennia have been lost or minimized. Even the stories of those closest to us—our mothers, grandmothers, and great-grandmothers—may be largely unknown. How many of us can even name them accurately?

The Native Americans I live among here in the Southwest are strongly connected to their ancestors, whom they invoke in rituals for help and wisdom. Hindus across the globe also acknowledge and honor their ancestors. It is a deeply human impulse to live in awareness of our forebears after they are gone. My work as a counselor has convinced me that many grandmas have ascended to sainthood in the memories and hearts of their granddaughters! The Holy Women in this book come to us over centuries through scripture and Christian history. Scripture speaks of them as part of the communion of saints, a great cloud of witnesses. Psychology recognizes that we are attracted to archetypal energy—mother energy, healer energy, warrior energy. So we may say these spiritual ancestors, mothers, sisters are multi-valented, magnetizing us in many ways, perhaps as saints, perhaps as archetypes. We sense their attraction even if we may not be able to easily explain it.

To me, they are Holy Women kissed by God, overflowing with creativity. I wanted these women to have the autonomy to speak to us in their own voices telling us of God's kiss. That kiss opened each one to follow her inner call: whether to write her own story, lead an army, or found a monastery. All was in response to that powerful kiss. This outpouring of Spirit caused young women to see visions and old women to dream dreams, to work wonders[1] through singing, dancing, painting, writing ...

I wrote this book because these stories of Holy Women and my own journey are also stories of your journey. Each is delicately shaped with nuances that reveal us as the unique and precious individuals we are. When our sacred journeys are thus put beside theirs, as I invite you to do, it is clear—our walk together, whether in the here and now or across centuries, is filled with rich meaning and blessing for ourselves and the world around us, if only we stop and attend.

And so, to begin.

Women's stories we find in scripture, tradition, and history often seem to be mere snippets, leaving layers of meaning unarticulated. The earliest come from times before stories were written down. These early tales were intended to instruct, motivate, and even entertain, which is why they have survived. Such tales were often not literal. Some had a basis in history, but often what impresses us is their spiritual, mythic, archetypal, and psychological meanings. The renowned storyteller Elie Wiesel wrote, "In literature, Rebbe, certain things are true though they didn't happen, while others are not, even if they did."[2]

Archaeologists and Jewish rabbis understand a process of taking known fragments, fitting them together, and envisioning the rest. Archaeologists conjure a complete pot from broken shards. Rabbis do the same with scraps of documents to come up with what might be the rest of a lost story, a process they call midrash. The Hebrew root of midrash is darash, which means to seek, search, or demand. That search often begins with questioning a story. And the questioning itself becomes a way to draw more and more stories out of the original.[3] And so, as I wrote the book, when I wondered what was between the lines of a story, I imagined being invited into cahoots with the Spirit to see what would emerge. Often it was a new spin on an old story, a burst of creativity.

We know that Miriam sang and danced, Brigid wrote poetry, Hildegard composed music and commissioned the painting of her visions, Teresa of Avila described her interior castle—all were overflowing with creative juice!

I will leave the dancing to Miriam in the desert with her tambourine! My dance has been a series of incredible pilgrimages over decades. Would it be fair to include the path that led me into and out of the convent? I think so, because every pilgrimage begins with a story. A love story called me into that life and later, called me out. The story of Jesus led me to the Holy Land, the story of Mary called me to Medjugorje in Bosnia and Herzegovina, the Black Madonna called me to France, and so it continued—to Italy, Mexico, Spain, the Czech Republic, Austria, Hungary, and finally Ireland. Someone once said that pilgrimage is extroverted mysticism and that mysticism is introverted pilgrimage.[4] Whether we consider the inner life or the outer life, we each are certainly on our own pilgrimage.

The Holy Women I met along the way were often writers. For me, the itch to write isn't new. Over the years, I've often written daily, filling dozens of notebooks, reflecting on my life and the meaning of events, feelings, and relationships, but always for my own enlightenment, not to share with others, not for publication.

Then I had a dream. It was brief and to the point. Jesus spoke.

He asked only one question: "Who are you besides who you are?" I answered, "A writer." I was mildly disappointed. I wanted the answer to be "an artist," but I said to myself, *You've never dreamed of Jesus before. This is important. You have work to do.* It was a dream I had to notice.

Within days, I began writing my entire life story with the urgency of a river torrentially carrying away whatever was loose in its path. In the midst of it, I wondered: was it really okay to follow where this path was leading me, beyond where I had ever gone before? Then I remembered a dramatic incident from my pilgrimage to Medjugorje. A priest gave me a valuable gift he himself treasured with the words "I know my gifts had been given to me for someone else."

I was flabbergasted. At the time, the memory jolted me. Was I to believe my life could be a conduit of wisdom for others? The answer came soon after in a journaled prayer. The words that flowed onto the page were like words from a loving mother: "I have brought you here with great love. You are being born."

Then, it all clicked. I knew my life story wanted to be written as urgently as a baby wants to be born. There was no holding back. I was ready to trust beyond my fear. I could even trust what I didn't know I didn't know.[5]

And, as has often happened in my life, one thing followed another. My life was busy. It was hectic being a wife and mother, meeting household demands, and working stressful jobs. Who had time for art? It was a very minimal part of my life. Then I had a series of crises: breast cancer, divorce ... and with the departure of my only son, an empty nest.

Well, I then had an extra room in the house. That was the beginning. In that empty room, I began to paint. The surprise was when I was pulled off to draw my grandmother's portrait. I wanted to paint, but it was as if Grandma was right there telling me to draw! I started drawing portraits. I'd never done that before. Over the next few weeks, I drew other members of my family until I had twelve. Then I stopped. It felt like I had finished whatever that urge was all about. Hadn't planned it, but there they were. I sat looking at them, wondering. Twelve. Slowly, an idea formed. I had been writing memories of these loved ones over many years. My journals were filled with stories, and now twelve drawings were here on my drawing board for a reason. ... I decided the family would enjoy a Christmas calendar of portraits and anecdotes.

I set to work. As I put together that calendar, it occurred to me that I had much more to say about these people and my life, more than would fit into a few lines of caption. That "much more" became my first book, *Chasing God*. In the process of writing it, my inner and outer lives were carried by an intense creative force.

Chasing God chronicled my closest family. Now these years later, *Kissed by God—Holy Women Create!* has chronicled mothers and sisters from across the centuries. Like the first book, this new one is not just history or theology or scripture study but rather is spun of spirituality and creativity, processes that are not strictly logical. And, of course, what is presented here is not comprehensive. Other people have written entire books about these women. My hope is to convey the uniqueness of each one as I know her, a close friend who is now reaching out to you.

God has hovered at every turn as I traveled with these Holy Women. I soon realized that, like me, they also journeyed without a map, always on new ground, going they knew not where but often guided by inspiration, intuition, dreams.

This book began as I painted my subjects. They gently revealed they were important archetypes I recognized in myself. One by one, they showed up on my canvases. Each attracted me, called me in her own way to tell her story. I had no plan except to continue to follow where I was led. Why have I painted these Holy Women? On some level I can't explain; I was magnetized by each one's spirit. I felt attracted to their love of God—I wanted that too. I started painting them, wanting to capture them on my canvas. I wanted their essence, the beauty of each one's soul as God saw it, deeper than physical beauty. I wanted to see who they were, to overhear their conversations, to bring them into my life as friends, sisters, and perhaps as trailblazers urging and leading me to new life.

Painting them was an experience of walking a path that appeared before my feet with each step. I had no plan. I painted, then wrote poems and prayers, made a calendar. Only gradually did I see the same process that led to my first book. One step has simply followed another: first journals, then art, a calendar, and finally a book.

This book is an invitation to you, the reader, and a welcome to them, our spiritual ancestors and archetypes who have graciously visited us. The spiritual world is crowded with helpers. Irish tradition places them just on the other side, hovering at the thin places between the worlds.

I understand from the paintings now on the walls of my home that these helpers are at my side, eager to comfort and guide and heal me, to mentor me—yes—but mostly to be my friends. And they invite me to think about befriending the archetypes they represent as well.

About Archetypes

A few words about archetypes. The term comes from Carl Jung, an early student of the psyche and colleague of Sigmund Freud. Jung said archetypes refer to inherited ideas that carry a sort of energy and are present in us all. He believed they arise from ancient experiences of the human race. He found the same themes in folktales and myths of many cultures and times as well as in the dreams of his clients, often expressed by figures and symbols.[6,7]

Since we each arrive born of a mother, the mother archetype is one of the deepest. Many stories of a great mother figure portray her characteristics. This royal and often divine figure will take care of us, her children, because she is wise and powerful, able to set up powerful forces on our behalf. That is what good mothers do: they take care of us. However, all archetypes also have a shadow side. For example, the mother can hover or control too much.

The deepest relationships we can imagine are the connection of mother to child and the joining of lovers. The pivotal experience of marriage gives rise to the lover or bride archetype. Fairy tales set the stage for these emotional expectations and, of course, from childhood we have heard of gods falling in love with humans and vice versa in Greek and Roman stories.

So to us, in our day and time, a mythic understanding of divine and human love is familiar.

Much earlier, in ancient Jewish and Christian scripture, a concept of bridal spirituality arose.[8] However, it was the thirteenth-century sermons of St. Bernard of Clairvaux on the Song of Songs that brought the bridal metaphor to prominence. The spirituality of men's orders at that time often had military overtones urging them to soldier on bravely and suffer for God. When Bernard offered his advice to male and female monastics, and indeed, to all Christians, to "anoint and bejewel themselves inwardly and ready themselves in every way for the kiss of Christ ... mystical union with God,"[9] that was a move in a new direction and led to the golden age of Christian mysticism.

Bernard's writing about the soul as feminine, a bride in relation to God, validated women who had long been left in the shadow of fallen Eve. The period following this teaching was a flowering of mysticism among monastics. One can imagine the lightening and delight of the male monastics to sense themselves so loved by God. Traditionally, church ministries were carried on exclusively by men. In this time of the blossoming of bridal spirituality, religious women spent what might have been ministerial time in contemplation. Those long hours no doubt led some to visionary episodes.[10]

The lover/bridal archetype may be resisted, of course, if we prefer to think of ourselves as instruments of God's peace, as stewards or servants or perhaps even students rather than brides. If thinking of myself as bride suggests subjugation, passivity, or even abuse, that truly signals a need for healing and not celebration.

If, however, it is the language of mystical/bridal love that is troublesome, it may be helpful to remember the times in which these women lived. Even now, we stumble on God language. In earlier centuries, God was exclusively spoken of in male terms as father, king, or lover.[11] For a mystic to use the bridal language might avoid accusations of heresy. Language was important. Today, we may understand the bridal love language as a way to approximate a reality beyond words, beyond naming, an attempt to name the God beyond all names, beyond all gender.

You will be invited as you read this book to reflect on your own archetypes, whether mother or lover or many others. You may wonder, as you do, why you are attracted to certain of these women more than others. Jungian David Richo explains:

> There is a reason for this. It is because they represent and personify one's own untapped potential. They had and gave the very gifts that are in us, too.... One way to know our apostolate in the world is to consider which ones we

most admire. They are the ones to imitate and invoke as patrons ... Admiration is a gift of discernment. It points to our life purpose, our destiny, and to our assisting forces ever visibly or invisibly surrounding us.[12]

One can get in touch with an archetype in creative work as I did, or in a dream. If you meet an archetype in a dream, you are likely to remember it. The dream will seem to have been a journey away from daily life, to another place or time, perhaps like a mythic tale. Even years later, the dream will carry much feeling and a sense of the truth of your life's unfolding and continued guidance.

But if you can't remember even one dream in your life, it doesn't matter. You have been called by the Holy Women—or you would not be reading this book. It is less important to understand than to respond. So enter their stories and think about their lives. What does this attraction say about what is at work in you?

In retrospect, it seems the most natural thing in the world for one thing to lead to another. First a chase, then a kiss, and we all know that means fertility. Perhaps the most creative thing a woman or man can do is to bring forth new life, whether of body, mind, or spirit. And so, together let us welcome the amazing light of their lives to shine into our own, that we may attend and come closer to that same great Light. In this process, perhaps like me, through their stories and my midrash, you will recognize that you also have been kissed by God.

Overview of Chapters

You will see that each Holy Woman has her own chapter made up of three segments. The first part is her story and the second describes how she showed up in my life. Then the chapter ends with a suggested exercise that gives you a chance to respond to what struck you. The Holy Women chapters are followed by a brief conclusion—**Holy Women, Create!**—an invitation to take inspiration from the Holy Women and open to the Creative Spirit in your own life.

Although the many chapters of this book are rich with words from our Holy Women, I hope they are only the appetizer, and you will be eager for even more nourishment. The next part of the book, **Readings by and About Holy Women Kissed by God,** addresses in a small way that happy possibility! Although the readings there are not comprehensive, in them you will find more stories and inspiration from their own hand or written by others about them. Enjoy!

Next you will find **Readings Contributed by Retreatants 2015–16.** As I present my retreats based on the Holy Women, I see those gathered before me pouring out their own creative responses to these our foremothers in Spirit. May the Spirit speak to you through their words also, our companion Holy Women of today who have certainly also been kissed by God. Their contributions are gathered here for you. May you feel welcomed to a wide and deep sisterhood with us all! (If you feel so moved, you are invited to send anything you might write and would like to share. Find contact information at www.artfromheartnsoul.net) Our sisterhood can continue to grow!

The last chapter, **Responding to the Holy Women: Exercises,** is made up of an assortment of exercises that can be used with any one of the Holy Women or focused on several of them together. For example, all the Holy Women of Scripture can be drawn into a conversation together, as I did in "Holy Women of Scripture Meet" on page 63.

How to Use This Book

First of all, this book can be used by one individual or by a group. In either case, you may think of the time you devote to it as an at-home retreat at the feet of these Holy Women. Consider where you can be comfortable and undisturbed while you read and reflect. A candle and art or other symbols may help set the mood, if you don't already have such a corner in your life. Be sure to have a journal and pen too. A break from the keyboard will make for a more leisurely experience as you read and perhaps jot down thoughts that present themselves. Even one particular word may strike you. I like to collect these "magic words" and have a ready store to draw from when a poem seems to want to be written!

Perhaps you already have a spiritual practice of writing or making simple art pieces. You will find exercises here to help you discover what is trying to evolve within you. Knowing what these women have meant to others can help you respond to the same Spirit that called them.

God's gentle kiss in these pages may also move you to express something not easily captured except by quietly opening to reflect. No experience or skill is needed, just a quiet corner and your willingness to hear and respond to the Spirit. You will know what calls you; attend to it. You are invited to follow the Spirit that has already gently guided you to this sacred time.

Journaling

I define the journal as a letter of introduction from your everyday self to your deeper self and a record of their conversation with each other, the world of events, and other people.

The journal is not a diary simply recording events day by day. Journaling is a process. It starts when you realize there is something your deeper self wants to communicate—and there always is! There are parts of you that want to be heard without judgment. Perhaps it's the part that feels uncomfortable following an exchange with a family member or someone at work, but exactly what you've experienced isn't very clear. You may be reluctant to express to anyone else what seems vague. However, when you write what the deeper self has to say to you, you move toward clarity, and sometimes the process takes courage!

Date every entry, including the year. Write until you feel you have said what you have to say, then read over what you have written. If other thoughts come to mind, add them, or you may decide to adjust what you wrote, explaining to yourself what you really meant. But remember, it's okay to be vague. Life is often filled with ambiguities! Something new and subtle may be emerging. Notice how you feel and write that as well as any new insights you have.

If you have a trusted friend who can listen without commenting or offering advice, you might read your journal entry to him/her. Hearing your own words deepens the journaling process. Read what you have written word for word without explaining references to your listener. This process is for you, not for the enlightenment of your listener; it is an opportunity to really hear yourself. When you do, emotions, memories, insights, even dreams may come up that you hadn't noticed as you were writing: something you knew was there but hadn't been able to get in touch with until hearing your own voice. If you have a spiritual director, that individual will be trained to listen in a receptive way and can be an ideal listener for your journal entry.

The last step in the journaling process is for you to reflect and maybe write about what the process was like for you. As an outcome of your journaling experience, you may decide there is an action you want to take. For example, perhaps you can gently sidestep a difficult situation, or better yet, have a conversation with someone to clear up an issue. You will soon see that there are many possible outcomes to consider and choices beyond what you might have originally imagined.

As you can see, uninterrupted time and privacy are essential to this kind of journaling. For practical reasons it's best to dedicate a notebook just for this purpose, rather than writing on loose sheets of paper. The notebook will be more convenient to review over time. For further ideas, Julia Cameron's book *The Artist's Way* is helpful for beginners. An in-depth guide is *At a Journal Workshop* by Ira Progoff, which can be studied for certification.

Collage

A simple collage can be very revealing, not only of conscious thoughts but also of new realizations and perhaps intuitions. A number of exercises in this book suggest collage.

Here are some simple instructions.

Gather your materials: newspapers or other paper approximately that size, a supply of white copy paper, colored markers, glue sticks, scissors, a pile of old magazines, and perhaps some found objects like bits of ribbon or dried leaves. When you are ready, play some relaxing music that won't distract you. Then, with no advance plan, tear out at least twelve images that strike you. Work quickly so logic doesn't take over! If you like, draw and color some of your own images on plain paper. You can also do that with words, but focus on images and keep words to a minimum. Cut or tear them out in various sizes and then arrange your pieces on the paper and glue them down. You may decide to add found objects that feel right. Enjoy the process.

Then sit back and let the collage speak to you. You might find some synchronicities if you notice the printed newspaper article underneath your image! (Someone defined coincidences as God's way of remaining anonymous!) For example, one happened to a retreatant when she collaged a picture of a large old-fashioned chair and then noticed she had covered up the image of a beautiful young woman. This retreatant had been wheelchair bound for a number of years and the image gave her much food for thought.

When you are ready, write what the images say to you. You can ask them questions and imagine their responses as well. Don't worry if it doesn't make sense … it may make sense later.

When you finish your collage, as you do with your journal entries, date it, including the year. Post the collage and live with it for a while. You may be surprised to have a dream related to it. If you're inspired, you could do another page and add the dream to the original collage, being sure to date it as well. You may want to keep the collage and return to it in the future. One woman I know made one every year on her birthday. The images gave her a record of her inner growth and change over time, which amplified her journal work.

My hope and prayer is that you sense the hospitality of our women gathered together across the centuries, kissed by God and blessed. As you read, may you be nurtured with time to think, reflect, pray, and create. Let the journey begin.

Will you join hands with the Holy Women reaching out to you? They await!

Holy Women
of Scripture

Miriam

1445 BCE

We first meet Miriam on the banks of the Nile where the Jews were slaves in Egypt. She is the sister of Moses and Aaron, all three acknowledged as prophets in scripture.[1] The most familiar of stories about her describes her role in saving Moses from death, along with all the other Jewish baby boys, when Pharaoh hoped to quell a rebellion by decimating the male population.[2] Another well-known story describes her triumphant dance after the miraculous escape of her people through the Sea of Reeds.[3]

A side of Miriam I gradually discovered as I researched this book was her prophetic role as a leader. Only her brothers could officially carry the title of prophet, so Miriam's gifts were overshadowed. Ironically, though, according to one Jewish scholar, Miriam was prophesying before her brothers were even born. When the girl was only five, she foretold that her mother would carry a son who would become a great leader and free their people from slavery.[4] This, of course, was Moses.

The story of Miriam's precocious prophetic gifts in a rabbinic midrash expansion of the Torah shows that Miriam was highly esteemed in her people's ancient lore. Midrashic tales always carry important truths: in Miriam's case, we learn that she was respected and admired even at a very young age.

Preceding page: *Miriam,* acrylic on canvas, by the author.

In Hebrew, Miriam's name is related to the notion of "bitterness."[5] One can only imagine how enslavement for a century could embitter a people. Another name given for Miriam is *Puah,* a term associated with midwifery. According to tradition, both Miriam and her mother were midwives ordered to kill Jewish infants at the time of the Pharaoh's proclamation.

But they found ways around his command, explaining, "The Hebrew women are not like the Egyptian women. They are robust and give birth before the midwife arrives."[6] So these clever women were honored for their role in the culture and their dedication to protecting new life. Midrashic tradition teaches that because they stood at the threshold of life and death, they found great rewards from God, who "established households for them."[7]

The word *puah* is associated with the cooing or whispering one might do to calm a baby. In her article "Miriam: Midrash and Aggadah," Tamar Meir writes that puah, Miriam's way of speaking, reveals her character. Her gentle cooing to a baby and crying for her brothers' suffering suggest sensitivity and tenderness. On the other hand, Miriam was also capable of verbal assertion, aggression, and even insolence in troubling situations. According to tradition, God rewarded her fiery response to Pharaoh's demands, blessing her progeny with sages and kings, among them the Tribe of Judah and David himself.[8]

It is clear that Miriam was considered one of the three shepherds of her people, along with Moses and Aaron, during their forty years wandering in the desert. And she cared for Israel's needs in the wilderness beyond her midwife skills. Legend tells us that abundant fresh water followed Miriam as her weary people crossed the desert:

> The itinerant well was first opened by Moses striking the rock with his staff at Horeb, but then the well provided water through song and did not remain at Horeb but became a rolling rock accompanying the traveling pilgrims to provide fresh water for the people and their cattle and sheep. Miriam's song in service to her people opens the well again and again ... and made the desert bloom with green pastures and beautifully scented flowers. So in addition

to being the one to inspire celebration at the moment of freedom through song and dance, Miriam is also the one to provide her people with a source of refreshment in the desert heat and dryness. So long as she lived, there was a fountain of living water to sustain the people.[9,10]

We have considered Miriam here through the lens of her Jewish tradition, but early Christians honored her as well. We know from the Book of Acts and letters of the apostles that women held ministerial roles in those long-ago days. In addition to scripture, we know from the history of Eastern and Western churches during the first centuries of Christianity that they ordained deaconesses as well as deacons. Ordination prayers for the women asked that they be blessed with spiritual gifts of prophetic Jewish women, including Miriam.

Until the end of the fifth century, women were ordained specifically to minister to and evangelize other women in certain parts of the Roman Empire where men were prohibited from entering the household. Deaconesses also assisted in anointing women baptized by immersion since the convert would be naked in the water. The prevalence of ordained deaconesses varied between the Eastern and Western church with more likelihood of such ministries found in the east.[11]

This early ordination ceremony for deaconesses begins with the bishop's laying on of hands:

Each begins by invoking God and acknowledging divine providence, then looks for antecedents ... of the office in Israelite religion, and finally asks for appropriate gifts of the Spirit to make the person worthy of the office.... As examples of women with spiritual gifts, the prayer cites Miriam (Ex 15:20–21), Deborah (Judg 4–5), Anna (either 1 Sam 1:1–2:10 or Luke 2:36–38), and Hulda (2 Kgs 22:14–20).[12]

An interesting detail in this source mentions that Pope Gelasius sent a letter to bishops in southern Italy and Sicily in 494 CE forbidding women priests. We can conclude there perhaps were ordinations of women presbyters as well as deaconesses during that period.[13]

Somewhere over the long centuries of church history, ordained women were dropped from the hierarchy of the clergy and have not been reinstated since. Miriam, too, in her last days was forced to the edge of the camp for criticizing Moses's leadership. Nevertheless, she kept the love and support of her Jewish community. The people:

> ... refused to continue their journey until she was brought in again. When she died, [they] refused to go on until she was properly buried. The text tries to present her as anonymous, silent, ineffective, excluded, disobedient and justifiably punished. Tradition remembers her for her courage, candor, initiative, spirit, her ability to inspire loyalty, and her quality of leadership, which included musical gifts. Miriam is one of the matriarchs, a heroine of the tradition.[14]

May we find our own prophetic gifts in our time as Miriam did in hers. Let us care for our community as she cared for hers. And may we come to the end of our lives richly blessed. "Miriam died ... [her] soul drawn out by God's kiss."[15] May we, Holy Women Kissed by God, at the end of our journey join our sister Miriam in the cloud of witnesses with great joy in God's embrace.

Discovering Miriam

As a child in Catholic grade school, I heard the Old Testament stories of the trouble the Jews had in Egypt. Having been taken slaves by Pharaoh, as time passed they became embittered and restless. The Pharaoh knew it would take drastic measures to control them. I'd already heard some bloody Bible stories, but it still seemed impossible that the Pharaoh would kill off little baby boys just because he didn't like the Jews!

I could completely understand an older sister saving her baby

Prophet Miriam
by Marcy Hall.

brother because at nine years old, I had a baby brother. I'd waited a long time for him, so I knew how Miriam felt about Moses. His big sister would definitely go into action to save him.

I don't remember if my teacher explained how Miriam was able to pull this off. But I had my theory.

She was probably about my age at the time I heard the story, and young slave girls certainly would have been considered even less significant than slave boys; otherwise, Pharaoh would have gone after them too. So who would pay any attention to what Miriam was up to? Even three thousand years later, I knew little girls like me were deemed less important than boys.

Miriam was confident she wouldn't be noticed as she carried out her crafty plan to keep little Moses safe. Her mom was in on the scheme and hid the baby in a basket among the reeds along the Nile while Miriam watched from nearby. Miriam kept her eyes open as she waited for Pharaoh's daughter, who often bathed there with her women. Moses was a very cute and cuddly baby. Miriam had seen everyone admiring him so she knew the princess would too, and she didn't want there to be any obstacle to the royal daughter taking the child for herself.

She remembered how her mother's friends suffered when their babies were taken. Baby Moses had to be kept safe! And Miriam was close enough to womanhood to know that this royal woman would need the help of a wet nurse.

Soon the princess and her entourage arrived. Miriam smiled as she saw the princess's delight with the baby, and politely approached. "Your highness, would you like to invite a wet nurse to feed your new child?"[16] It was the most natural solution in the world ... and Pharaoh's daughter never learned that the baby's nurse was his own mother!

From those early days of Bible history in grade school, I knew I liked Miriam, but I seldom thought of her unless there was a scripture reading about her at church. I hadn't even thought of her when I began painting Holy Women a few years ago. Yet after I painted a number of them, a beautiful, blissful face showed up on my canvas. Her eyes were closed, head tipped back as though an invisible lover might have just kissed her. She held a tambourine, and I imagined she was catching her breath after a wild, ecstatic dance.

I usually knew who my subjects were as I painted these women, but this one puzzled me. Finally, I titled the painting The Visitor. I didn't know if she was the visitor or if she had been visited, but the title was as close as I could come to what the piece seemed to be about.

Only after I started writing about these creative women did I think of Miriam. Among their ranks, I'd found some artists and many writers, herbalists, weavers, musicians, and composers—but no dancers.

Then I remembered the other story, of Miriam leading a jubilant dance as Moses led the Jews out of Egypt.[17] I recognized her. My painting was definitely Miriam!

This was Miriam grown—a mystic and a prophet during the years Moses was a trusted leader close to Pharaoh's throne.

Then the trouble started. The Egyptian ruler discovered the Jews had fled into the desert. This wasn't just the aimless wandering of a lost people—which Pharaoh had seen before—so it didn't take him long to set out in hot pursuit with an army, horses, and six hundred first-class chariots and charioteers. Thus began the great escape of the Israelites known throughout history as the Exodus.[18]

As the Egyptians began to catch up with them, the Jews were terrified. Miriam describes the heart-stopping escape.

Miriam Remembers

I was running for my life! Scared to death!
Breathless, trembling ...
My heart pounded as I leapt, stumbling in the piles of wet
*   sand ...*
The column of God's light was right ahead of us,
leading into the sea,
the path into the sea!!
and then,
and then ...
we hurled ourselves headlong into it ...

but I couldn't understand ...
my bare feet were running on warm, dry sand ...

Ah, and I never will forget that flight
*   from Egypt.*
We followed our God, the Light ...
the column of fire ...

right into the sea ...
the path that opened in the sea.
So much like our lives ... the sea ...
tumultuous ...
always moving,
but it could carry us too ...
That time, though,

we weren't to be carried.
We were on dry land!
How could it be?

As we ran for our lives,
the sea crashed into itself at our very heels.
And the Egyptians, so close,
Were suddenly in total confusion!
Water frothed on all sides.
Everywhere, the sea raged.
The men unhorsed, terrified ... flailing,
Metal helmets torn from their heads,
swords ripped from their hands
by terrifying waves.
They struggled,
then disappeared ...
drifting to the floor of the sea ...
yes, horses too ... horses snorting,
splashing,
drowning.

But we were safe.
We had trusted our God.
He saved us.
We were safe.
How could it be?
Our feet on dry land.
Breathless, trembling, yes.
But our feet were on soft desert sand,
dry sand.

And I had my tambourine ...
My precious tambourine.
It was warm against my heart.
I closed my eyes,
slowly moving to its rhythm,

fingers tingling,

toes tingling ...
I began swirling,
laughing,
leading the women,
our hearts bursting with joy
in the nearness of God.

We raised our voices slowly,
then gathered to a great crescendo,
a mighty roar.
We sang:
"Horse and chariot,
horse and chariot ...
horse and chariot ...
horse and chariot,
You cast into the sea ..."[19]
I will never forget that night ...
God so close.

After the music stopped,
quiet descended upon me ...
filling the place now empty
of all that had burst out
in music and dance.

Silence fell gently like moonlight,
surrounding me,
embracing me.
I sat motionless, still,
somehow outside of time.

Then,
gently,
the voice of God spoke,
without sound
in that silence,
coming from far away,
but heard in my heart:

"Peace, daughter."

Yes, peace.

We were all at peace
in that night,
in our God's night,
in the safety of His presence.[20]

Responding to Miriam

Associations/archetypes: prophetess, outsider, child, midwife, wise
woman/elder, pilgrim, Jewess, Exodus, Red Sea, tambourine, dance,
big sister, leader, well, water, Moses.

Miriam represents one who comes to help the vulnerable and suffering. Unlike many of the Holy Women, she has no church named
after her, but there is a house for homeless women inspired by the
story of Moses. Have you ever thought of him as a homeless child
found there in the Nile among the bull rushes? A hospital, too, bears
her name. It serves indigent Jewish immigrants, reminding us of
her people, slaves fleeing Egypt with only the clothes on their back.

As a child, Miriam saved her baby brother's life, a brother who
had been abandoned to die because Jews were captives, foreigners in
Egypt. Perhaps you have seen photos of children among displaced
refugees today, also unwelcome on foreign shores. Perhaps you
remember yourself as a child or as a big sister.

Imagine being with Miriam, both of you quite young, in the
midst of such chaos. Let this imagining be like a dream you make
up as you go along; allow it to become real in your mind: Hot
Egyptian sun. Tall reeds. Perhaps alligators. You feel you may be
watched ... do you whisper? What does Miriam say to you? What
is your conversation?

In your imagination, you both are clever, and you are brave

problem solvers. What are you able to do despite your vulnerability and fear? Are parts of the problem too big for you to solve? Imagine you find a helper to turn to. What happens? How do you feel?

Sit quietly in the presence of the Spirit and listen. Does the meditation shift to today, to something in your present life? Allow this reflection to continue to unfold as you make it vivid in your imagination. When you are ready, journal about it. Don't be surprised if more details, meanings, memories, and associations occur to you as you write. Be attentive to your inner response. End with what you have to say to the Spirit.

If your inner journey wants to go in a completely different direction, allow it, perhaps returning to the suggestions here as you proceed. End with what you have to say to the Spirit.

Then ask: "Is there an action you are inviting me to take?"

Mary

Early CE

Commemorated December 8

Mary of Nazareth, the mother of Jesus, is paradoxically one of the best-known and least-known women in history. Christian scripture names her (sometimes unidentified) only twenty-three times,[1] not counting the "woman clothed with the sun" mentioned in the Book of Revelation.[2] Interestingly, seventeen of these mentions are in Jesus's infancy narrative. Little is known about Mary's later life.

Although the focus of Christianity is on the life of Jesus, from the earliest days and through the centuries Mary as his mother has been honored by Roman Catholics, Eastern and Oriental Orthodox Christians, Lutherans, Anglicans, and Muslims.

When Mary was born in the world of ancient Israel, oral tradition prevailed. The few surviving written documents that became part of the biblical canon were based on memory and often incomplete due to accidents of history or, in some cases, authorial intent. Perhaps Mary's later life was described in lost documents that would have filled out the scant information we find in scripture, but without them, we are left to speculate. Nevertheless, in the early centuries of Christianity, Mary was well known among Jews, and starting in the seventh century by followers of Islam as well.

Mary was, of course, a Jewish woman and is understood as such by Jews today, who regard her simply as the mother of Jesus. Followers of Jesus who knew Mary in her lifetime, mostly Jews, likely saw her as a strong personality. Her contemporaries may have witnessed her going into action at the wedding feast of Cana, the occasion of Jesus's first miracle. When Mary pointed out an

---

Preceding page: *Mother and Child*, acrylic and mixed media
on canvas, by the author.

The Nativity by William Blake portrays Jesus on a
shaft of light arriving into the arms of Elizabeth as
Mary swoons in the arms of Joseph. 1799–1800,
copper image in Philadelphia Museum of Art.
Photo by the author.

embarrassing wine shortage to her son, Jesus seemingly rebuffed
her, saying, "Woman, what is that to me and to you? My hour is
not yet come."[3] I can just see her giving him one of those "mother
looks" and then simply directing the servants, "Do whatever he tells
you"[4] knowing full well that her son had a compassionate heart
and would see to the wine problem.

Mary was part of Jesus's life and death. She also had a place in
the Upper Room at Pentecost with his brethren, the eleven apostles,
and the other women when "they were filled with the Holy Spirit."[5]
What happened to Mary later becomes sketchy. Some sources
maintain she lived in Ephesus in Turkey and was miraculously taken
up into heaven from there.[6] Then she disappears from scripture.

Christian scripture, that is. In the seventh century, as Islam
grew out of Judaism and Christianity, it became apparent that
Mohammed and his followers had absorbed the spirit of these
earlier traditions and a high regard for Mary as well. We know she
was and remains a prominent figure in Islam. To this day, evidence
of devotion to her can be seen in the Hagia Sophia mosque in
Istanbul. Verses from the Koran about Mary are inscribed on its
walls,[7] attesting to her honored place in Islam.[8]

Queen of Poland, a portrayal of Our Lady of Czestochowa, acrylic and mixed media on wood, by the author.

Not all the words honoring Mary in Islam are written on the wall of a mosque. An entire chapter of the Koran is dedicated to her.[9] She is mentioned in the Koran fifty times, and she is the only woman mentioned in the Muslim holy book.[10]

Mary has another distinction in Islam. She is the sole woman Muslims consider to be a prophet.[11] One remembers that her predecessor, Miriam, struggled for that role. At the time of the Exodus, she was forced to the edge of the camp, subservient to her brothers, Moses and Aaron. In the Koran, Mary holds the prophetic role without dispute because she has accepted the Angel Gabriel's invitation and prophecy about the coming of Jesus.

Jesus's birth in the Koran is in contrast with the story told in Christian tradition. In Christian apocrypha, Mary gave birth without pain.[12] In the Islamic version, she suffers. As the story goes, the birth pangs become so severe that Allah tells her to grasp a palm tree. When she does, she shakes it with such violence that date palms fall on her, seemingly a sweet gift from Allah.[13]

The issue of Mary's marital status comes up in both Islamic and Christian stories, however. Being unmarried and with child was a serious problem for observant Jews who had become Christians and for Muslims as well. In the Islamic version of Jesus's birth, the problem is settled by the infant himself. Once in the cradle, Jesus speaks up, foretelling incidents about his life, the first of many prophecies. His phenomenal precocity dissipates all questions about the circumstances of his birth.[14] Christian scripture describes the pregnant Mary betrothed to Joseph. He knows well the child isn't his and considers quietly putting their betrothal aside to protect her reputation. But he is stopped by the dream of an angel who tells him the child is conceived by the Spirit of God.[15] Mary is held in high esteem in both traditions despite starting out as an unmarried mother.

It seems Muslim as well as Christian women empathized with Mary's childbearing struggles. Through the centuries, they visited Christian as well as Muslim Marian shrines, including baths in Jerusalem that she reputedly visited. Muslim women who bathe there ask her intercession to cure barrenness.[16] Mary, the compassionate mother is sought out, since she was believed by Christians and Muslims to be the most powerful of all saints, able to grant favors to her devotees.

Mary's reputation as a powerful mother eager to help her children has persisted over the centuries. Many claims of

The image of Our Lady of Guadalupe is well known in the Americas, having been carried here by conquistadors and added to by the story of Juan Diego in Mexico, mantled in stars and roses. My painting *Guadalupe 2* remains a woman of color, a simple archetypal woman of the earth with only one rose and one star. That is all she needs.

miraculous Marian appearances have been made, perhaps the most familiar to Christians being those in Fatima in Portugal, Lourdes in France, and Medjugorje in Bosnia-Herzegovina. The merciful archetypal mother who visits the world is a bodhisattva in the Buddhist tradition of Kuan Yin, "an enlightened person who keeps coming back to earth to help others find the light,"[17] refusing to enter nirvana in order to save others, allowing them to enter first. That Mary is believed to visit the earth demonstrates the expansiveness of her unconditional love, which cannot be confined but overflows every boundary to reach all her earthly children of whatever persuasion.

A contemporary Sufi mystic writes of Mary the Divine Feminine that he experiences as a protective patroness, the Queen of Heaven, and the Queen of all Saints. (See Appendix, page 209). Many traditional Christian icons also present Mary as queen and even as archetypal Black Madonna.

We see in the persistent claims of visions that the historical Mary has been transformed into something much larger. She carries the energy of the feminine divine, a very deeply held universal archetype. Archeologists believe the first image representing divinity was the small figure of the Venus of Willendorf. Her round shape promised that she could provide sustenance, like a good mother. This artifact is believed to date back to 28,000 BCE.[18]

The feminine divine was honored in the tales of earliest known cultures. The ancient goddess was a triple goddess: virgin, mother, and wise old woman or queen, representing woman in all her life roles. Mary also gradually became known in these roles, first of all as "Ever Virgin."[19] Although virginity is a physical condition, when it is considered metaphorically, it can suggest "spiritual intactness in the midst of the vicissitudes of human transformation."[20] If indeed Mary had children other than Jesus, as some assume from reference to "the brothers and sisters of Jesus" in scripture,[21] the concept of Mary's virginity as intactness is helpful.

Also helpful is the understanding of the virgin warrior goddess archetype in classical stories. These archetypes present woman sufficient unto herself. Mary "Ever Virgin" is a concept that deserves consideration for its spiritual and symbolic meaning. The scriptural story that the Holy Spirit had come upon her[22] is a clear message. No man had caused this momentous event in her life. Mary's consent was made freely and independently. With it began her powerful role as mother, one who creates and nurtures. However, since Mary carries the virgin archetype as well as the mother archetype, sensual femininity has often been minimized in her religious images. Fortunately, some medieval sculptures survive that portray her nursing the child Jesus. They testify to Mary's full human motherhood, enriching the archetype.

Another aspect of the mother archetype often minimized is its dark side. The mother can be destructive as well as beneficent. Mary is not viewed as destructive, but is connected to death as well as birth; she held Jesus's dead body on Calvary. When it comes to archetypes, one picture can be worth a thousand words. Anyone who has looked at Michelangelo's *Pietà*[23] has seen Mary present at death, a mother in grief. Another piece of art,

Our Lady of Perpetual Help, a Byzantine icon.

a fifteenth-century icon, gives us a sense of the mother's role as companion through suffering and even death. She is present without denial or overprotection. David Richo, a Jungian student of Mary, shares the story behind a familiar Byzantine icon:

A universally revered icon is that of "Our Lady of Perpetual Help." It depicts a pious legend that the child Jesus was visited by two angels of truth who showed him the instruments of his future suffering and death. He was frightened and leaped into his mother's arms so quickly that one of his sandals began to fall off. Mary holds him in the safety of her embrace but does not dismiss the angels with the thorns and spear. In the picture, we notice that Jesus is held in such a way as to be able to see the givens of his life *and* still feel safe. Mary holds him/ourselves in a way that grants stability but does not deny the dark options in human reality.... Help is perpetually available as a reliable grace so we can live through the predicaments of our lives ... [and] share in the redemption of our universe.[24]

So we see Mary has a connection with death, although she traditionally carries the light side of the archetypes of the triple goddess. Because over millennia she has been named "Ever Virgin" and "without sin," several other aspects of the feminine archetype are missing. The complete feminine archetype would include darkness, earthiness, passion, and sexuality. The Black Madonnas we are learning about today may signify that connection with darkness through nature:

> The black is that of the fertile black earth. The dark also represents the mystery of a reality that is still deeply unconscious. The mother god Isis was black too. In alchemy, the symbolic process of transformation of the leaden ego into the golden Self, begins with *nigredo*, the blackness. Darkness is so often the connection between living archetypal images that meet, as for example, suffering and resurrection.[25]

The Black Madonna is connected to the dark night, to what is not yet born, still in the darkness of the womb. There will be pain at the time of birth, and one reflects that one must also die, another painful transition at which the mother is present. The old gives way to the new through suffering. The dark side of the mother archetype is maternal energy obscured in shadow, beyond words, impossible to imagine yet not to be feared. Darkness is the mystery of what is yet unknown.[26]

Mary remains a historical Christian figure across cultures, but she also carries an energy, a presence that resonates with the feminine divine. In the eighth century, St. Andrew of Crete, first deacon of the Hagia Sophia Cathedral, wrote: "Mary is a statue sculpted by God as an image of a divine archetype."[27] She has become mythic, known as the Mother of God over the centuries of Christianity. In Jungian thought:

> To say that is to say she is the feminine energy that brings to birth in us a consciousness of our deepest reality, i.e., divinity. The motherhood of Jesus is an allegory of that stature and destiny in all of us. It is already and always in us but awaits consciousness."[28]

Just as we understand Jesus as more than a historical figure, his life and teachings bringing to us religious and mystical meaning, the same is true of his mother, Mary.

The Black Madonna

Woman of the garden,
You are black and you are beautiful.
The one the lover sings among the lilies.
The one enveloped by night under the stars,
The moon at your feet,
The aurora borealis your mantle.
You are mystery,
Coming from the deep, returning to eternity.
Regal, yet simple, of the people.
Close as earth,
Musky as a lover's breath in the darkness,
You hold me.
In the sightless dark, I awake in your embrace.
Living and moving safely in You,
Rocked in your womb,
You nourish me, guide me,
Without seeing or knowing,
Enfolding me in your warmth,
Like dark and fragrant earth.

You are my mother.[29]

Discovering Mary

I've always been able to relate to Mary as a loving, protective mother. I know what a good mom is like because in my family, I had one. She protected me. Still, when I found myself in certain frightening situations, I knew she was powerless to help.

Mary, though, was never powerless. She was the all-powerful Queen of Heaven and Mother of Mercy. I can still recite by heart the prayer I had learned in Catholic grade school:

Remember, O Most Gracious Virgin Mary, that never was it known, that anyone who fled to thy protection, implored thy help, or sought thy intercession was left unaided. Inspired with this confidence, I fly unto thee, O Virgin of Virgins, my Mother. To thee I come, before thee I stand, sinful and sorrowful. O Mother of the Word incarnate, despise not my petitions, but in thy mercy hear and answer me. Amen.

One night when I was sixteen, I was walking home alone in the dark through unfamiliar streets, sometimes followed by strange cars. It wasn't a life-threatening situation, but I didn't know that at the time. Vulnerable and afraid, I turned to Mary for the protection she promised.

Years later, I *was* in a life-threatening situation. My husband and I were among other inexperienced sailors visiting the Cyclades islands of Greece in a small boat. As we sailed in the Mediterranean, I saw many outcroppings of rock, each bearing a small shrine to Mary to protect against shipwreck. I took them as curious but touching aspects of the culture.

We stopped at Santorini, Ios, and Tinos, all gems in the glorious aquamarine ocean, impressively beautiful. Then we were ready to return to the mainland, amply rewarded for our adventure among the hospitable Greeks. So far our crossing between islands had been smooth. But shortly after we set sail, as my husband and I stood on deck holding hands, we noticed that the ocean's calm surface was swelling into waves.

Within a very short time, dangerous winds came up. Suddenly the sea was a wild and frothing thing. The boat seemed to rear up, and it was hard to tell whether we were standing in rain or a deluge of water from the roiling sea. I grabbed the deck's guard rail as my feet slipped on the wet surface.

The crew leader saw me stumble and quickly gathered us all into the cabin. We gingerly seated ourselves. As clouds ominously darkened the sky, we watched through watery portholes, hoping we were safe.

The wind became a gale howling around us, and our anxiety increased. Soon water was seeping through the planks of the deck down below. The captain, calm but commanding, gave an order: "All passengers! You are to immediately lie down on the floor."

The crew scurried among us, moving to the deck. We watched nervously as they tied themselves to chairs that blocked our way out, as if they were determined to protect us at all cost. Meanwhile, cavernous waves, one after another, crashed against our little boat, pitching it side to side.

I was terrified. I clenched my husband's hand, closed my eyes, and thought of our eleven-year-old son. We had left him with my parents. *Will I ever see him again?* The thought was too much: *This must be what death is like.*

Then I thought of all those little shrines to Mary on every prominent rock. Mary! The protector of those at sea! My mind raced ... I could pray to her, beg her help. I could promise to do something to help mothers and children when I got home. I could give special help. I could counsel them, make donations to family agencies. I begged her. I prayed the *Memorare*.

Gradually, as if coming out of turbulence in a plane, the floor under us stopped lurching. The sea slowly calmed. Sitting up now, we could see shore in the distance. It seemed to take a long time to cross the watery expanse to port in Piraeus, but we made it. It took me a while to calm down after such terror. Shaking, but filled with gratitude, we disembarked. When all of us were securely on the dock, our captain addressed us. "You have been brave and most cooperative sailors, and I thank you for that. This has been a very rough crossing. Here on shore, they report that ships have crashed off Crete in eighteen-foot waves not far from where we have just sailed."

I could hardly breathe. I turned, gasping great sobs into my husband's shoulder. Thank God we were safe! As we rounded up our gear to leave, the captain wished each of us Godspeed on our travels. When he came to me, he took my hand in both of his and bowed slightly, looking at me kindly with tears in his eyes. I noticed then a small medal fixed to his lapel. It glinted in the light: a blue, white, and gold image of Mary.

Once home, I made the promised donation. And my counseling practice gently morphed into services for women and children. My retreats and workshops filled with women. Sometimes I wondered how my unplanned specialization had materialized that way. Then, gradually, it occurred to me that when I made my promises to Mary, I had received my life back—my entire life! That was the deal. In God's plan, my life would go on. My part of the deal was to follow the path right in front of me.

These days, I know that my near-death experience in the Greek islands was something of a new birth through Mary. I understood Mary as the mother of new life.

Only years later, after a tough divorce and subsequent remarriage, did I begin to understand that the mother also stands at the place between life and death. It was one thing to rattle off the *Memorare* or the last words of the *Hail Mary:* "Holy Mary, Mother of God, pray for us sinners, now and at the hour of our death." It was a completely other thing to understand the depth of meaning in those ancient prayers.

Jerry and I had been married less than seven years when his heart problems became critical. We'd been through a series of dangerous surgeries—multiple stents, bypasses, valve replacement—but kept trying to live a normal life despite his noticeable decline. His short-term memory loss got to the point that he couldn't keep track of his complicated medical regime. So I started going with him to the doctor's office. We both pretended it was just an excuse to have lunch together on a weekday. I tried to be inconspicuous as I took notes on what the doctor told us and wrote down all of Jerry's meds. I knew he was embarrassed, but my brave husband made light of it. He joked, "Nothing like a little congestive heart failure to bring a couple together!" It was fine. I wasn't going anywhere.

Then, our first grandchild Hannah was born ... in Spokane. Kelly and Christie had been in Washington for a while, close to her family as they began married life. I had waited a long time for that baby. My son and his wife had courted for several years. My younger sisters and many friends had become grandmothers long since. I was very ready to be one too! And having only one son, the arrival of a little girl was the icing on the cake. But Spokane felt so far away.

Jerry had his opinion about what I should do. "You get on the plane and go see that baby! I just wish I could go, but you can't miss her baptism!"

I knew not to argue with him, but I was torn. I wanted to go but worried about leaving him. He hated that his health had deteriorated so much. I could see frustration and regret in his eyes. It was very tough for him to accept that he needed me.

All my thoughts and feelings churned as I stood there silently, not sure what to say. I knew he wanted to meet this lovely new member of our family as much as I did. Finally, he reached out, putting his hands on my shoulders, turning me to face him.

"Shirley, I want you to go." He shook me a little. I leaned into him, resting my head on his broad chest. With mixed feelings, at his insistence, I agreed.

Although still anxious about him, I got away for a few days. Oh, and the joy of that beautiful little child! I wanted to bring her home with me ... but at least, I had many photos to share with Jerry, the new grandpa.

As the autumn months passed, Jer didn't feel better. His problems got worse as Thanksgiving came and went—a lonely, painful time. Every day, I saw more clearly his increasing need to have me at his side. As Christmas approached, we missed the kids but knew there was no possibility we could visit them. Just getting off the plane in Spokane to a lungful of cold air could send Jerry's heart into a fatal spasm.

I called Kelly. "Could you kids bring the baby home for Christmas? Jer isn't up to the trip, but he would dearly love to meet Hannah." They quickly agreed. They understood: Jerry was failing, and it was tough for me.

Christmas was joyful and bittersweet. I'll never forget the happiness in Jerry's eyes and smile as he held little Hannah for the first time. And I never forgot my sad realization of how sick he was on Christmas morning. When it was time to leave for church, he came from the bedroom in robe and slippers to sit quietly in his chair, obviously weak. Tears filled my eyes as I stood in the doorway looking at him. Had he ever missed Mass on Christmas before? I knew the answer to my own question. It scared me. Suddenly the worst seemed just ahead.

A few days later, he went into the hospital and, to my alarm, was immediately admitted to the intensive care unit. He had multiple problems. He couldn't breathe. Was it pneumonia? Was it a lung infection? Did he have Legionnaires's Disease?[i] Did he need surgery on his lungs? A pulmonary surgeon proposed it. Jer had been on blood thinners for what seemed like forever. And I had already seen the aftermath of anesthesia following earlier prolonged surgeries: confusion, weakness, and long, slow recovery. I was frightened by the risk. The surgeon suggesting it to me seemed nervous himself.

Over the months, I had found strong support in Jerry's cardiologist. We had both trusted and respected him through all our daunting decisions. He knew that the pulmonary surgeon would be discussing Jer's best option with me. Now, when I reported it, his face told me what he thought and felt before I even heard his words: "Shirley, it could be dangerous." That settled it; no surgery.

The days in the hospital stretched on, turning into weeks, the weeks approaching a month. Jerry's heart slowed, palpitated, then raced. His kidneys started to fail. On top of it all, his ability to breathe was alarmingly unstable. Despite the volumes of paperwork he had filled out about his care preferences, he was put on a ventilator, not once or twice but three times, each followed by days of disorientation. We gave our doctor permission to keep trying to help, even with the ventilator. We both trusted his judgment that there was still hope.

For nearly a month in the ICU, Jerry struggled not only physically but with the chaos in his mind. It was excruciating to watch. My worst fear was that his thoughts would never be clear again, that he'd wind up confused, helpless, and weak in a nursing home, not able to recognize me. Each time he was disoriented, I wondered

---

i   Legionnaire's disease was a dangerous and highly contagious virus, thought in those days to have somehow originated at a gathering of American Legion conventioneers.

if he could come back. I went home late those nights, exhausted and worried.

Then one morning after the latest crisis, I walked into his room to a cheery "Hi, sweetheart!"

My heart skipped a beat! He was coherent. Thank God! I sank down in my chair, hitching it as close to his bed as his IV stand would allow. He saw my eyes fill with tears as he reached for my hand. The first words out of his mouth were "I love you, Shirley."

That made me cry some more, and then laugh with relief that he was back! I don't know what I babbled, but then I could see he was eager to talk.

He launched right in. "Shirley, I don't want that ventilator again. I know the doctor has tried to work with my problems all this time, and I understand how you feel too." Already winded by the few words, he stopped to take a breath. "But I really don't want the ventilator again! Remember, I signed all those papers about my wishes."

I gripped his hand and kissed it, not sure what to say.

His eyes were full of urgency. Voice dropping, he whispered, "Please."

I knew he meant it. Despite my anxiety, I managed to answer him. "I'm just so sorry you have gone through so much, and it breaks my heart."

His grip on my hand tightened. "I love you, Shirley."

I couldn't hold my tears back. "I love you, too ... and I will do what you say."

Just then, our doctor came in for rounds. His face lit up in a smile when he saw Jerry conscious and coherent for the first time in days. When he glanced at me, though, his expression changed to concern.

Jerry squeezed my hand as if to assure me that he knew I was too choked up to speak. He repeated to the doctor what he had said to me just minutes before, almost word for word. The hard reality was his that heart, lungs, and kidneys were closing down. We all knew that.

The doctor listened carefully. After a pause, he reached over and placed a hand on Jer's shoulder. His smile was kindly. "I know this has been tough for you, Jerry. We've all been waiting for you to be able to talk with us again. And Shirley has been right here."

I could see my husband's face relax. Then the doctor asked, "Okay if I check you out?" Jer nodded. He took his blood pressure, listened to his heart, looked at his chart, asked some questions. Satisfied, he glanced at me, then turned back to Jerry. "Today, you are very clear. Jerry, we will respect your preferences. No more ventilator. You understand what will happen if you can't get your breath?"

Jerry nodded. He was a dentist. Our doctor knew that. His training had included at least two years of medical school. He understood the process his body would go through unable to breathe without mechanical help. Neither Jer nor I had any questions.

We had been fully informed about all the protocols of his care over the excruciating weeks in the ICU as each complication had arisen.

"Good ... It's important that I've been able to hear this from you, Jerry." He went on to clarify some points about orders he would leave for staff, closed his notes, then paused. The eyes of the two men met. When he reached out to shake Jerry's hand, I could hardly breathe. Then he turned. My face told him exactly how I felt in that moment. He took a quick step to grip my hands with crushing intensity. And somehow, it reassured me.

After the conversation, Jer was exhausted and lapsed into a light sleep. I closed my eyes too, sliding down into the bedside chair. I hadn't slept well and was tired but I couldn't rest. We needed to respect Jerry's wishes, but I couldn't take it in. What had just happened? I couldn't absorb it. Then, suddenly, a discomforting thought arose. This was real! Jer could die at any moment without that ventilator, and I didn't know what to do. I knew he wanted to be cremated, but I had no idea how to handle things. In the midst of this crisis, I had been so lost in my own fear and sadness that I hadn't thought beyond the moment, hadn't thought anything through ... I'd completely lost track of ...

I couldn't bring myself to say the words, even to myself.

I pushed myself out of the chair and quietly hurried out of the room. The nurse at the desk immediately stood, alert to the possibility Jer had fallen into another crisis. When I spoke, my voice seemed to come out of someone else. "It's okay—Jerry is sleeping, but please call the social worker. I need to talk with her right away."

Of course, the hospital dealt with these matters routinely. The social worker had all the information I needed. I just hoped I could keep it straight in my stressed state of mind. Her explanation was detailed in a folder she was patiently reviewing with me when there was an insistent tap on the door. The charge nurse, not waiting for a reply, pushed in and took my arm. "Shirley, the doctor needs you in Jerry's room."

My heart leapt into my throat as I half-ran the few steps down the hall, the nurse still holding my elbow. In the room, Jer's bed was surrounded by a half dozen nurses and respiratory therapists. He was in distress. They were all trying to help him breathe. I'd never seen so many tubes and unfamiliar devices. The doctor motioned me to stand at his right side. He held what looked like an empty gallon milk bottle with a hose attached. He moved it into position near Jerry's mouth. "Now, Jerry, I want you to take a deep breath." As I leaned over to see what was going on, Jerry clamped his lips together. The doctor turned to look at me, an expression of astonishment on his face.

What could I say? Jerry was a stubborn Irishman—and he didn't want to do this.

The doctor's face was tense. He continued manipulating medical devices I couldn't name and directing therapists and nurses as they stood ready to assist. I couldn't take my eyes off my husband. His breath seemed to be slowing and sounded muffled.

Finally, I looked up. Only one nurse and the doctor were with me. One by one, the medical staff had quietly left the room. Our doctor slowly turned to me, eyes wet, squeezed my shoulder, and then moved to the door.

The nurse at my side smoothed the sheets around Jer. He seemed to be unconscious. She gently whispered to me, "If you need anything, I'll be right outside," then quietly let herself out of the room.

In that moment, I realized with a rush how much I had wanted to be alone with my husband, to hold him. Now that we were alone it felt like we were the only two people on the face of the earth. He was so precious. But so many tubes were coming out of him! I didn't want to hurt him! Then some voice of reason told me I couldn't hurt him at this point. If a tube came out, it didn't matter. I kicked off my shoes and climbed onto the bed.

My dear husband. It was a relief to finally get my arms around him. I closed my eyes and held him close, rocking him, rocking him ... and then gently started singing. "How Great Thou Art" ... "Amazing Grace" ... "Ave Maria" ... "Lullaby and Good Night" ... "Sleep My Child" ... "You Made Me Love You, I Didn't Want to Do It" ... "My Wild Irish Rose" ... "Take Me Home Again Kathleen" ... "Danny Boy" ... "When the Saints Come Marching In" ... "Black Bird, Bye-Bye."

I don't know how long I sang. Over and over: hymns, lullabies, love songs, Irish songs, songs I knew he liked, one song after another. It was my privilege to accompany this good man on his journey in the best way I could. I sang and sang. I could tell his breath was changing; sometimes it was uneven, sometimes interrupted by a little shudder. I wondered if he could hear me singing him to sleep—I hoped so. I knew how much he loved *Ave Maria*, and I sang it over and over from my heart, a little surprised that I didn't choke up. It ended, "Pray for us now and at the hour of our death."

When did I ever learn that song? Were there angels in the room ready to assist his spirit into God's arms? It seemed so to me ... I kept singing. Or maybe I was the angel, carrying Mother energy to him for his passage into new life? All I knew was that I was with him and it was a privilege, a sacred time.

It was years before I understood that experience. I had felt the Mother's presence as Jerry passed from life to death, but I didn't comprehend it. God was mothering, birthing in such a mysterious way.

Then, during a retreat, it came to me. It was rainy and green that spring in Washington State, with new life bursting out all over. The focus of the retreat was on archetypes, the Mother prominent among them. During our days together, the facilitator[ii] invited us to explore this powerful archetype in many ways. We meditated, walked the labyrinth, made collages, and journaled.

---

ii   This retreat was led by Christine Valters Paintner, PhD, in Seattle, Washington, on the theme of archetypes. She is a Benedictine oblate and online abbess of Abbey of the Arts, a program for Monks in the World.

A portrayal of the mother archetype: *The Nativity,* a painting
in Old St. Patrick's Church, Galway, Ireland.
Artist unknown; photo by the author.

By birth order in my family, I am the oldest sister: "assistant
Mom" in my growing up years. As a girl, my strong protective side
emerged. I definitely had maternal inclinations. I wouldn't have
called it a persona then, but as I matured I understood that part
of me. The birth of my son was where my heart had truly wanted
and needed to go. I knew motherhood was part of my call. It had
been a grace.

Finally, on the last day of retreat, after thoughtful discussion
and prayer, the leader invited us to body prayer, moving to music in
any way we chose. Feeling a bit self-conscious in the group, I closed
my eyes as an ethereal *Ave Maria* filled the room. Though it was a
chanted version that was new to me, it was somehow familiar and
very sweet. I stood there swaying to the soft music and then quietly
stepped to a corner.

The simple gesture of crossing my arms surprised me. It took
me back to the warmth of holding my newborn son, a time of
great joy. As the gentle chant continued, something slowly opened
inside me. Flooded with joy and tears, I rocked from one foot to
the other and crooned a lullaby to my precious infant son as I had

done so many years before. I had picked up the haunting melody of an unforgettable song I'd known all my life.

Then something shifted as I moved with the music. I was no longer holding my baby, but was transported to the hospital room holding Jerry. My arms were around my husband as I sang him across the threshold from life to death on his journey to the other side of the veil. As I moved to the music, I felt that I, too, was slipping to a place outside time.

Holding my husband as he made his transition to his home with God and holding my infant, newly arrived from the mystery of the not yet born, were the same! The Holy Mother was with me in exactly the same way. I knew it viscerally, in my body, as I moved to that music. The Holy Mother stands at the bridge between life and death as well as between the darkness of the womb and life in the world. It all seemed so natural—because it is.

Only later did I consider that Mary held newborn Jesus and then held him at his death. She holds all of us in the same way, from birth to death. A thirteenth-century Gaelic hymn says it all:

> There is no hound in fleetness or in chase,
> Nor wind nor rapid river,
> As quick as the mother of Christ to the bed of the dying.[30]

Life and death are part of the divine plan, and the loving Mother attends to it, as she attended to Gabriel on the day that brought God to the world in a new way. Birth and death are thin places where we encounter the presence of the Holy Mother.

I knew that day on retreat that I would never fear death again—a great gift. I knew the Holy Mother would hold me as she will hold each and every one of her children in her loving embrace on the day of their journey home.

Responding to Mary, the Mother of Jesus

Associations/archetypes: virgin, mother, unwed mother, lover, wise woman/elder, Jewess, mother bereaved of child, angels, marriage feast, refugee, taking child to temple, filled with Spirit, lily, stable, carpenter, donkey, star, three kings

Choose a Mary story you like, referring to the scripture references that appear in the endnotes for this chapter if you wish. Imagine the story spinning out at length as if it were happening to you in current times. What is happening? Describe it in your journal, including your thoughts and feelings as well as dialogue. What are some possible outcomes of your story?

Now sit at Mary's feet and talk to her. This conversation may turn into a prayer or poem in your own words.

When you are finished, wait in silence for a bit. Then reread what you have written. As you do, circle or underline at least ten words that seem to vibrate a little on the page ... those that catch your interest. If you want to, add any of your favorite juicy words as you read along.

Now pick just one word and write a sentence using it; this may be the first line of a poem.

Skip a line on your page so that what you are now writing is double spaced and pick another word. It doesn't have to be the next one in your journal entry—any word you like will do. Follow your intuition! Write another sentence or line using that word. Continue the process until you have ten lines or sentences, double spaced.

Read over what you have. You can add new lines, rearrange, break up, or repeat lines you have written, or take part of one line and add it to another. You can reverse the order of the whole thing, putting the last line first and first line last. And you can go back to add new words that help you see, hear, taste, smell, and feel what you have written. Play with it until it pleases you. Then sit back and check in with Mary to see if she has anything she'd like to add. If so, add it.

Now you are ready to write a one-line clincher to close. Maybe

Pietà by Michelangelo, 1499.

it will be a one-sentence prayer, but it doesn't have to be. Your poem could end with an irreverent chuckle like this: "That's my story and I'm stickin' to it! Amen!"

Mary Magdalene

Early CE

Commemorated July 22

Mary Magdalene has been known throughout most of Christian history as a repentant prostitute. She is possibly the most misjudged woman in scripture. Even a cursory reading of the New Testament reveals a bevy of women named Mary. In early centuries, various commentators tended to conflate their identities and then wax eloquent about the message their interpretation conveyed. Finally, in the late sixth century, Pope Gregory I gave a homily on Luke's version of the unnamed "repentant woman," identifying her as Mary Magdalene. That homily solidified her identity as a prostitute.[1]

Rosemary Radford Reuther, a prominent contemporary theologian, remarks:

> The misinterpretation seems to come about primarily from a rhetorical tendency to reduce the complexity of "Marys" in the New Testament to a simple dualism: the ever virgin mother and the repentant sinner. For the first five centuries no writer misinterpreted Mary Magdalene as a prostitute. Rather she was seen as a leading disciple.[2]

There is no confusion about that. In the Easter stories, it is Mary Magdalene who encounters Jesus at the tomb and is sent to tell the apostles. Later writers, artists, and theologians, including Reuther, testify that she is thus an "apostle to the apostles."[3] Contemporary scripture scholar Miriam Therese Winter agrees.

Both in the New Testament and Gnostic writings she is por-

Preceding page: *Magdalene's Chalice*, acrylic
and mixed media on canvas, by the author.

trayed as the spiritual companion of Jesus who alone
understood the mysteries of
his message and who interpreted these to the others,
including the male apostles,
some of whom resented her
status and the special love
Jesus had for her.[4]

This portrayal of Mag-
dalene as companion goes
back to the first commentary
on the Canticle of Canticles
(Song of Songs) written by
Hippolytus, an early bishop
of Rome. As early as 170–235,
he understood Magdalene as
the Bride of Solomon's love
song to his beloved.

He describes Magdalene
as she seeks Christ in the
garden in the words of the
Canticle: "By night, I sought
him whom my soul loveth."
He then quotes the Easter
story: "The women came by
night to see the sepulcher."
Then Hippolytus uses the

A panel from an altarpiece, *St. Mary Magdalene Preaching*, dated 1515–20 from the Netherlandish (Brussels). Almost hidden in the background behind a tree is the boat referred to on page 41. The piece is in the Philadelphia Museum of Art.
Photo by the author.

words of the Bride: "I sought him and found him not." He continues
in the Bride's words: "The watchmen that go about the city found
me." She asks: "Saw ye him whom my soul loveth?" The watchmen's
reply is given to the Easter angels guarding Jesus's tomb: "Whom do
you seek? Jesus of Nazareth? See he has risen." Then the multiple
watchmen of the Canticle become the singular gardener of the
gospel account. As the scripture continues, Magdalene speaks to
Jesus, not a gardener. When he says her name, she cries, "Rabboni,"
having found him. At the end of the encounter, Hippolytus again

uses the language of the Bride: "I found him whom my soul loveth and ... would not let him go."[5]

The connection Hippolytus made in the third century between the lover in the Canticle and Mary Magdalene is still reflected in readings used today in Catholic liturgical celebration. A hymn from the Canticle forms part of the liturgy of Magdalene's feast day on July 22. It celebrates her passionate and undying love for Christ, and allegorically, the love of the Church for Christ:

> Set me as a seal upon thine heart, as a seal upon thine arm: for love is strong as death; jealousy is cruel as the grave: the coals thereof are coals of fire, which hath a most vehement flame. ... Many waters cannot quench love, neither can the floods drown it.[6, 7]

In Hippolytus's thought, the Easter garden is also Eden. Genesis is the place of Eve's temptation and fall, but in this context, Magdalene's recognition of Jesus is the remedy for Eve's fault.[8] Thus Magdalene as the reformed Eve began to be seen as a penitent offering hope to sinners.[9]

In the second century this view of Magdalene gradually constellated into her three archetypes: strong independent woman leader/apostle; lover of Jesus; and penitent, "one who has loved much and been forgiven much."[10]

Magdalene's role as apostle began through her commission from Jesus on Resurrection morning to go tell the others, but her mission continued beyond that first assignment.

I learned many stories about her role in early Christianity while on a pilgrimage to the Black Madonna sites in Europe. These traditional stories survived not because they are exclusively based on history but because they are spoken about in a poetic, intuitive way that points at truth and enriches knowledge of life beyond mere reporting of facts.

A modern-day monk describes how he came to understand this way of knowing:

> As a monk, we sang the psalms and read scripture out loud, five hours a day. So when I went to Yale to get a Ph.D. in

New Testament, I was stunned by the academization of all of this and especially by the privileging of history—as if somehow, if we could get the history right then everything would be ok. And that was quite a contrast from living within, in fact, a living tradition in which scripture was almost kinetically inhabited. You bowed and scraped and genuflected and sang scripture. The notion of scripture as being a cadaver that one performs an autopsy on—as opposed to a living body with which one danced—was stunning to me. And I have never completely bought it. I have never bought the premise of modernity that history is the only way of knowing.[11]

I was about to be introduced to such knowing when I arrived at the Church of Les Saintes-Maries-de-la-Mer in the legendary "cradle of Christianity in France."[12] It was a hot July day on the Feast of St. Sara. Magdalene's post-Resurrection story begins here:

Mary Clopas [mother of James the Less and Joses], Mary Salome [Mother of James the Great of Compostela and John], Mary Magdalene, Martha and Lazarus and perhaps servants arrived from Palestine in a frail bark without sails or oars.[13]

More details were available from the local pastor of the church:

According to one legend, Sara, the Queen of the Gypsies, was already in the Camargue in the first century when the boat full of Marys arrived ... [and she] waded into the sea to greet them ... In another version a woman known as Sarah of Egypt ... came as a servant with the Marys on the boat as they fled persecution.[14]

Was Sarah one of the unnamed women with Mary and Martha at Christ's tomb? No one really knew. Nevertheless, the ancient legend was still powerful for the throngs of gypsies surrounding us that day on the Camargue. It was an unforgettable spectacle. Fully garbed caballeros reenacted the mythical arrival, galloping their steeds into a frothing sea to bring Black Sara's barque, arriving with the Marys, safely to shore. Then, with much solemnity, Black Sara's statue was taken to the church and dressed in a gown for veneration by each person in the crowd.

Gypsy celebration for Sara aside, for me—curiously enough—the day was filled with a sense of Mary Magdalene. The site of this gypsy festival was close to Marseilles. Ancient church tradition held that after Pentecost, she and Lazarus had gone to Ephesus with Mary, Jesus's mother, and then later continued on to Marseilles as the first evangelists to the area.[15] The region of Marseilles was one of a number of French sites associated with Magdalene's relics over centuries.[16]

Here in Saintes-Maries-de-la-Mer, we were so close not just to Marseilles but to Sainte Baume! Magdalene was believed to have lived there in a cave among rocks after retiring from the arduous work of teaching and preaching, her mission from Jesus. Had she spent the last thirty years[17] of her life here, a penitential hermit? Was her energy in the very earth where we stood? Something had drawn pilgrims here for centuries. Was it the hope that Magdalene's contrite femininity meant even great sinners could be forgiven? We are left to wonder.

Meanwhile, St. Baume is still a busy stop along the well-populated route to San Diego de Compostela.[18, 19]

I had certainly focused on Magdalene as a model penitent when she was presented to me as such in long-ago parochial school, but in later life what attracted me to her was how much she loved Jesus. In grade school, we knew nothing about Hippolytus, but fortunately, many followed Hippolytus's lead and focused on Magdalene's archetype as lover as well as apostle:

> The suggestion of love between Christ and Mary Magdalene had been celebrated by the Gnostics in the second century. The apocryphal Gospel of Mary portrays her as a supreme initiate into Christ's mysteries and the teacher of the other apostles, while the Gnostic Gospel of Philip sees the union of man and woman as a symbol of healing and peace ... [it] dwells on the relationship of Christ and the Magdalene, who, it says, was often kissed by him.[20]

Christine Bourgeault, a contemporary Episcopal priest and scripture scholar, proposes that theirs was a unifying, mystical love because Mary understood Jesus's teachings and was able to "deeply absorb and integrate his spiritual methodology. She had learned the secret of unbroken union with him across the realms."[21]

Bourgeault explains their connection across the mysterious gulf between the death of Jesus and his meeting with her on Resurrection morning.

> It is ... love holding vigil when everyone else has gone home ... their hearts stretched taut to accommodate the vast distance that has suddenly opened up between them.... And it is love that remains there for those entire three days ... holding his tether like falcon and falconer as he descends into the underworld. The sheer tenacity of her presence is not the result of ordinary human courage.... It is an act of substituted love, as instant by instant she gives herself that he might be well. For those three days she holds in her own heart all that death has left unresolved in him—the swirling events of that final week, the anguish of betrayal and abandonment, the wrenching final "My God, my God, why have you abandoned me?" She takes his anguish into her own heart, so that he might travel freely to accomplish the cosmic task he has been given to do ...
>
> So it is on the morning of resurrection, her firmness drawing his circle ... she recognizes that he has ... ended where he begun. She is the last person he sees before he leaves the human realm and the first person he sees upon returning... Then with a forceful, "Go and tell the others," he sends her forth.[22]

Bougeault goes on to say that she is "not proposing that the whole sacred drama of Christ's Passion and resurrection ... is only a love song ... [but] that it is also, among other things, a love song."[23]

Magdalene is thus named as an archetype of the divine wisdom, or of the divine feminine "based on traditional wisdom teachings on the human soul as a bridge between the visible and invisible realms laid out in the gospels of Thomas, Mary Magdalene and Philip."[24]

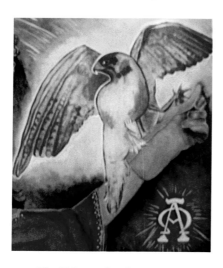

The Falconer by the author.

This is Bougeault's frame of reference in explicating Mary Magdalene.

The complete feminine divine archetype, psychologically speaking, would include a wise woman leader, which fits the apostolic Magdalene. When one speculates on how long she might have lived,[25] she also emerges as a mature elder, an archetypal wise woman, offering inspiration to older women often held in low esteem by their various cultures.

Magdalene as feminine archetypal lover is dramatized in ancient commentaries from Hippolytus and explored in newly discovered documents Bourgeault studied. The early characterization of Magdalene as whore by the sixth century bishop no doubt was intended to suggest a simple dyptic (typically a two-panel painting, perhaps hinged) with the Virgin Mary on one side and the Magdalene on the other[26]—under whom were subsumed the other nonvirgins (sinners or not) found in early scriptures.

Contemporary mariologist and author Marina Warner explains how thought about Mary in those times impacted how Magdalene was considered:

> The rise of the cult of Mary Magdalene through the high middle ages and the Counter Reformation kept pace with the growth of belief in the Immaculate Conception of the Virgin. For the more Mary was held to be free of all taint of sin, actual and original, the less the ordinary sinner could turn to her for consolation in his weakness, and the more he needed the individual saints whose own lapses held out hope for him.[27]

Thus we see Mary Magdalene with the potential dark side of feminine sexuality projected onto her. The projection acknowledges a human capacity to misuse sexuality, while at the same time offering the possibility for repentance.

An aspect of the feminine divine archetype that is still lacking is that of the ancient triple goddess: maiden-mother-crone. This is the archetype of a complete woman, fully sensual and virtuous, integrated as virgin, lover, mother, leader, and wise elder capable of standing on her own even surrounded by loved ones, but not defined exclusively or prohibitively by any relationship or role.

We can only approach this multi-valented figure by considering her archetypal attributes one by one. With Magdalene, we have a choice: strong female leader, lover, or penitent, forgiven because she loved much.

About Love

Why delight in empty days?
When the end of
Love's song kills
all joy?

Kiss that limit
in your soul—

that sweet healing kiss
will push wide
the gentle door
of your heart

to Love's avalanche.[28]

Discovering Magdalene

My acquaintance with Mary Magdalene began before the 1960s and the Vatican Council. During those same grade school years when I met Miriam in Bible study, Magdalene's story was part of the gospel read in church. I wasn't clear if she was the woman we learned about who had been caught in adultery, but I did learn that Jesus chased seven devils out of her.[29] The adultery part was both impressive and scary to me. I was waking up to new sexual feelings as adolescent hormones raged.

The nuns in our school weren't from Ireland, where shelters for unwed mothers were run by nuns. Nevertheless, I'd heard of "the Magdalenes," and though I wasn't sure of all the details, I definitely got the drift that it wouldn't be a good thing to be one or to live in one of those places for pregnant girls. Their hormones had probably raged too!

At the end of the Catholic school day each Friday, the nuns marched us across the street to the church confessional. I was afraid of that little dark box and of any mortal sin that could send me right to hell. The nuns talked to us about purity and coached us not to be alone with boys. It was nothing clinical like today's sex education, but the message was perhaps more ominous for its vague questions about "touching," "how many times," and "alone or with others," which were all part of the weekly preparation for confession.

So when I heard about Mary Magdalene being forgiven and getting all those devils out of her, I figured she was a saint I could consult for help. My mother had often told me that when I wanted something I was like a devil after a soul. Even as a twelve-year-old, I knew I was plenty determined. I wondered if I might resemble a devil in some other ways I didn't know about. If the devil of determination was in me, who else might be there? I decided I was definitely a Mary Magdalene case!

I liked Mother Mary, sure—all of us girls did. We each aspired to be the lucky one chosen by the nuns to place the crown of flowers on her statue during the annual parish May Crowning procession. Mary, the Blessed Mother, as she was called, was Jesus's mother, after all, but I didn't feel maternal as a girl. I think I'd already had a bit too much babysitting of younger siblings as an assistant Mom. For me, maternal feelings came much later. So I didn't really identify with Mary. She was just way too good. No, Magdalene suited me better.

Over time, I gradually began to sort out her stories. Scripture studies after the Vatican Council made it clear that she was not the adulterous woman about to be stoned, or the sister of Martha at Bethany. A woman who suffered infirmities? Yes, perhaps. The scriptures did mention demons. Would the writers of those ancient documents speak of demons instead of depression? Psychology developed much later, of course ... and psychological problems certainly can be devilish!

Mary Magdalene is specifically identified on only three occasions in the canon: as one of the women following Jesus who supported his ministry from their own means;[30] as one of those present at Jesus's death on Calvary;[31] and—most notably—as the first to meet Jesus on Resurrection morning.[32]

She is one of many women named Mary in the stories about Jesus, attesting to the widespread admiration of Miriam, the sister of Moses, an illustrious ancestor. Among them all, Mary of Magdala heads the list,[33] according to biblical scholar Miriam Therese Winter.

> Tradition supports her leadership role, both in the New Testament and in the Gnostic writings. In several Gnostic gospels, she is portrayed as the spiritual companion of Jesus who alone understood the mysteries of his message and who interpreted these to the others, including the male apostles, some of whom resented her status and the special love Jesus had for her. One can only wonder if the strength of this latter tradition was in some way the basis for discrediting Mary and her historicity.[34]

When I learned this part of Mary Magdalene's story, I saw her in the same tradition as her prophetic ancestor Miriam, also a woman forced to the edge of the camp by the leaders of her time. Then I read Susan Haskins's study of Magdalene, which documents her many evolutions in two thousand years of ecclesiastical and cultural history.[35] I understood that one aspect of this woman, her penitence, was magnified and that her role as a leader, a powerful woman loved by Jesus, was largely obscured. Biblical scholars since the Vatican Council have "restored Mary Magdalene to her New Testament role as chief female disciple, and apostle to the apostles. ... The woman so long regarded as the penitent sinner has been shown in her true light."[36]

Such revisionist studies have been encouraging for women who clearly have been excluded from full participation and leadership in secular and religious institutions since before the time of Jesus. The struggle continues today.

As a Roman Catholic woman with a lifelong awareness of a call from God but no aspiration for ordination, I shocked myself when I attended an Episcopal church. A recently baptized friend, Darlene, had invited me to her Sunday service.

As the liturgy started, four fully vested women walked confidently and joyfully to the altar to lead us in prayer and the breaking of the bread. I suddenly had tears in my eyes and a large lump in my throat. It was hard to breathe! Their smiles and grace were so right, there at the altar of God. My heart overflowed with feelings I remembered from my own vows years earlier. While I had never consciously desired ordination, that day with Darlene I celebrated those Episcopal women. And at the same moment, I was saddened that girls in my Catholic diocese are not permitted even to assist at the altar. That spot is reserved for males.

Imagine my surprise and delight at recent speculation about Leonardo DaVinci's famous painting The Last Supper. Did the artist intend the beloved disciple at Jesus's side to be Magdalene, not John?[37] I always wanted to be a favorite of Jesus, like John. I wanted that seat next to him and my head on his shoulder. Better yet if that figure was Magdalene. So yes, for reasons other than my youthfully mistaken devotion to Mary Magdalene for sexual guidance, I now see her as a powerful woman Jesus loved, a woman to emulate for her strength.

When I painted her, we became even better acquainted. Immediately her graceful femininity came to the fore on my canvas. She was beautiful, her face as lovely as her spirit in God's eyes. I knew the painting's title was to be Magdalene's Chalice. She would have had her place among the women preparing the Passover meal, setting the table, cooking the food, polishing the chalice. Magdalene, Jesus's mother, and the other women would have been there at table sharing the cup of blessing. The chalice is, to me, a significant symbol of communing with Jesus and with each other. Along with the chalice, an ointment jar had to appear in the painting. Whether or not Magdalene anointed Jesus's feet, scripture tells us she was among the women who anointed his body for burial.

As soon as Sabbath ended, she hurried back to the garden at dawn, worried about the gravesite. Light had been fading when Jesus's body was quickly sealed away. There had been no time to anoint him with herbs and fragrant oils. But now she carried her ointment jars and bags of dried flowers. Just as she met a stranger dressed in white, she could see that the tomb was empty.

A panel from an altarpiece of *Saint Mary Magdalene* by Ambrosio Bergognone 1515, Lombardy, Italy, portrays her with the oil of anointing and long flowing hair. Philadelphia Museum of Art. Photo by the author.

Shocked and frightened, she cried, "Where have you laid him?" Then, with one word, he calmed her: "Mary!" And so she was the first to meet Jesus, thinking he was the gardener.

And so he is ... the one who tends us in this earthly garden, a place of life, fecundity, growth, and beauty. May the greenery of Magdalene's Chalice awaken us to our own encounter with the Divine Gardener she met that joyful day!

Responding to Mary Magdalene

Associations/archetypes: lover, teacher, apostle, penitent, seeker, leader, wise woman/elder, priestess, garden, falcon, chalice, ointment, one who keeps vigil, maligned woman, forced to the edge of camp

Mary Magdalene had a great love for Jesus. It probably started the first time she saw him in the midst of a crowd and heard his profound invitation to love. Perhaps he spoke the words of the Book of Revelation "I stand at the door and knock. If anyone hears my voice and opens the door, I will enter and dine with him."[38]

Magdalene began a young girl, a virgin, as all women do. Was her heart yearning for love? Had she become disconnected from her true heart's longing somewhere along the way? Had she fallen into the dark side of her love energy, carelessly wasting what was so precious? Was that why Jesus's presence and invitation magnetized all her energies? This woman did not hold back. She had to open the door—her heart was flung open! Whatever she was doing in her life stopped. She plunged headlong into Jesus's presence, arms loaded with luxurious oils to lavish on her beloved. Who could resist such outpouring? There are always faults and failures along the path of love, but they can be forgiven. Jesus told her: "You have been forgiven much because you have loved much."[39]

Although Luke does not name the woman, we can consider Magdalene the lover archetype in this story, as Hippolytus did putting the words of the Bride from the Song of Songs into her mouth. Once she found that other who drew her very soul, all else fell aside. She sought him whom her heart loved, giving all to this itinerant prophet who went about doing good. On darker days, she suffered when he suffered, and was excruciated as all lovers are when they are separated. Did she internalize Jesus's vision so completely that she carried it to others in her last years as teacher and wise elder?

How do you see yourself as lover? Are you the innocent, still searching? Or are you the disconnected, not having found the one your heart loves, letting what is precious slip away? Do you see yourself as committed to the good of the one you love as to your own wishes? Have giving and receiving love taught you to love yourself and God more deeply?

Perhaps your commitment has been to a single or vowed life where your generative energies are spent in service through love. Or perhaps you have lost your life partner and know what it means to suffer grief, defined by some as love that has no place to make its home.

Whatever your chosen life walk or stage—maiden, mother, or crone—reflect on what love means to you. Sit quietly at the feet of Magdalene and listen to what the Spirit may say. Then write in your journal.

The Samaritan Woman

Early CE

The story of Jesus and the Samaritan woman is precious for several reasons: It is the only mention we have of this woman in the scriptures. Their conversation is the longest Jesus had with a solitary woman in the entire New Testament. And this woman was an outsider.[1] We don't know if she was historical or intended by the author to represent all outsiders. Either way, if we take a look at her times and culture, we can understand more deeply the meaning of her appearance in this unique story about Jesus.

We know that Jesus had his frustrations in trying to get his message across to the stiff-necked Jews, so maybe it was a welcome break for him to be in Samaria and meet this receptive woman. Jesus wanted to bring the outsiders in, to welcome them. He said, "The hour is coming, and is now here, when true worshipers will worship the Father in Spirit and truth; and indeed the Father seeks such people to worship him. God is Spirit and those who worship him must worship in Spirit and truth."[2] This was Jesus's way of telling her their ancient disagreement about where to worship was no longer a reason for them to be estranged, as the Jews and Samaritans had been. It was a message of unity: they could join together as true worshipers of the God of Spirit and truth.

The rigid formality of rabbinic dictates may well have been the reason Jesus usually spoke very briefly to women when he was at home. The scriptures record him speaking to women on twelve occasions, excepting Resurrection appearances,[3] but in few words. Was this because rabbis were to avoid conversation with women,

---

Preceding page: *At the Well,* acrylic
and mixed media on canvas, by the author.

especially married women? Perhaps. No woman Jesus spoke with was identified as married.[4]

Jesus specifically said that the Samaritan woman was not married to the man she was with at that time. It's not clear just what her status was. Had she been in a Levirate marriage[5] and was her final husband now elderly and impotent, thus not able to meet the letter of the law about a husband's duty? Perhaps. In Mark's gospel, Jesus answered a question posed by a group of Sadducees who described a woman who was widowed, then given to her brother-in-law according to Levirate marriage law:

> Their first born son would be considered to be the son of the deceased husband. In this case, they [the Sadducees] imagined that seven brothers-in-law married her in succession without having a son. This Jewish law is found in Deuteronomy, a book of the Torah familiar to the Samaritans. In it, the woman was not allowed to refuse to marry any of the brothers, even if she despised some of them. Levirate marriage often involved serial rape.[6]

One scripture scholar wonders why Jesus didn't take the opportunity to preach on the unfairness of the Levirate marriage. Maybe he did,

> but his words might not have been considered significant, thus the Gospel writers might not have recorded Jesus's comments. Alternately, they might have recorded Jesus's criticism of Levirate marriage in the original, autograph (sic) copy of their Gospels. However, a later copyist might have deleted the passage. As archeologists are fond of saying; "Absence of proof is not proof of absence."[7]

Others question whether the scriptures selected in the canon reflect the events of Jesus's life so much as they frame the Christian story for particular evangelization purposes.[8]

Jesus's few exchanges with women in scripture may mean that women weren't typically present in the market or public places where Jesus taught. More likely, it just meant male authors in their time and place paid little attention to women who did, of course, attend synagogue and some of their encounters with Jesus were in the precincts of their place of prayer.

When one considers the entire New Testament, including not just the four gospels but the Acts of the Apostles and their letters, it only mentions about forty women by name, a few of them not followers but figures known through the historian Josephus and others.[9] Anyone who reads through the gospel stories will notice there are many unnamed women too:

> ...the woman who anoints Jesus in all four gospels ... the Jewish women said to have been present at the crucifixion ... the women who travel with Susanna, Johanna, and Mary Magdala and support [Jesus] financially ... the women on the way of the cross who praise the breasts and uterus of his mother, the women of Jerusalem who lament Jesus on the same occasion; the women accompanying the male disciples in Jerusalem after the resurrection ...[10]

Certainly some of these writers intended the unnamed women to stand for all those who loved Jesus, bravely staying near him to then end, then continuing in faith at the side of the disciples.

Among the unnamed women is the woman of Samaria, the woman at the well. She has remained "un-sainted" and unnamed in Roman Catholicism, just a generic Samaritan woman. Despite her anonymity and all the uncertainties surrounding Jesus's exchanges with women, the story of this plucky woman at the well has been included in liturgical readings since the days of the early church. Her story was told because of its meaning—she stood, an outsider who came to faith in Jesus—the embodiment of many who followed. In that sense, it is true.

As history unfolded, Eastern Orthodoxy, Byzantine Catholicism, and other rites emerged from the church of Rome. In these dispensations, we discover the Samaritan woman had finally been named. She was baptized[11] as St. Photine, "the luminous one," thus both named and raised to sainthood. She is also called St. Photina. Eastern Orthodoxy sometimes calls her St. Svetlana, another name that means "light," "shining," "luminescence," "pure," "blessed," and "holy," Svetlana being found commonly in Russia, Bulgaria, Macedonia, Serbia, and Belarus.[12]

The Eastern Orthodox tradition honors St. Photina by teaching a lengthy history of her life after she met Jesus. Her brothers and extended family as well as their disputes with Emperor Nero are also part of the chronicle.

One tale, perhaps based more on legend than history, claims that St. Photina preached to one hundred slave girls of Nero's daughter Domnina, and converted all of them. Nero was upset and began serious persecution of Photina and her clan, especially when his daughter ordered the empire's gold to be sold and proceeds given to the poor.[13] After surviving torture, Photina died when Nero had her thrown down a well.[14]

It seems to me this heroic Samaritan woman, who immediately after her encounter with Jesus proselytized her neighbors, deserves to be named and acknowledged as a saint, whether the stories about her later life are historic or not. She is the only women in our present scriptural canon portrayed in a lengthy dialog with Jesus and deserves her place because of what she represents in Christian tradition, if not because of testimony of ancient documents. This open-minded outsider portrays a seeker and eager convert who led her people to the God of Spirit and truth through Jesus. She was an apostle of the first order.

Discovering the Samaritan Woman

The women followers of Jesus have been close to me for a long time, but I didn't always know it. As I think of them now, I remember walking past mosaics of many Holy Women in a narrow stairway of the church of Our Lady of Montserrat in Spain. It was a dreamlike experience to glimpse them surrounding me, life size and glinting beautifully in blue and gold mosaic.

I jostled between them and the sea of pilgrims climbing to venerate the Black Madonna statue smiling down from the cupola above us: St. Anne, St. Elizabeth, the early martyrs Catherine, Agnes, Margaret. Was St. Scholastica here? Likely, since she was St. Benedict's sister and this was a Benedictine monastery. What about Magdalene, or the Samaritan Woman? I reared back from the walls, hoping to recognize more women, to get a full view, perhaps a photo, but I was too close to see them clearly. I never did get that photo, but I will not forget how it felt to be surrounded by that phalanx of feminine energy on my way to the Mother.

I'll never know if the woman of Samaria was there, but she has long since become immortalized in my heart. She showed up on one of the most painful days of my life.

We had been married twenty years that summer. I thought we'd never kept anything from each other. I didn't know that all was not well in my marriage. Then my husband made a revelation so sudden and shattering that it terrified me. I was stunned, in free fall, with nothing to hold on to ... as though the ground had disappeared from beneath my feet.

After the first few days of confusion, we tried to talk. We didn't get far. I felt like I was talking to a stranger I'd never seen before. Our warm connectedness had been severed with one blow. Tears flooded me every time I tried to speak. Finally, I got a few words out. "I don't understand any of this. We need to talk to someone."

Bob sat silently for a long moment, then leaned back with a sigh. "I know you want me to come with you, and I will. But not now. First, I want to go away for a while."

"Go away?" Another shock.

"Yeah, to California. I need to know how I really feel before I can do any counseling with you."

I was stunned again. My mind raced to stay ahead of an avalanche of questions. Where would he go? What would he do? When would he know how he felt about me and our marriage? Twenty years of security with him suddenly and painfully went up like a puff of smoke.

He went.

All I could do was hang on. In the meantime, I tried to cope by just putting one foot in front of the other to get through the day, and at the same time coping with my son's questions. It was only late at night that I could be alone. Often I sat at the kitchen table, lonely in the quiet house, poring over the newspaper. I couldn't ignore the frightening questions in my mind: What if Bob disappeared, never to return from California? Would that actually happen? I hadn't heard from him since he'd left. His silence did not portend well.

I had to make some practical decisions. I moved a yellow marker down the "Help Wanted: Professional/Administrative" columns. Then, pushing the paper away, I laid my head down on my arms and cried.

The nice little box that was my life had been thrown on the floor where it shattered into a million pieces. How would I ever put it together again? My trust in Bob was ruined. Maybe I couldn't trust God either. *Where are You now, God? Are You gone too?*

The question hung there in the emptiness of the cold kitchen. Maybe He was. I couldn't stop sobbing.[15]

Gradually I realized that a peaceful quietness was coming over me. I took a deep breath, feeling my body begin to relax. It was a relief. Even my tense stomach gradually calmed down. I hadn't been able to eat; I had always carried my stress that way since I was a kid.

I stood to stretch, then wondered ... Could I even eat something? I did feel a little empty.

Sliding my chair away from the table, I went to the counter, found a loaf of bread, a plate, and a napkin. Then I stood there, knife full of peanut butter. Something happened. The quiet peace suddenly felt like the presence of a dear and close friend, almost as though a loving arm were wrapped around my shoulders, a warm cheek next to mine.

She gently whispered in my ear, "God is close to the broken hearted, the crushed in spirit He saves."[16]

A wave of warmth slowly spread over me, beginning in my heart. I somehow knew who was with me. It was the woman Jesus met at the well. I couldn't see her, but I knew she was graceful, beautiful, smiling, and standing right next to me in my kitchen. There was a little note of laughter in her voice when she spoke again: "I always had trouble with men too!"

At that moment, I was far from a realization that came much later—that in the big plan, the task Bob and I had come together to accomplish was complete. Now, years later, I understand that the Samaritan woman had herself lived in terrific turmoil when she met Jesus. She understood me.

This woman was an outsider but had the mind of a seeker. As she came to draw water in her Samaritan village, Jesus sat alone by the well and asked her for a drink. She was amazed he spoke to her, a woman and a Samaritan—she knew well that Jews were hostile to Samaritans. As she stood there looking at him, he told her, "If you knew the gift of God, if you knew who it is who is asking this of you, you would have asked me for a drink, and I would have given you living water."[17]

He had no bucket and the well was deep. Jesus's next words were even more mystifying. "Whoever drinks the water that I can give will never thirst again; for the water I give becomes an inner spring welling up to eternal life."[18]

She understood what thirst was and knew her own deep neediness. Jesus saw into her heart, knew all that was unspoken there, but offered no challenge to her. Instead, he quietly suggested she get her husband.

Then came the moment of truth. She said she has no husband. Jesus knew she had had five husbands.[19] Certainly my feelings of abandonment were nothing compared to hers. What would it be like to go through five separations? Samaritans and Jews both took their marriage rules from the Torah, which gave men permission to divorce but not women. These rules also required a widow to marry her brother-in-law.

What had happened to this unfortunate woman? Was she married at twelve or thirteen to a man old enough to be her father who then divorced her? Or perhaps she was barren and a disappointment to her husband? Or did the husband prefer a slave girl to his wife? Was he impotent? Was she widowed and passed to one brother-in-law after another? Or was she too beautiful, too intelligent, and the husbands insecure? That she was intelligent and a good listener is evident in this meeting with Jesus, but intelligence wasn't necessarily a desirable wifely quality in a culture where women could easily be abandoned if the husband decided to reject them.

I treasured my encounter with this brave woman at the well. Whatever she had endured, her encounter with Jesus strengthened her. She recognized him as a prophet, the awaited messiah, and spread the news until many more believed in him.[20]

She took me, too, beyond the day of our meeting over peanut butter to an encounter with Jesus. As he had promised her "living water, an inner spring welling up to eternal life," he soon promised me, "I am always with you." And so it has been.

It was a few years later that I painted the woman at the well that appears on the first page of this chapter. I wanted her to be as beautiful as I imagined her soul was to God. She sat there, a rapt listener, looking intently at me out of her canvas ... as she would have looked at Jesus, entranced, unmoving, in no hurry to run back home with her large jar of water. She sits in a golden doorway surrounded by roses and greenery, an inviting natural setting, a liminal place between everyday needs and the mansions that Jesus promises await us in His father's house.

If you look closely at the painting, you will see pages from a missal my mother gave me when I took first vows as a Franciscan nun. They tell the story of the woman at the well, one page printed in Latin, the facing page printed in English. Behind the bank of roses, you can also see sheet music for *Liebestraum*, a song of love, to recall what passed between her and Jesus that day. It was a great outpouring of love. It changed her life.

Responding to the Samaritan Woman

Associations/archetypes: lover, seeker, leader, listener, wise woman, apostle, outsider, questioner/challenger, well, water, unnamed, many times wed

This woman at the well makes only one appearance in scripture, but it is a rich one.

Her one-to-one meeting with Jesus is the only lengthy conversation he had with a woman that we find there. In the exchange, we learn she had had five husbands and was with a sixth man, although not married to him. Think about her culture. She likely was married very young, by her father's arranging and with little choice. What happened after that? Was she widowed young? Did her husband decide to divorce her because she was barren? For other reasons? Did she really want to marry a brother-in-law now? Was this another relationship about which she had no choice?

Imagine her confiding to you, "Yes, I had problems with men." That likely meant the problems came up with husbands ... but perhaps not just with husbands, but her father and brothers-in-law as well. Do you think she was braced to have a problem with Jesus too when he spoke to her, a Samaritan, at the well?

Most of us have had some problems with men: fathers, brothers, husbands, sons, employers, clergy, colleagues, or supposed friends. Imagine sitting down at your kitchen table with this Samaritan woman for a chat over a glass of wine from the vineyards of Samaria. We know she was a good listener and a wise woman with an open mind. Tell her the whole story. Then listen. What does she have to tell you? Does she also tell you something about Jesus? What do you learn from her thoughts and feelings? As women, do you have struggles in common? Are women always "outsiders"? Invite Jesus to join you. What is your three-way conversation?

For men reading this meditation, consider the struggles you have had with women in your life. Have your intentions ever been misunderstood or doubted by a woman as Jesus initially was in this episode? If so, how did it resolve? Have you felt frustrated that misogyny in the culture can play out negatively for you and the women you love? When you are in a group of women, do you feel yourself an outsider? Enter the conversation with this woman and Jesus; then listen to what they have to say to you.

Journal about this reflection. End by writing a prayer that captures a bit of your heartfelt response. You may want to share it with a spiritual director, friend, sister, brother, or husband/wife/partner.

Holy Women of Scripture Meet

*As I reflected on the four Holy Women of Scripture I'd painted,
they fell into conversation in my imagination. Mary, the mother of
Jesus, Mary Magdalene, Miriam, and the Samaritan Woman—were
they acquainted? Well, of course, Miriam's days during the Exodus
were long past by the time her two namesakes came along. However,
it is interesting to speculate what the other three might have to
say to each other. Their conversation is my version of midrash, a
process Hasidic rabbis used, taking scriptures and putting them
together in new ways to teach a lesson.*

Miriam: Yes, we are joined in spirit, all women of the desert, yes.
Like me, you grew up knowing about my powerful brother Moses.
And how he led us to our very own land, out of the brutal desert,
out of our abandonment ... to our homeland.

Mary: Well, Miriam, I'm named for you, right along with half the
women of Israel! (All laugh.) I loved the idea of you as my Big Sister
of the Victory Dance that night—we never forget. Every year, we
relive our escape! And Miriam, as Moses's baby gaze went right to
your heart, I too saw in my infant the promise of Great Things!
My heart still rejoices just knowing my God called me to raise this
precious son. His eyes spoke to me from the first time I held him
to my breast ... and I was never the same.

Samaritan Woman (to Mary and Miriam): I know something about that gaze! And like you both, I'll ever forget it. That day at the well, this man of your people sat looking at me. I pulled my veil across my face and tried to hurry filling my water jar. To my complete amazement, he spoke: "Please bring me a drink." I too felt a stranger. We Samaritans were like dirt among you Chosen Ones, the People of God ...

I was almost afraid to turn around, but I stole a quick glance. His eyes, I'll never forget. His smile—and he definitely was a Jew. I could hardly speak. It was a moment that changed my life. I'll never forget. I was so afraid at first. Would someone see us?

We Samaritans were despised, shunned among you Chosen Ones, the People of God ...

Trembling, I sat down on the edge of the well ...Would I be stoned for talking with him? The thought terrified me ... and then he told me my whole life ... this prophet!

(She glances toward Magdalene.) Well, you, Magdalene, you understand ...

Magdalene: Yes, I do! That gaze fell on me too. The same gaze you (turning to Mary) recognized in him when he was so very young. And I was very young when I first saw him in our town. The crowd bustled around him, elbowing to get closer, perhaps to see a miracle. That was what captured my imagination. I was just a kid and had heard the old stories about our healers and prophets, of course. But here was this man, right in our village. My sister and I kept to the edge of the crowd. Our brother was around there someplace too, Lazarus—always wandering around.

But that was just the beginning, that day Jesus first came ... we later all got to know each other very well.

Mary: Do you remember that wedding? We were all there. It was Joseph's nephew, you know, on the side of my in-laws? (Magdalene laughs in remembrance!)

Mary continues: Yes, poor planning. They ran out of wine!

Miriam (breaking in): Hey, a good thing there was water around! Remember my story? Lots of fortuitous water, first baby brother floating in the Nile, and later the rest of us running for our lives across the Sea of Reeds. Our God does provide, even with those in-laws of yours, Mary!

Magdalene (laughs remembering): Yes, that was about the time I broke in on that Pharisee's party and washed Jesus's feet. That guy had no manners! Hmm, I've never really thought about the water like this before ...

Samaritan Woman: Well, nobody ever wrote down the end of my story, but Jesus did pour water over my head and bring me into the family. You all know that. And how welcomed I felt to be part of one big family with you at Passover.

Mary: Yes, yes ... like one big family at Passover for years (touching the Samaritan, smiling). Remember how we all would dance and sing? "Horse and chariot ..." our skirts flying, our tambourines a celebration?

All: Yes yes! Amen! Amen! Alleluia!

Holy Monastery
Women

Brigid

451–525 CE

Commemorated February 1

St. Brigid of Ireland is believed to have been born in 451 and to have lived approximately seventy-four years.[1] Before we begin Brigid's life story, the first we have of an Irish saint—and a woman at that—we need to put ourselves back in time. Modern scholar Dara Molloy tells us the Celts lived on their forested island in an undeveloped natural world. They settled on the coasts and near lakes and rivers because the center of their island was basically untamed forest.[2] To them, a forest wasn't a business opportunity of some kind as it might be to us. It was forest primeval, a place of mystery and sacred presence.

You may have heard the Celts worshiped trees. Well, certainly the oak was greatly valued, but for its strength and steadiness, not necessarily for its divinity. Perhaps the ancients connected with the mystery of the Divine through those trees in the darkness of the forest primeval. It seems possible to me.

Besides the wildness of the land in Brigid's day, we need to remember it was a time before stories were written down. The Irish, even now, are known for their gift of gab, imagination, and storytelling. In the fifth century, the Druids, an educated class of the Celts, memorized and passed down lengthy tales, genealogies, and even histories. When many of them became Christian and some of them monks, the storytelling tradition continued over centuries, often taking on new content and losing some of the old, of course.[3] The Christian Irish tales, like Aesop's fables, were intended for instruction and motivation while at the same time

Preceding page: *Brigid of Ireland*, acrylic
and mixed media on canvas, by the author.

providing entertainment—which is why they have survived.

The earliest Brigid stories date as far back as one hundred years after her death. We know from these early sources that she was born to a woman slave named Brocca and baptized by St. Patrick. When Brocca became pregnant, her owner, a chieftain, sold her to a Druid priest. The chieftain's other bondswoman/wife became jealous and threatened to leave. But this would deprive the chieftain of her dowry, so it was Brocca who had to leave.[4] (We see here why Brigid has been named as a helper to broken families.)

An amusing early anecdote is told about Christian baby Brigid. When her adoptive Druid daddy tried to feed her, she repeatedly spit out her breakfast. After a bit of this, he somehow found a white cow with red ears to provide her milk. Maybe well-meaning, devout monks in later time spun this breakfast episode to emphasize the Christian side of Brigid's story—who knows? It is, however, one of many "milk" stories about her and the reason why milk and white cows with red ears are associated with her.

Even her birth was a milk story. A mysterious prophecy had foretold that Brocca's child would be born neither within nor outside a house. And so it came to pass! Her very pregnant mother was carrying buckets of milk on February 1, the day of Imbolc, the beginning of Celtic spring. Brigid must have been in a hurry to arrive because she was born just as her mother had one foot in the house and one on the threshold. Of course, the milk went everywhere. But a kindly neighbor woman was on hand to help. Amid the excitement, there was no time to run and boil water, so the mother's helper used what was at hand to wash the newly arrived baby Brigid: milk![5]

The little girl spent her early years at her mother's side. By the time she was about ten, Brigid was back in her father's household as a slave. She quickly exhausted his patience, however, by giving away to the poor the treasures she found among his household belongings. Finally, he decided to sell her to someone else. That required the king's permission, so they set off to obtain it. Upon arrival, Brigid was left in the carriage while her father went to speak with the king.

Meanwhile a ragged man spotted Brigid in the rich carriage. She listened as he told her the story of his starving children. Touched

Brigid of Kildare by Marcy Hall.

with pity, Brigid gave him the only thing of value in the carriage: her father's bejeweled golden sword. Both knew it was sure to be worth plenty! Then her father returned. I can just see him taking her by the ear and marching her into the king's palace. When this ten-year-old, with wisdom and grace beyond her years, spoke, the king was taken aback. "If I had your power and wealth, I would give it all to the Lord," she told the king.

Apprehensive, the king turned to her father: "It is not for us to deal with this maiden, for her merit before God is higher than ours."[6] He freed Brigid, and his words have lived on after him.

So Brigid's young life continued. In a few years, she grew into a beauty. Her brothers noticed and started thinking of all the things they could do with the generous bride price they might get for such a girl. However, God had already given Brigid other ideas. In what we can only imagine was a violent episode, the brothers attempted to drag her off to a rich suitor. She managed to struggle free, then turned and said, "It is unlikely that anyone would ask for a blind girl." Before they could stop her, she scratched out one of her eyes. The brothers gave up. When Brigid was satisfied that she had secured her future, she healed her eye with one touch, and the story ends.[7]

The storyteller may well have intended to set Brigid in the company of saints already known to the new Irish Christians: early virgin martyrs who faced forcible marriages. For me, the dramatic story just emphasizes Brigid's good sense. She knew she literally needed two good eyes to focus on her vision. Establishing monasteries all over Ireland to serve the poor, the ill, and the forsaken while managing the creation of illuminated scriptures would take everything she could give, including good eyesight!

It wasn't long before Brigid made her vows before the bishop and many onlookers. Everyone present saw flames rise from her head as she repeated the words of the ritual. Did the bishop think of the Pentecostal fire that fell on Jesus's early followers gathered in the Upper Room? As observers today, we might. Whatever his thoughts, that day he granted Brigid unusual canonical authority similar to his own. The story suggests—and from the vantage point of history, we can see— that Brigid indeed lived out an extraordinary call from God.

Interestingly enough, although a nun vowed to celibacy and never a mother, Brigid was strongly associated not just with milk but with motherhood. An early telling of the life of Brigid maintains there was a young cleric in her monastery whom she treated like a foster son. She had taken him in, concerned for his spiritual as well as physical welfare. Since it is said that St. Brigid invented whistling, I imagine this young lad was a bit of a trickster who got on famously with his playful foster mom. He may well have sought her advice about his need for a soul friend, an *Anam Cara,* the Irish term for it—a special friend, a serious friend, one to turn to, one with whom to share one's heart, spiritual needs, and prayer.[8]

She said, "Go forth and eat nothing until you get a soul-friend, for anyone without a soul-friend is like a body without a head; is like the water of a polluted lake, neither good for drinking nor for washing. That is the person without a soul-friend."[9]

We have seen that St. Brigid has been the subject of many stories over time. She has been portrayed in many images as well, some of which may touch you as an individual and some of them less so, for reasons we can't always explain. As we go beyond what is obvious in the story or image, however, we may uncover other layers of meaning and perhaps find inspiration.

Generic holy card images that could pass for any saint or abbess don't do justice to the unique spirit that was Brigid's. And perhaps ancient images carried over from the Celtic goddess Brigid aren't the whole story either. The goddess was considered a patron of poets, for example.[10] Is the goddess behind it, then, when our saint is shown with sheets of vellum or a book? I think our Brigid deserves her own standing as poet and artist.

After all, she attracted many scholarly artists to her monastery to create a poetry of scripture in illuminated manuscripts of vellum and gold. And many poems and prayers are attributed to Brigid herself. She certainly wrote some of them.

In one early prayer, she wants to throw a great party for God and his family.

> I should like a great lake of finest ale
> For the King of kings.
> I should like a table of the choicest food
> For the family of heaven.
> Let the ale be made from the fruits of faith,
> And the food be forgiving love.
> I should welcome the poor to my feast,
> For they are God's children.
> I should welcome the sick to my feast,
> For they are God's joy.
> Let the poor sit with Jesus at the highest place,
> And the sick dance with the angels.
> God bless the poor,
> God bless the sick,
> And bless our human race.
> God bless our food,
> God bless our drink,
> All homes, O God, embrace.[11]

She certainly knew how to celebrate! This was no tea party—Brigid would serve a lake of ale. Forget our little champagne fountains. And as for the entertainment she has in mind? How about dancing with angels? Dancing meant music around her as well as in her heart. For the party, surely she ordered a Celtic melody and the rhythm of flute and drum, and certainly the angelic sweetness of the harp.

This enchanting instrument comes up early in Brigid's stories. We've already seen her in trouble with her family for her generosity. If Brigid was a trial to them, she was a trial to local chieftains and kings too when it came to getting what she wanted for the poor, the enslaved, and the imprisoned.

In the harp story, music wins a prisoner's freedom. It begins when Brigid heard about a man unjustly imprisoned by a nearby king. She made it her business to track down the king. And when she did, she marched right up to his door.

Well, as luck would have it, he wasn't home, but his family was there, including three children. They all knew Brigid by reputation and welcomed her warmly. We can imagine her settling into a chair by the fire with a cup of tea and looking around. The king's home was large, made for entertaining. Several harps were lined up near her chair, as if arrayed for a party. The children told her the harpers were gone but if she gave them her special blessing, they would play for her. These were very young children, but bless them she did! And though the children had never touched harps before, they played like angels.

When the king returned, the children rushed to him, bursting with the story of the miraculous music. Hearing that Brigid's blessing had released torrents of intricate and beautiful music from their tiny fingers, the king was amazed and touched. He turned to Brigid. "Sister, will you bless me too, like the children?"

Brigid hesitated a moment, then replied. "Well, yes—but there is one condition. You must release the innocent man you have imprisoned here." After the miracle of the music, he couldn't say no. And the rest of the story? The children grew up to be harpers ... and the calling continued down the family line. The harpers of their posterity were known as the bards of the kings.[12]

When I painted Brigid with a harp, I didn't know this story. I only knew that harps were generally associated with Ireland. The image that really puzzled me, however, was the wolf. Was I thinking of Irish wolfhounds, or had I seen one with her in some other painting? I didn't know, didn't remember.

Only now have I learned the story of Brigid and the wolf, sometimes called a fox. In it, the king, perhaps this same long-suffering king we've met before, had a pet wolf, quite a marvelous animal that entertained the king's guests with its tricks. All was fine until one day, someone at the castle carelessly left a door open. The wolf wandered out, away from the king's grounds.

Night was approaching. In the fading light, an alarmed neighbor saw the animal in his garden. Thinking it was a wild wolf, he panicked and shot it! When the king heard what happened, he was furious. He ordered the man thrown into prison to await imminent death.

Brigid heard about the unfortunate prisoner. In hopes of getting to the enraged king before he could act, she rushed to her carriage. Rain fell as she raced along the darkening trail, cartwheels splashing through mud and gravel.

To her surprise, out of the gray mist a young wolf suddenly leaped onto the seat beside her. She jumped with fright. But instead of attacking, the animal quietly rested its paw on her knee. By the time they got to the castle, Brigid and the wolf were friends.

Once in the ornate drawing room hung with priceless tapestries, Brigid bowed and approached the king's throne, the wolf slightly behind her. The king knew Brigid, of course, but not why she had come on such a dark, wet night.

She explained. "I heard of your lost wolf, my king, and have brought you another." With that, she stepped aside and the wolf came into view. The king may well have been incredulous at Brigid's naïveté. His pet wolf had been trained by his court fool to perform many amazing tricks. This wild wolf could never be a replacement! As if on cue, Brigid's wolf moved to the center of the room and began showing off antics far beyond the imagination of everyone present, including the king.

Brigid must have been a bit surprised herself when she realized the king's lost pet had just been outdone by her still-damp wolf before the eyes of the entire court. I can imagine her smiling at the king in her courteous way and saying, "Now you see, my king, because of this wolf, you have indeed suffered no loss."

And that is how Brigid arrived at the king's door with a wolf and left with a free man.[13]

Today when I look at the wolf in my painting, I ask Brigid's help to stay as focused on my calling in life as she was on hers. And I slip in a little request for the kind of aid that came to her through unforeseen circumstances. Not that I want a wolf in my lap, but there might be something to simply starting out with trust on a dark and stormy night!

As you can see from the many tales we have about her, Brigid was well known in her day. People saw her charity to the poor, which began long before she took the veil. Once she was living her vowed religious life, many women noticed the good she did and joined her. Soon the nuns had a housing crisis.

From what we know of Brigid, it didn't take long for her to step up to her responsibilities. To start a monastery, she needed housing and land. All land was held by the king, perhaps the same king who freed her from slavery to her father or the king who owned the wolf—we don't know. But we do know Brigid repeatedly approached whomever was in charge.

As the story goes, one fine day she was standing right next to him, the royal master of all he surveyed: a forest full of kindling to collect and wild berries to pick, a lake full of fish, and fertile land for gardens. She praised the king's land, then quietly suggested it would be a perfect spot for a convent. He quickly told her he wouldn't be giving any of it to her.

I can imagine Brigid saying a quick prayer and turning back to the king, undaunted.

"Of course, my dear king, and forgive me for speaking again ... but I know your kind heart and was just wondering if you could spare a little tiny plot. Let's say the size of what my cloak will cover?"

Could she be joking? He took a closer look at her disarming smile. He was kind, but he also wanted to be rid of her and on his way, out of this conversation!

"Well, all right, little sister, but let's be quick about it."

Brigid was quick. She whipped off her cape, handing the corners to her four sisters.

To the king's surprise, each ran in a different direction and the cape grew immediately until it covered acres of his royal land.

The king was alarmed. Brigid saw his fear, but also knew he didn't realize the needs of the poor. She quietly observed, "My cloak is covering your entire kingdom because of your stinginess to the poor."

Suddenly very uncomfortable, the king remembered the little

slave girl who had reproached him so long ago. Was this young woman standing before him the same child he had freed that day, still remarking on his wealth? Was his entire kingdom to be lost to her in this moment? He didn't want that.

"Dear Brigid, call your sisters back. I will give you a goodly plot of land."

Brigid did so. She smiled as she thanked him and gathered up her cape. It occurred to her that perhaps the mere sight of her cape would be enough if she ever had to deal with this king again. As it turned out, she didn't need to. Before long, the king became Christian and a helper to the poor. He also commissioned a convent to be built for Brigid, maybe just to be on the safe side![14]

So, today we may see paintings of Brigid, cloak wrapped around her as she holds a little house or chapel in her arms, a symbol of her many monasteries. Her most famous foundation was built on the site of a revered oak tree. The oak, still the national tree of Ireland, was sacred to the ancients. The name "Kildare Monastery" came from the Celtic words for Church of the Oak.[15] It grew to be a large double monastery housing both men and women. Such monasteries were common for centuries before separate monasteries were mandated.

Kildare Monastery was an amazing place, a center of learning that became a cathedral city. And here is a tribute to Brigid's creativity: her community produced the celebrated Book of Kildare, an illustrated manuscript rivaling the famous Book of Kells, likely created about 300 years later in 800 CE. The Kildare manuscript disappeared, unfortunately, sometime during the Protestant Reformation in the 1500s.[16]

So far we've been talking about the Irish stories of St. Brigid. The Scots also have a long history of devotion to her. Many places in Scotland are named after her, including the Outer Hebrides Islands. One of their tales says Brigid was a serving maid at the house where the pregnant Mary and Joseph sought shelter when they came to pay taxes, and Brigid found them a corner in the stable. In another story, Brigid sees herself in a vision serving Mary and the Child Jesus in Bethlehem.[17] Because of these stories, the Scots prayed for her to fill an empty cradle, or to put her hand of peace on the troubled hearts of women.

St. Bride by John Duncan, 1913.
National Gallery of Scotland, Edinburgh.

A fascinating Scottish painting by John Duncan imagines how Brigid traveled to the land of Jesus's birth. Brigid, or Bride as she was sometimes called in Scotland, is perfectly composed on her way to be Mary's midwife and wet nurse for baby Jesus. In the painting, she looks to be a very young teenager. Lounging in midair, she wears a simple white gown, her long hair flows in the breeze, and her hands are piously folded as the angels carry her, supporting her under shoulders and knees. The angels' robes are decorated with scenes from the life of Jesus and even a portrait of the artist with the three magi.

This painting from the early twentieth century is engaging and a bit humorous. It sets the fanciful image of Brigid being carried by angels in contrast to realistic birds and seals, natural to Scotland's waters.

The Scots called Brigid "Mary of the Gaels," comparing her with

Brigid, collage by the author.
Since Brigid stood at the juncture
between the old Celtic religion and
Christianity, she is sometimes said
to be the bridge between them and
so the symbol of the bridge appears
in her iconography and
in this collage.

Mary, Jesus's mother. They think of her as a sort of foster mother, in the mother role in a mystical sense. For them, the foster mother or father could be a stronger connection to a child than that of the blood parent. In the Scottish stories, Brigid promises to be Jesus's mother, claiming God as her father, Jesus her son, and the Spirit her tutor.[18] We don't know whether Brigid ever set foot in Scotland but certainly her fame had traveled there.

Her contemporaries and those who followed knew she was a prodigious worker, founding the first women's religious houses all over Ireland. Both she and St. Patrick crisscrossed their small island, leaving many monasteries and convents in their wake. They were coworkers and friends, and no doubt were sometimes weary from their travels.

As one story goes, she and Patrick had recently arrived in a monastery town where people were clamoring to hear him speak. As his sermon went on, Brigid fell asleep. We don't know from the story if Patrick noticed or not, but we do learn that in her nap, Brigid dreamed. In her dream, a field was being plowed by four plows and produced a great harvest. When Brigid awoke, she described her dream to Patrick. He interpreted it, suggesting that the four plows represented the four gospels and the bountiful harvest symbolized the faith that grew and ripened among the people through their shared ministry.[19] Her recounting of the dream and Patrick's response sound like an exchange that could happen between soul friends today.

Brigid is one of the great monastic founders among our other Holy Women—Hildegard of Bingen, Clare of Assisi, and Teresa of Avila. She deserves her place there as she not only established a chain of monasteries, but also because she created the first rule of life for women for her nuns.[20] Her rule dictated daily prayer and specific directions on how to serve others in the name of God.

When Brigid died in 525, she was buried in Kildare. Later raids by the Norsemen meant her remains had to be moved. In an interesting turn of events, she was placed in the very tomb of Patrick and another prominent Irish saint, Columba.[21] You can't get much closer than that to a friend! Today they remain in Down Cathedral, the patron saints of Ireland whose churches honor them with stained glass and statues, right up there with Jesus and Mary.

Let us pray for strength and eagerness to serve in our day as St. Brigid did in hers.

May she dance among us all, Holy Women, kissed by our God!

Brigid

I am one who knows wine from milk,
blood from water.
I am one who blesses, nourishes, heals.
Where all is green, all is beauty.
Bridge the old and the new with me
Girded for the road.

I am one who blesses, nourishes, heals.
I am one who knows the Spirit is upon me.
Bridge the old and the new with me
Girded for the road.
Ever ancient, ever new.

I am one who knows the Spirit is upon me,
Where all is green, all is beauty.
Ever ancient, ever new.
I am one who knows wine from milk,
blood from water.[22]

Discovering Brigid

It took a Celtic spirituality pilgrimage to Ireland to introduce me to Brigid. I'd painted her before the trip, but why? I didn't know. I just felt drawn to put something on canvas so I could see for myself who she was. And why so large? At 36 by 24 inches, this was far bigger than most of my paintings. Maybe I sensed that she was important, like an ancestor, a great-great-great grandmother perhaps? Or maybe I was just remembering tales of the Goddess Brigid, so like the fairy stories I loved. One thing I did know the day I first touched a paintbrush to her image was that she needed lots of room.

Some of my decisions about how to present her were easy. Her gown needed to be green. In my mind's eye I saw her standing in a wood under moon and stars with a harp under her arm. We all know the color green is associated with Ireland, as perhaps is the harp, but other than that, I had no idea about the other elements. Why did those trees need to be licked by flames? Why did a wolf need to stand at her left hand? I didn't even know how to paint a wolf! Was I thinking of Irish wolfhounds?

Only when I began researching Brigid did I learn Ireland was covered with forest in her day and that Kildare, the monastery she founded, was named for an ancient oak on the site.[23] Only then did I read stories about the wolf, and about unexplained flashes of fire at her birth and later when she made monastic vows.[24]

As a girl, all I knew about Brigid was that she was Irish and her name was among the saints. But what I knew about being Irish was that it meant celebration, special treats, music, and fun. Every year on St. Patrick's Day, Dad insisted on a dinner of corned beef and cabbage, and we kids could break our Lenten fast with candy. I remember visiting Mom in the hospital the day after my brother's birth. She opened her gift box of chocolates, smiled, and let me have my pick, a coconut creme. (If he'd been born a few hours later, he would have been among the legions of Irish boys named Patrick!)

I was ten that year and had a gang of school friends. We spent recess teaching each other how to dance the Irish jig. Later when we were in high school, we learned to sing "Piping Tim of Galway" in harmony for a music competition. And, of course, I loved my Irish grandma, who could play "Danny Boy," "When Irish Eyes are Smiling," "Peg of My Heart," and "My Wild Irish Rose" by ear on the piano while I sang along. Sometimes she even danced with me. When I was a young teen nervous about my first prom, she taught me how to waltz while she counted "one-two-three, one-two-three."

Celebratory Irish music thrilled me, for sure. But besides that, I didn't know why the sound of bagpipes always gave me a lump in my throat and chills. Weren't they from Scotland rather than Ireland?

On my way to the pilgrimage in Ireland, I'd decided to spend an extra couple of days in Scotland. I'd long heard about the famous military Tattoo, a traditional annual gathering of the clans displaying their regalia amid much playing of bagpipes and ceremonial marching in front of the ancient Edinburgh castle. That was an opportunity I didn't want to miss—a chance for lots of goosebumps!

Afterward, walking back to my hotel, I noticed a local auto repair shop prominently displaying a sign: Cunningham Auto Service! What was this all about? I knew for a fact that my Irish forebears came to the United States from Kilkenny in Ireland.

When I got home, I researched Cunninghams and found plenty of information about Scottish Cunninghams. Name variations included Cunegan, Conyngham, and Coineagan. But then why did my family emigrate from Ireland? Soon I was into history. I read about Scottish tenant farmers pushed off their land by landlords working with the English, who wanted to take over sheep pastures for the profitable wool trade. I came up with a theory: many Scots were displaced in the upheaval, pushed to the southern edge of the country. Likely some were pushed right over the sea to Ireland! Historians called this exile the Highland Clearances.[25] Maybe my Scottish Cunninghams were forced off that land and years later, in the devastating Irish potato famine, migrated to America with the others, decimating what was left of the Irish population—those who hadn't starved. Kilkenny was a primary departure point for those headed to the United States.

So, I concluded I was Scotch-Irish and that explained my bagpipe chills. Their plaintive sound was emotionally wired into a tribal memory I hadn't known I had. That we carry vestiges of experience from our forebears in some deep places of spirit has always seemed likely to me. I wondered about how those memories are playing out in my day and time as masses of people are migrating in many areas of our world. The prayer in my heart is "Let there be gentleness, let there be kindness." All of us in the United States, excepting the indigenous peoples, have been immigrants.

The surprises in Scotland didn't dilute my enthusiasm for the Celtic pilgrimage I was about to begin. I was ready to love Ireland and would soon learn that many Scots also honored Brigid.

Like many pilgrims, I had known more about St. Patrick than St. Brigid when I arrived. Once truly in Ireland, however, I discovered that like Patrick, Brigid was everywhere. She was in every church, memorialized in stained glass and statues, right up front with Patrick. I found out they and St. Colomba are the three patron saints of Ireland, even purported to be buried together.[26]

As I began the pilgrimage, I wondered again about St. Brigid as an ancient ancestor. She had dreams full of portents, even discussing them with St. Patrick.[27] Hadn't my Irish grandma swirled tea leaves in a saucer and smiled at me wisely, promising love and adventure? Hadn't she told me what my dreams meant? And hadn't I had years of significant dreams? I could identify with St. Brigid, this woman of portents and dreams.

The journey to Brigid put me on the path of a powerful Holy Woman held in high regard by the Irish, Scots, and Welsh. I walked in her footsteps, amazed at her prodigious spirit and work founding many monasteries. Brigid's love of God and devotion to serving all his children are embedded in her history and continue to inspire the devotion of her followers in Ireland and beyond to this day.

Responding to Brigid

Associations/archetypes: child, virgin, healer, fire, water, wells, milk, cow, wolf, ale, threshold, sword, harp, illuminated manuscripts, nurse/midwife to Jesus, poetess, goddess, nature mystic, generosity, hospitality, determination, Patrick, cape/mantle, abbess, Kildare

Consider the stories you have read here about Brigid's persistence in helping others in need. Begin a conversation with her about her mission to replace the king's wolf and gain freedom for the unfortunate neighbor who had mistakenly shot it.

Ask Brigid what her thoughts and feelings were as she rushed in an open carriage through that torrential night over rocks and mud to save the man's life. Did the king have a reputation for such injustice and cruelty? Was she praying for self-restraint when she entered his sumptuous castle and saw how he lived among the poor?

Continue the story by writing your questions with your dominant hand and her answers with your nondominant hand. Keep the conversation going back and forth between you until you fill at least a couple of pages, even if it feels awkward and the words don't seem to make sense.

When you finish, still using your nondominant hand, do a simple drawing using colored markers. Your image might be of Brigid, or the wolf, or the king, or something completely different arising from the dialog between you. It may even happen that what you think of seems unrelated. Let come whatever wants to come.

After you work for a while, ask yourself, "What else wants to be here? What else is needed?" It may be a color, a shape, or some words. Or your conversation may be calling you to come back to make an adjustment or add a detail. Be open to your intuition. Then read all that you've written. Finally, journal a bit about what this process of exploration has been like for you. What reactions or questions came up?

When you think you are finished, post your nondominant hand story and drawing where you can sit quietly and look at them. Ask Brigid's help to see a gift in this experience and thank her for whatever you may have realized.

Hildegard

1098–1179 CE

Commemorated September 17

We have much more solid history about St. Hildegard of Bingen, born in 1098, than we have about St. Brigid, born seven centuries before and whose stories have come down through oral tradition. Much of Hildegard's twelfth-century writing, art, and music survive thanks to safekeeping by her nuns when Germany was bombed during World War II.[1] Hildegard's visionary work is richly spiritual, mythical, archetypal, and psychological, as we shall see.

A child of noble parents, Hildegard, the youngest of ten, was dedicated to the church when she was only eight years old. Such practices were common in medieval times and perhaps a precedent to what we know today as tithing 10 percent of one's income to a church. Little Hildegard was given into the care of an anchoress, a noblewoman named Jutta von Spanheim. Jutta lived as a solitary in a cell attached to a monastery, rather than in the usual society of a convent. The call to a life in solitude with God has been known since the ancient times of Hebrew prophets and the early Christian desert fathers and mothers.

By the twelfth century, monastic orders had created the means to live a hermetic life without going to a desert. Among the early Benedictines, a nun became an anchoress with a rite symbolizing her death to the world. She received the last anointing, extreme unction, and was sprinkled with ashes, and then the door of her cell was sealed from outside. The anchorage had interior windows so food could be passed through and those inside could participate in community prayer or spiritual ministry. An unsealed door gave

---

Preceding page: *Hildegard of Bingen,* acrylic on canvas, by the author.

access to the monastery when doctors or servants were needed.[2]

Life in an anchorage was not a customary choice for children, but Hildegard's parents knew their child had visions—or what we might call clairvoyant experiences—before she was six. It was a time when church authorities viewed the healing powers of midwives or wise women with suspicion. The notion of direct access to God or finding the sacred in nature was considered verging on heretical.[3] Witch hunts of the Inquisition hadn't yet begun, but suppression was in the air. Hildegard's parents could have worried about their little girl's safety. And what could be safer than an anchorage?

Hildegard was in good hands with the magistra Jutta, a highly respected spiritual leader who educated incoming candidates in the Benedictine way of life. As magistra, she was consulted by disciples, both within the monastery and from without. Under her tutelage, Hildegard studied and completed her preparation to take religious vows at age sixteen. Throughout her early years, she confided the secret of her visions only to Jutta and a learned monk, Volmar.[4]

Why the secrecy? Hildegard was very young. She worried that she was deceiving herself. And no doubt she feared criticism because her visions were not like the more personal revelations of other mystics. Hildegard's cosmic visions were filled with the vastness of the universe, "theological content that was directed to the church at large,"[5] to all people.

And so Hildegard lived in the anchorage into her forties until Jutta died. She had led an observant monastic life like the other nuns, and when they elected her abbess she continued to do so. Despite years spent in seclusion, she knew the problems of her times and understood her role. Abbots and abbesses were traditionally considered trusted advisors. She knew she would be involved with powerful rulers of church and state.

Within a few years, Hildegard broke the silence surrounding her visions. She had been very, very hesitant to reveal them, but finally one broke through her reluctance. A powerful voice came to her: "Say and write what you see and hear."[6] The voice became even more urgent: "Cry out therefore, and write thus!"[7]

This insistent voice marked the beginning of Hildegard's work in documenting her visions in her first book, *Scivias* (Know the Ways of God), which took her ten years to complete. To help clarify the written meaning of her revelations, she dictated their images to be painted into mandala-like illustrations she called "illuminations." She wanted to represent her revelations visually as well as with the text of her manuscripts.

Illuminated manuscripts were not new; they had been created in monasteries perhaps as early as the fifth century, their texts richly emblazoned in brilliant gold and colorful script filled with images. However, Hildegard's illuminations were so named because she consistently spoke of "the Living Light who illumines all darkness"[8] in her visions. She hoped to capture something of that great light. These precious illuminations "gave birth to new symbolic forms and pictures which were unknown in the Middle Ages."[9] Her illuminated manuscripts were uniquely her own and we are fortunate to still have them today.

Hildegard likely directed others to create these illustrations, but she wrote every word of her treatises by her own hand. No scribe took dictation. Hildegard's accomplishment is all the more amazing in that she wrote her complex and lengthy works in Latin rather than her native German. While she had been exposed to Latin as she chanted the office and prayed the liturgy, she had no formal instruction in it. But she needed to write in Latin, the liturgical language.[10] She knew her words from Spirit about the ways of God would be read by churchmen of power.

One of Hildegard's central themes in *Scivias* is found in a word she invented: "viriditas." She meant the term to convey that the Holy Spirit was the source of all life or "greening power" and that Jesus was "Greenness Incarnate," God's freshness deep down in all that grows on the earth and in each person.[11]

She wrote many books, but her masterpiece is *Scivias*, which established her identity as a nature mystic. In her visions, she saw God's light, which she called the "Living Light," shining in the human heart, and a second light that bathed all creation. This double light enabled her to see the transparency of all creation, to see all things in God and God in all things as revealed each spring when everything turns green. Hildegard saw that God's continuous creation also goes on in the human heart, where his bright light is preserved in those formed in his image and likeness.[12]

Hildegard understood that where God's spirit and the human

spirit meet, they produce the fecundity she named viriditas. Thus Hildegard weaves together two great stories: God's presence in history and in the entire cosmos—including humankind: both continually changing, evolving, and growing. I tried to capture a sense of Hildegard's spirit when I painted her surrounded by greening creation, the way she understood the divine, the ongoing revelation of God.

From childhood, she was drawn to learn the healing use of herbs, no doubt in part because of mystical experiences in nature. She describes how she heard God speak in this lovely little song:

> I am the breeze that nurtures all things green.
> I encourage blossoms to flourish with ripening fruits.
> I am the rain coming from the dew
> that causes the grasses to laugh
> with the joy of life.[13]

If God in the rain makes the grasses laugh with joy, Hildegard's spirit had to be full of joy. She herself had blossomed in the nurturing touch of the divine. God's ongoing revelation to her was that we are all invited to bloom and be fruitful.

Her first illumination, the introduction to the *Scivias*, has been titled *Hildegard's Awakening: A Self Portrait.*

Hildegard is shown writing about her visions with flames over her head reminiscent of the Pentecost presence of the Holy Spirit, which she names the "Living Flame of God." Seated in a church structure with her teacher, spiritual director, and friend, the monk Volmar,[14] she hears a heavenly voice telling her to convey "the marvelousness of God" in her "own way of speaking":

> Behold in the forty-third year of my temporal journey, when I grasped at a heavenly vision with great fear and trembling attention, I saw the greatest brilliance. In it a voice from heaven was saying to me: "O weak person, you who are both ashes of ashes and decaying of decaying, speak and write what you see and hear. But you are shy about speaking and simple in explaining and unskilled about writing those things. So speak and write those things not according to

Hildegard's Awakening: A Self-Portrait
by Hildegard of Bingen, Plate 2,
Illuminations of Hildegard of Bingen
by Matthew Fox.

human speech or human inventiveness but according to the extent that you see and hear those things in the heavens above in the marvelousness of God. Bring to light those things by way of explanation. Be like a listener who understands the words of his or her own teacher but explains them in one's own way of speaking, willingly, plainly and instructively. So you too, O woman, speak those things which you see and hear. Write those things not according to yourself or by the standards of another person, but according to the will of the one knowing, the one who sees and arranges all things in the secrets of his own mysteries."[15]

I painted Hildegard at her writing desk, where I imagined her delight at reliving her visions. Was her heart enraptured as she attended to the voice that commanded her to do this work? I think so. I can see her, feather pen in hand, inviting us to be "feather(s) on the breath of God"[16] with her. Hildegard's first illumination is collaged in the lower left of my painting. .

Another of Hildegard's illuminations has as its theme Creation and the Creator. It pictures God enthroned, resting his feet on a shell that appears to float on a pool of water. Hildegard tells us that "every faithful soul is a throne of God if it reverences God wisely."[17] The image conveys that God is centered in us, as if seated on the throne of the heart. Hildegard tells us that we are all capable of being such homes for God. We also notice here the shell and water, common symbols of the feminine, an enlightening addition to this creation vision. Hildegard reports that she saw:

> ... an extraordinarily beautiful young woman ... wearing shoes which seemed of purest gold [whom] the whole creation called "Lady." The image spoke to a human person of sapphire blue and said, "Dominion is yours on the day of your power in the radiance of the saints. I have brought you forth from my own womb before the daystar." And then Hildegard heard a voice tell her, "The young woman whom you see is Love. She has her tent in eternity. For when God wanted to create the world, he bent down with

The Creator's Glory, Creation's Glory, Plate 8, Illuminations of Hildegard of Bingen by Matthew Fox.

the most tender love. He provided for everything that was necessary, just like a father who prepares an inheritance for his child and with the zeal of love makes all his possessions available. ... For it was love which was the source of this creation in the beginning when God said: 'Let it be!' And it was. As though in the blinking of an eye, the whole creation was formed through love." Continuing her story, Hildegard celebrates Psalm 110, "The right hand of God embraces all creatures and is especially extended over peoples, kingdoms, and all goods. And that is why it stands written in scripture: 'The Lord says to my lord: "Sit at my right hand."'" But why does the whole creation call this maiden "Lady"? Because it was from her that all creation proceeded, since love was the first. She made everything."

This is an astounding and exciting statement from Hildegard—that womanly love birthed all creation.[18]

We can consider this "Lady" an archetype for the divine feminine aspect of the Creator, as she is not identified in any personal way. Historian Barbara Newman, in studying many of Hildegard's poems, songs, and prayers about Mary and Eve, sees them also as functioning more like archetypes than individuals.

There is a strikingly impersonal quality to her lyrics: she (Hildegard) cared as little for the "personality" of Mary as she cared for the psychology of Eve. Both women are larger than life, not individuals but cosmic theophanies of the feminine; and the purpose of the feminine is to manifest God in the world.[19]

That the feminine divine can bring forth all of creation through her own womb is an ancient archetypal idea. The first image we have of a divine female, the Venus of Willendorf, looks not only well-nourished but perhaps pregnant. This figurine carries the same energy Hildegard describes as veriditas, the "greening": fecundity, fertility, the capacity to give life—all feminine prerogatives.

Hildegard's ability to give life through her many accomplishments flowed directly from her visions and her conviction that she was to teach what they revealed. But the process was not an easy one for her. Early on, disturbed by a vision, she wrote to her contemporary Bernard of Clairvaux for guidance about what she should reveal. He responded, "[W]hen learning and the anointing (which reveals all things to you) are within, what advice could we possibly give?"[20] He was impressed and went so far as to present her work to the Synod of Trier convened by Pope Eugene III. The pope was equally moved. He read from Hildegard's *Scivias* to the gathering of bishops. And best of all, he set her mind at ease by encouraging her to continue writing. [21]

She certainly did. Hildegard wrote book-length mystical treatises, poems, and prayers as well as letters to popes, cardinals, bishops, abbots, kings, emperors, nuns, and monks. She was involved in the political, ecclesiastical, and intellectual currents of her time.

In addition to her prodigious written output, Hildegard composed an opera and more than sixty-nine musical pieces with text[22] that, like her writings, are still accessible today.

As her fame and holiness grew, Hildegard founded many monasteries and nurtured the spirituality of their communities. She also moved beyond intimate circles to become a public preacher, teacher, and prophet, consulted by simple and prominent people alike in her day. Because of her extensive work and Pope Eugene's attention, her visions were documented. She was called, even in her day, the Sybil of the Rhine.[23]

By any standard, Hil-

Hildegard of Bingen, icon by Marcy Hall. The crosier she holds represents her authority as abbess and suggests that her influence was equal to that of clerical and political leaders of her time, a singular role for a woman.

degard's creative outpouring marks her as a significant author, composer, and theologian, an unusual woman coming out of the Middle Ages when few women could read or write. In 2014, she was named a Doctor of the Church,[24] joining the small minority of women so recognized among several hundred men. The other Holy Women are Catherine of Sienna and Teresa of Avila, both honored in 1970, and Thérèse of Lisieux, recognized in 1997. These three were immortalized in a Catholic church stained glass window. It remains to an enterprising artist to portray Hildegard with them, and perhaps that will be on my agenda soon!

Women Doctors of the Church portrays St. Edith Stein
(Teresa Benedicta of the Cross), St. Teresa of Avila,
St. Thérèse of Lisieux, and St. Catherine of Sienna.
St. Edith was a doctor of philosophy but was not
formally known as a Woman Doctor of the Church.
St. Thérèse of Lisieux Church, Montauk, New York,
was dedicated in 2007, before St. Hildegard was
named a Doctor of the Church. Window by master
craftsman Paul Coulaz.

St. Hildegard Strolls Through the Garden

Luminous morning, Hildegard gazes at
the array of blooms, holding in her heart
the young boy with a mysterious rash, the woman
reaching menopause, the newly minted widower,
and the black abbey cat with digestive issues who wandered
in one night and stayed. New complaints arrive each day.

She gathers bunches of dandelions, their yellow
profusion a welcome sight in the monastery garden,
red clover, nettle, fennel, sprigs of parsley to boil later in wine.

She glances to make sure none of her sisters are
peering around pillars, slips off her worn leather shoes
to relish the freshness between her toes,

face upturned to the rising sun, she sings lucida materia,
matrix of light, words to the Virgin, makes a mental
note to return to the scriptorium to write that image down.

When the church bells ring for Lauds, she hesitates just a
moment, knowing her morning praise has already begun,
wanting to linger in this space where the dew still clings.

At the end of her life, she met with a terrible obstinacy,
from the hierarchy came a ban on receiving
bread and wine and her cherished singing.

She now clips a single rose, medicine for a broken heart,
which she will sip slowly in tea, along with her favorite spelt
biscuits, and offer some to the widower

grieving for his own lost beloved,
they smile together softly at this act of holy communion
and the music rising among blades of grass.[25]

Discovering Hildegard

My familiarity with and admiration for Hildegard began only in recent years. Her story, unlike those of Miriam, Mary, Magdalene, the Samaritan woman, and Thérèse of Lisieux, wasn't commonly known in the years of my Catholic schooling.

She was no doubt familiar to the Benedictine order since she was part of their history, but only came to wider notice when she was recognized as a saint and honored as a Doctor of the Church in 2012. I first heard of her when I read Matthew Fox's *Original Blessing* in 1985. I was very attracted to women mystics and he introduced her to me, not only as a mystic but also as a writer, artist, composer, healer, and herbalist[26]—an amazing woman, certainly kissed by God. As happened to many of the Holy Women I've studied, Hildegard's visions gradually demanded to be expressed despite her inner struggles to keep them secret. Fortunately for us, she followed the urging of the Spirit and her confessor,[27] and so we have both written and visual descriptions of her visions.

I had to know about her, so I studied her *Illuminations* as Hildegard called them: mandala-like paintings portraying her inner life with God. I found recordings of her music quite by happenstance when I was on a Black Madonna pilgrimage in France and bought a collection of authentic music from Chartres Cathedral. Only when I began studying these Holy Women did I discover some of Hildegard's songs included in the album. Since then, I've played them as I painted her and the other Holy Women, and play them even now as I write.

Has Hildegard been at my elbow whispering encouragement and excitement? I think so. Recently, someone asked me why I painted her left-handed. I hadn't noticed. Had I caught some of her energy? Was her influence on me so powerful that I painted her left-handed because I'm left-handed? I do know that painting these Holy Women was simply a process of following where I was led and walking a path that appeared before me as I walked it. I had no plan. The beautiful faces just arrived, one by one.

So I learned about Hildegard. It struck me that although an amazing visionary, she was also an eminently practical woman, well versed in the arts of gardening and herbalism. She was an abbess, a recognized healer, musician, and manager of property and people. She lived to the ripe old age of eighty-one and has been called the "Grandmother of the Rhineland mystics."[28]

That title got me thinking. She was German. Hildegard's practicality reminded me of my own German grandmother, who lived to age eighty-four and was a milliner before her marriage. Grandma had taken art lessons, could play the piano by ear, and knew how to cook. I'm supposing all women of her era learned to sew, crochet, and knit because ready-made clothes from catalogs were new and expensive in the early 1900s. So she made all the clothes for her children, including winter coats. She also made and used her own soap, knew how to dress and cook poultry and small game, and planted the annual garden, cultivated it and the trees and vines, and then preserved the year's fruit and vegetable crops.

A small pasture for sheep and cows ran along the edge of the family lot, not far from the house. As a little girl, I perched on the fence watching my young uncles shear sheep. Later, in the barn, I'd sit on a stool to play with the kitten who lived there, a mouse catcher. My youngest uncle, about ten years old, would milk the cows, sometimes squirting milk into the kitten's mouth to entertain me. When I wasn't paying attention and he squirted me as well, I'd decide it was time for me to carry the bucket of milk to Grandma's dry kitchen. I never could understand how she separated cream from that milk and then mysteriously churned it into butter.

Just a visit to my grandparents was an educational event. If the next day was Saturday, I'd watch as those same uncles, just boys themselves, killed a chicken or duck for Sunday dinner. Grandma let me stand next to her at the counter afterward when she pulled out the "innards," as she called them. I watched the whole process with big eyes! She had told me what to expect, but nevertheless, I still remember those innards. At the time, her calm smile and crinkling eyes were reassuring enough that I was willing to help her pull feathers off the birds. But when she singed them over an open flame, the pungent smell sent me out of her busy kitchen. It was her workplace most of the time, cooking for her ten children.

When I read that Hildegard was the youngest of ten children and had been given to the church as a tithe, I thought again of my own family. My mother was one of ten. One of her sisters left for the convent at age sixteen. Our family tree recorded nuns on both my mother's and father's sides going back several generations. As a child, I was told that years ago, it was very common for at least one child from a family to become a priest or nun. It was clearly a point of pride. I learned later that in years past only the oldest son could inherit family property, which might mean the next son went to seminary or monastery, or perhaps into the army. Women didn't inherit at all and were expected to be dependent on their husbands.

The attitude of Hildegard's family about having their own in religion was recognizable to me. I remembered my grandparents telling me that our family had someone praying for us all the time. As a child, I didn't know that in the history of monastic orders, wealthy families sometimes gave bequests to convents for elaborate memorial altars with the stipulation that relatives buried there be remembered in perpetual prayer by the monks or nuns.

Hildegard was a reformer in her day, followed by another German reformer four hundred years later, Martin Luther. His teachings caused the split between his followers and the Roman Catholic Church, the ripples of which flowed down the centuries to my own mother's life.

Those ripples began when my maternal grandfather migrated from Germany as a devout Catholic boy of sixteen. He soon met a nice Lutheran girl. Church law specifies that a Catholic marriage can only be made between two Catholics, if there are special permissions or dispensations.[29] So my grandmother became Catholic to marry Grandpa, to her own mother's great displeasure—I remember a lot of tiptoeing around great-grandmother when I was a child. My mother, of course, had seen the tiptoeing all her growing-up years.

And wouldn't you know it? My mother fell in love with a Lutheran. All was well—at first. Her fiancé agreed to be baptized Catholic, but at the last minute changed his mind. When Grandpa heard about it, he sent my mother away, heartbroken, to live with relatives in another state. Although Luther lived in sixteenth-century Germany, feeling about the split from Catholicism still ran strong in the early twentieth century in the American Midwest.

From my adult perspective, I've wondered if there wasn't a certain wisdom in his decision. Maybe on some level, Grandpa was less worried about his daughter "falling away," as they said, to become Lutheran than he was that she would live with the intergenerational stress a mixed marriage could cause as had happened to him. Well meaning though his decision was, I'm not sure my mother ever forgave him for disrupting her life.

Despite the vicissitudes of my mother's first romance, she soon married my father, had five children, was widowed young, then married again. This time she married a widower with ten children and became part of a large German farm family. So my grandmother wasn't the only matron to manage a property and many people; my mother had the same responsibility. I remember visiting during those years. It wasn't unusual for thirty-five family members to be seated at the table on an ordinary Sunday.

As I reflect on my German family background, I can only admire the prodigious energy that must be part of the national DNA. It's easy to imagine Hildegard as an ancestor passing some of her staunch practicality down through the generations to us, and I'm impressed all over again with the Grandmother of the Rhineland Mystics.

I love her. Besides her considerable practical accomplishments, her spiritual gifts amaze me. Hildegard's dedication to opening her spirit to God deeply touched me and has drawn me to her. Since my family is filled with women of faith whose love of God and capability cannot be doubted, Hildegard also stands before me. She is a historical and archetypal woman, gifted and powerful, an abbess/ruler and sage—an ancestor in the cloud of witnesses, a towering presence among these Holy Women kissed by God.

Responding to Hildegard

Associations/archetypes: orphan, solitary, virgin, visionary, prophet, herbalist, healer, abbess, author, poet, playwright, artist, musician, composer, nature mystic, service, Doctor of the Church

Hildegard is one of two of our Holy Women who has had a planet named for her. Planet Hildegaria was identified by an astronomer in Heidelberg in 1918.[30] I wouldn't doubt that this German was pleased to honor his countrywoman in this way for her remarkable contributions to herbal medicine some seven centuries earlier.

It took the church a little longer to tune in to the extraordinary Hildegard; she was sainted and honored as a Doctor of the Church in 2012. About a century before that, the Abbey of St. Hildegard at Eibingen, Germany, was built on the site of her original abbey by Prince Karl Löwenstein, who gave the land and built the monastery for her Benedictine nuns in the early 1900s. A quick online search didn't reveal any churches named for her, but perhaps that will happen soon and even stained glass windows will be designed to honor her.

In the meantime, all of nature can remind us of Hildegard. Her garden became her pharmacy. If you have access to a garden, depending on the season, climate, and location, you may find many of her ingredients there: carnations, poppies, geraniums, roses, red clover, dandelions, aloe, lavender, various grasses, parsley, nettles, fennel, spelt, and myrrh. Simple recipes using these plants for teas can be found online.

In want of a garden, a visit to a local flower shop or nursery may do. In want of a flower shop or nursery, consider the craft shop's beautiful imitations. A little rose or lavender oil is likely to be in a health food store's pharmacy too.

Not easy to get out and about? You could create a bouquet by finding pictures of flowers in magazines or online and then collaging them into an arrangement that pleases you.

Once you have it, think about the many meanings assigned to flowers: mature charm and glorious femininity to orchids; purity and sweetness to gardenias; joyfulness to bird of paradise; pride and beauty to carnations; love and innocence to roses.[31]

How do these qualities figure into stories of Hildegard and of your own life? We know that Hildegard used these and many more flowers for healing purposes. Do some of these flowers carry healing in your experience of them?

Then write about your creation, being sure to date it, including the year, and post it in your home where it can become a small shrine for Hildegard, perhaps lit with a candle for your prayer time.

Clare

1195–1253 CE

Commemorated August 12

Unlike the other Holy Monastic Women, St. Brigid of Ireland and St. Hildegard of Bingen, St. Clare of Assisi was born into a wealthy Italian family and raised in a stable environment. Stable, at least, until beautiful, noble teenage Clare heard the impassioned preaching of another young noble of Assisi, the radical upstart Giovanni di Pietro de Bernadone, known as Francesco.[1] Thus Chiara Offreduccio began the journey toward founding a religious order, the Poor Clares, that still exists today.[2,3]

In thirteenth-century Italy, her family took it for granted that gentle, quiet, obedient Clare would marry into nobility.[4] We can imagine the lavish wedding this would have occasioned in medieval Assisi. No doubt Francis's wealthy father would have been called upon to provide the rich fabrics for her gown and those of the women in her party, and even the fancy tunics for the men. Such was his role as fabric merchant. Yet Clare may well have had very mixed feelings about just such an eventuality.

Looking for signs of the transformation of this seemingly tractable young noblewoman into the abbess of the Poor Ladies of San Damiano, her biographers tell a story of her last day under her family's roof. It was Palm Sunday. During the previous week, she had heard a lenten sermon by Francis, on fire with God, urging simplicity and holiness in imitation of Jesus.[5] His words filled her with yearning—a longing like his own—for a joyous new life attained by imitating the poor and humble Jesus.

Now here she was again in the same ornate church with her friends,

---

Preceding page: *Clare of Assisi,* acrylic on canvas,
by the author. It portrays Clare in habit and veil
holding the host and ciborium.

Clare and Francis, an unidentified reproduction
found at the Franciscan Renewal Center, Scottsdale,
Arizona, likely to have been painted in the early
twentieth century. Photo by the author.

the other girls of nobility, all lined up to be admired in their finery.
It was time for the traditional ceremony of distributing blessed palm
fronds in remembrance of Jesus's entry into Jerusalem. When the
other girls ceremoniously rose in the pews to proceed to the sanctuary,
formally kiss the elaborately robed bishop's ring, and receive their palms,
Clare silently remained seated.[6] The bishop may well have assumed that
she, like Francis, had already decided on a path unlike his own, one
of simplicity. He, too, had heard the troubling young firebrand speak.

Many say that Clare and Francis were a love story in those days of
troubadours and courtly love. After all, it was a time of knighthood
and unconsummated passions. We are familiar with the tales of King
Arthur's Round Table of knights, and the two of them could neatly
fit into the template of these romantic legends in which the brave
young hero serves a beautiful and good lady.[7] However, with Clare
and Francis, the spiritual love underlying their story is what captures
us. And it began with as much excitement as any elopement.[8] On the
very evening of Palm Sunday, Clare took the first courageous step to
begin her new life. In the dark of night, she and another girl slipped
out the back door of her house and ran to an old church at the edge
of town: Portiuncula, "the little portion." Francis had repaired it, and
it now sheltered him and his friars.[9]

The brothers welcomed them joyfully. Francis presented Clare with a tunic, the same rough cloth that he and the others wore. Then, as she knelt in their midst, he cut her beautiful hair in a ritual of promise and renunciation.[10]

We don't know if Francis expected Clare to show up at his door, but once she arrived he was evidently keenly aware that her absence would soon be discovered—she would need protection from her family at once. He acted quickly, escorting Clare and her companion to sanctuary in a nearby Benedictine convent.[11] She probably had no inkling at the time that Francis would become her lifelong spiritual advisor.

As he expected, it wasn't long before Clare's family came for her, bursting into the usually serene monastery of women. What happened next, we do not know exactly, but it is clear that family uproar ensued. Did Clare's father chase her to the church and attempt to bodily carry her home? It sounds likely:

> Clare seized the altar cloth and in the same instant pulled off her own veil. Shorn of the beautiful hair that had attracted rich suitors, her bare head conveyed the irrevocability of her decision. She was Christ's bride now, living under his protection, and life would be one of continuing sacrifice, patterned after his. The family accepted defeat and left, but they returned a few weeks later, even angrier, because now Clare's sister Agnes had slipped away to join her. This time they were rougher, but again they were foiled: one source claims Agnes's body became so heavy no one could carry her.[12]

When it was safe, Francis moved her and her little community into the humble church of San Damiano for shelter. The plot of land there was just large enough for a small garden. In their enclosure, Clare and her sisters depended on alms the begging friars shared with them, what they could grow, and perhaps recompense for simple things they produced through the work of their hands. This version of poverty went beyond even that practiced by the begging friars.[13] Francis was sympathetic to Clare's needs. He, too, had had a tumultuous start, struggling against his own family and his bishop's urgings. The little poor man, "el poverello," desperate to dramatize his resolve to follow Jesus, had stood before the church doors and stripped off his rich clothes, standing naked before them all.[14] He made his point. Francis renounced the luxury of the church and all that his wealthy father had given him. Thus began his life of prayer, preaching, and service to the poor.

Clare, too, gave away all her belongings. Her gift was her understanding that nothing could fill her heart like the love of God: not riches, not any material thing. She was an impetuous teenager, a young girl in love with God—and who hasn't gone to extremes in the flush of first love? She had been kissed by God, filled to overflowing with the Spirit:

> Clare's life of poverty was not a grim, calculating handing over but rather a joyous easy, impatient flinging aside: lovers don't feel the cold, lovers don't care what they eat—and Clare was a lover, running full tilt toward her Beloved.[15]

She spoke of wanting to empty her heart of all desires, even for a warm blanket or food. Sometimes she fasted to the point of jeopardizing her health.

In these days of eating disorders, it is puzzling to put ourselves back into another time and culture to grasp what such behavior could have meant to these early mystics. We do know from testimony given during Clare's canonization process that Francis intervened more than once in her "mortification" practices. Maybe he played on the resonances of the word itself to remind her that the goal of fasting, or any penance, was to help her to live "in the world but not be of it"—not to literally leave it![16]

Clare's charism and gift of the spirit of poverty become clearer when we remember the context of convent life for women of early times, our Holy Monastic Women St. Brigid and St. Hildegard.

We have seen in the life of Brigid that the site of her first convent, Kildare, grew into a cathedral town. She was noted for founding a number of convents across Ireland on land given her by chieftains and kings. Later, Hildegard was raised from the age of four in a large Benedictine monastery at Bingen and lived there for many years of her long life. Similar to other great monasteries founded since the time of St. Benedict, it comprised extensive holdings. Such complexes, based on the saint's rule of life for men, were a world apart from the humble convents of Clare and her followers. The Poor Clares, as they later became known, had no guest houses, bakeries, breweries, or hospitals. Clare's call to poverty precluded elaborate ritual, collections of religious art, or owning any property.

In the very early days, the Poor Ladies of San Damiano, as they came to be known, received papal permission to live in intense poverty. But struggles arose when they were later legislated to follow a Benedictine rule of life written for men. That rule recommended "prudent leniency," and included warnings to potential new members about "the hard and austere realities" of the sisters' lives, referring primarily to their poverty. The rule of the monks mandated vows of stability, obedience and "monastic virtue," but there was no mention of poverty.[17]

Clare never inflicted on the other sisters the intense penitence and fasting she undertook for herself; the practices she prescribed were gentle. Her rule, the first for women in Western Christianity,[18] grew out of the way Clare guided her community of women over the years, and it was her joy and holiness that drew them to join her.

With her spirit of gentleness and joy, it is unlikely Clare ever thought of her life in any other terms. She advised her sisters to go "with swift pace, light step, unswerving feet, so that even your steps stir up no dust, may you go forward securely, joyfully, and swiftly, on the path of prudent happiness."[19]

In time, Pope Innocent IV composed a rule specifically for Clare, but it still wasn't what she considered a true reflection of her way of life. When she wrote her own rule, Clare asked that "the tenor of our life be thoroughly explained" to the new members of the convent. She went on: "If by divine inspiration, anyone should come to us desiring this life, the Abbess is required to seek the consent of all the sisters."[20] Her way of welcoming new members was not with a warning but with prayerful faith in the discernment of the entire community.

Clare's approach was based on her sureness that the Holy Spirit had brought the sisters together and would continue to guide them. Her rule specifies that "the abbess call her sisters together at least once a week and consult with them, 'for the Lord frequently reveals what is best to the least among us.'"[21] Clare was humble, an outcome of her deep faith in God. She knew that God could speak through each and all.

Her rule also stressed *discretio*, or discernment. When faced with greater decisions, Clare directed that "the whole community ... elect eight sisters 'from the more discerning ones' whose counsel the abbess 'should be always bound to use in those matters which our form of life requires.'"[22] No unilateral leadership decisions would be made in her community!

The flavor of Clare's guidance always emphasized the voluntary poverty that had opened her own prayer to God. She knew that such poverty, when lived in community, created a bond that was enviable among human relationships. When each one trusts that God provides, whatever comes is sufficient. It will simply be up to the community to distribute resources according to need. Trust, then, is the climate in such a supportive community because each member knows that what she has helped create will be there for her as well.[23, 24]

Clare's approach was one of collaboration and common sense rather than rigid rules and authoritarianism. She saw good in the sisters in her community, trusted their judgment and sincere commitment. Her confidence in God's guidance led her to coach them to step out in confidence too.

When one of the sisters was obliged to go out of the convent, Clare's rule offered some cautions, but nothing about fear of strangers or custody of the eyes, an older monastic practice of keeping one's eyes on the ground.[25] Rather, she urged her sisters to "praise God when you see beautiful trees, flowers, and bushes; always praise Him for and in all things when you see people and creatures."[26]

Legends and stories of miraculous deeds have followed Clare as they have Brigid and Hildegard, her companion monastery founders. There are tales of feeding and healing miracles. Some miracles involved safety from violence; like Brigid and Hildegard, and indeed all of the Holy Women here, Clare lived in a time of war.

One particularly dramatic story is documented in Clare's canonization record:

> Mercenary armies hired by warring nobles were terrorizing the countryside. At one point, soldiers scaled the walls of San Damiano by night and were inside the convent enclosure. Claire had the pyx containing the eucharist brought from the chapel to the entrance. There she knelt in fervent prayer tearfully begging God: "Lord, look upon

St. Clare with Monstrance, stained glass window at St. John Cantius Church, Chicago. Photo by Br. Michael-Francis, O.S.B., 2009.

these servants of yours, because I cannot protect them."[27]

She told her daughters she would be a hostage for them and that no harm would come to them as long as they stayed faithful.[28] Did Clare face the soldiers, holding the ciborium to an open window? Did they lose hold of their ladders and fall back, to the astonishment of the watching army? Details vary, but according to the record, the invaders left. This incident is the reason paintings of Clare often portray her holding a ciborium. Whatever happened, God acted.

A contemporary of Clare's, Mechthild of Magdeburg, said, "That prayer is powerful that a person makes with all her might."[29] Those words defined Clare, a Holy Woman capable of trusting God, letting go of all else, putting first her desire to be one with God, surrendering completely, and praying with a whole heart. Such was the life of this Holy Woman, kissed by God.

Francis

Hollowness of poverty,
Gaunt-framed friar,
Thou, now filled with fire,
Walk before me
Brown-robed,
Barefoot,
Thong-waisted,
Amongst the bird-thronged boughs,

Bearing
Wounds of brackish poorness,
Wounds of burning love,
Wounds of bleeding joy.
I follow.[30]

Discovering Clare

Until I began to research St. Clare as one of the Holy Women while I prepared a Kissed by God retreat, I didn't realize that it was her spirit of joy and single-minded pursuit of God that initially drew me into a Franciscan convent.

That story began when my grandfather died. I'd raced home from my out-of-state college to be with the family. Now, he was about to be buried.

Bleak, gray snow clouds hung low over the cemetery. I shivered a little sitting in the funeral home's shiny white car behind the hearse. It was comforting to be crowded there, knee to knee and shoulder to shoulder with Mom and Grandma, my brother and sisters, but I hadn't slept well the last nights and was tired from crying.

Shifting in the seat, I closed my eyes. In the restful stillness, I slipped into a quiet, inner place. Then, as if marching one by one, words slowly came into my mind: *What does it profit a man to gain the whole world and suffer the loss of his own soul?* In the silence, I turned the words over and over, examining them from all sides like facets of a gem. Loss of soul? Loss of one's true life?

Suddenly a rush of tears flooded me. I knew beyond doubt that my grandfather had lived his life faithfully. But what about me? What was missing? In that moment, I recognized a terrible yearning ... for what? For my own true life? For God? What was the life I so intensely longed for, the life that was uniquely mine?

I'd been thinking about entering the convent for a while. The School Sisters of Notre Dame had run my all-girls high school with efficiency and high standards. They let us know that with no boys around, we could be as smart as we really were—and we'd better be! I found plenty to admire in these women: the good they did, their dedication, their ideals. Their life was a special calling to serve. I appreciated the Notre Dame nuns I'd known throughout grade and high school, but it was the Franciscan Sisters, my Aunt Jean's order, who attracted me.

I'd resisted and resisted the idea, and never told my Mom or even my closest friends.[31]

I liked boys, clothes, high heels, lipstick, dances, and even secret cigarettes! I couldn't imagine giving them up at nineteen. Until now. When I finally told Mom, she said, "The sisters always seem so happy." I, too, had felt the peace and joy of these modern women whose unwavering pursuit was of God ... like Clare. I could feel Clare's joy leaping across the centuries when I was around them.

It was on the Feast of St. Clare, August 12, that I made my first vows in religion. That day, I stood in the church, smoothing my new veil and habit and ... then fell motionless. An ethereal song filled the vaulting cathedral. It took my breath away.

The courts of heaven are paved with stars,
glistening stars.
This is what love prepares for the bride,
glistening stars.
Oh, hide my life within your arms, in your embrace
Such love is God's mysterious gift, His love for me.[32]

With full heart, I spoke my vows yearning for that closeness with God.[33] It was a glorious day!

When the ceremony was over, the nun who had guided my spiritual preparation stood by my side. She quietly pressed something into my hand, smiled, and walked away. It was an illuminated holy card: *O taste, and see that the Lord is sweet: blessed is the man that hopeth in him,* the words of Psalm 34:9. Tears filled my eyes as that sweetness overflowed in my heart.

Now years later as I read about Clare, I understand that her gift of poverty meant she spent her life emptying her heart to make room for God, creating a vacuum that God would fill ... with joy. She wrote of it to a friend: "A hidden sweetness that God has reserved for those who love him."[34] The kiss of God!

Only now have I learned that Clare had paraphrased the words of the Psalm when she wrote them to her friend Princess Agnes of Bohemia. I knew nothing of the backstory of their friendship then. I had certainly experienced much closeness with the sisters I'd joined, some of whom are still very dear even now, so many years later. And I'd known Clare was close to her daughters in the new community. But I didn't know about her friendship with Agnes, had never read their affectionate letters that survive from the thirteenth century.[35] I tried to imagine the impossible distance those letters traveled from Assisi to what is now Prague.

Agnes had heard about Clare from Franciscan friars who somehow managed to cross the sea to preach in her father's kingdom. She was deeply moved by the story of her counterpart, also beautiful, wealthy, noble, and in love with God.

Agnes had undergone a dehumanizing process that had little to do with love. In the thirteenth century, young girls of noble families were promised in marriage even as children to bear male heirs, once old enough. Male succession was deemed essential for reasons of state alliance and inheritance. Agnes had undergone this empty betrothal repeatedly before her father agreed she could live her own life, one of charitable works.

Over time, Agnes built a hospital, hospice, friary, and convent in Prague. Her intent was that friars and nuns could serve the sick and dying. In 1234, Clare sent five nuns from San Damiano to the new convent. Seven young women of Bohemia, including Princess Agnes, soon joined them.[36] The loving relationship between Clare and Agnes had begun. They never met but corresponded for more than twenty years.

The last of the letters that remain from Clare, written just before her death, was a testament to her guidance and love of the younger woman:

> If I have not written to you as often as your soul—and mine
> as well—desire and long for, do not wonder, or think that
> the fire of love for you glows with less delight in the heart of
> your mother. No, this is the difficulty: the lack of messengers
> and the obvious dangers of the roads.[37]

113

On my vow day, I knew nothing of the friendship between Agnes and Clare. I only knew my heart was filled with sweetness. Only these many years later do I grasp Clare's promise of joy. It is a revelation, a stunning new kiss from God to learn the deep history of the words on the yellowing holy card still in my Bible.

Over the years since I left the structure of religious life, I have always thought of August 12 as the day I promised my life to God. It was very clear to me that my life had been set on a course. I never took back that promise—I just took it on the road! And that road had cataclysmic turning points. August 12, 1990, was the day my husband of twenty years made a revelation that essentially ended our marriage. Yes, the revelation described here in the chapter on the Samaritan Woman took place on that date.

That particular turn in the road has made me watchful of the calendar ... for blessings too. My one and only grandson was born on August 13, 2010—close enough! The very next year I had the biggest Clare surprise of my life. It was the year I visited Vienna, Budapest, and Prague.

Our tour of these three amazing cities included a day of leisure in Prague. We were on our own, free to roam the city. Our tour literature suggested a long list of options, but what caught my eye in the list was an art museum. It was within walking distance from our hotel, not far from the historic old town. Best of all, the day was sunny, just right for a stroll. We wended our way over cobblestoned streets to a small stone building.

The Prague National Museum stood unpretentiously in front of us. It didn't look like a museum. Well, whatever it was, we were going in.

Once inside, I was dazzled. The place was filled with medieval art: statuary, carvings, altar pieces, and paintings of the Madonna. This ancient art always transported me. Notes posted near the entrance said "Church of St. Agnes." At the time, the only St. Agnes I'd heard of was an early Christian martyr. As I read on, I learned I was indeed standing in a church, the very building that had been the original Poor Clare convent where Agnes lived with five sisters from San Damiano sent by Clare herself.[38]

I could only imagine the hardship of a lengthy sea crossing from Italy in the thirteenth century to this place in the present-day

Czech Republic. Those early women from San Damiano must have been hardy indeed.

This was my introduction to Agnes of Bohemia. Now I understood how this noblewoman had become a Poor Clare. She and her companions from Prague who joined the newly arrived Italian nuns had heard the invitation of the Spirit and felt the contagion of Clare's joy, even across miles.

The history blurb there in the museum said Agnes had provided land for a hospital about the same time the Poor Clares arrived from Italy. As I looked from the front door of this humble stone church across to the nearby buildings, I could see a multifloor complex. My map marked the spot with the symbol for a hospital. I looked again. From where I stood, I could see a gold cross glinting on the building's highest spire. The fine print on the map gave a bit of history: this modern Franciscan hospital was built on the site of one founded centuries ago by early friars.

My path had led me on this European journey ... right to the very first convent in old Bohemia filled with the first Poor Clares sent by Clare! I had to shake my head. One of the blessings of my mature years is to see more clearly the slow work of God in my life unfolding over time. It is a blessing and inspiration to realize I have been led at so many turns and continually surprised by the Spirit.

That we are joined in the Spirit and led by the Spirit is a truth I will never doubt. We are in a vast network and sisterhood of Holy Women named and unnamed in scripture and history, including our foremothers. All have been kissed by God and answered the call to create beauty on their path. Let us journey with them, the great cloud of witnesses, ready to be surprised again and again by Spirit.

Responding to Clare

Associations/archetypes: virgin, abbess, healer, mystic, lover, holy fool, nature, service, joy, poverty, fasting, bravery, Francis, light, Assisi

Imagine you are sitting with Clare. She tells you she sees Francis as a holy fool who can strip off his clothes in public to make a point. You know she admires his ability to see things as they are and speak the truths those in authority don't want to hear. Francis can play and be spontaneous, living in the moment with great vitality, not worrying about tomorrow. He is in love with God.

You quickly realize that Clare has the same "foolish" energy—she doesn't care what other people think either. She is joyfully in love with God, seeing His goodness in everything, in nature and in people and especially in her sisters. Her rule creates an atmosphere of freedom and trust among them.

The joy of God's closeness led to a kind of holy madness by our careful standards. Clare was so intent on filling herself with God that she had little concern for her own health. It never occurred to her to wonder whether it was safe to fast as much as she did. God's closeness filled her with trust and the realization that she wasn't just her body. Francis had to insist she moderate her behavior. She smiles as she recounts to you how lovingly he did that.

Ask her about the night she ran away to join Francis. Did she feel mischievous sneaking out of her father's house at night? And then, when Francis cut off her beautiful golden tresses ... how did she feel when she saw the pile of her hair on the floor at her feet? What does she tell you about that night?

Reflect on what you feel and how you think you and Clare are alike and different. Do you see the shadow of the fool in yourself at times, taking unwise chances or using poor judgment? Does the idea of the fool attract or repel you? Do you know why? What would happen if you experimented with the fool's freedom? Listen quietly for a few minutes to what Clare says to you.

When the conversation feels complete, write it in your journal. The next step is to look over your entry and choose a few words that capture your attention. End your writing by using them in a short prayer or poem. (See some ideas for how to write a poem in "Responding to Mary," page 35.)

P.S.: If you feel you need more of the fool energy in your life, you could add a little humor. www.laughfactory.com might be a good website to visit. Pick out a joke you like there and tell it to someone today. Make the intention that this small practice can be a spiritual ritual, to bring a little balance and lightness into the too-serious world. (For maximum effect, tell the joke in person, not just as an online "forward"!)

Teresa of Avila

1515–82 CE

Commemorated October 15

Teresa of Avila, a Spanish mystic of the sixteenth century, wrote a compelling love story of her journey with God that still teaches us today. Like all love stories, it had its ups and downs, twists and turns, but Teresa's wisdom, humor, energy, and courage continue to move and inspire us.

Teresa was born into the turmoil of the Reformation, Counter-Reformation, Spanish Inquisition, and Spain's entry into the New World.[1] The practical founder of monasteries, she was also a visionary. Of all the Holy Women we look at here, her life was the most imperiled; the bloody, devil-fearing Inquisition represented a mortal threat. In fact, she wrote in her autobiography that those who had such great fear of the devil frightened her more than the devil himself.[2] Despite the irony, she was in danger and knew it. Just as Joan of Arc, accused of hearing voices from the devil, was burned at the stake, Teresa could have suffered the same fate.[3]

There was another reason for her to fear the Inquisition. Not only was she a woman, but she came from a family of converted Jews. Both groups were suspected of heresy and demonic possession.

Teresa's backstory arises from Spanish history. In 1492, when Spain was finally able to overcome the Moors at Granada, the first to be exiled were the Jews. The only exceptions were those who converted to Christianity. Among these "conversos" was Teresa's grandfather, Juan Sanchez, who changed his name to Cepeda

---

Preceding page: *Teresa of Avila*, acrylic on canvas, by the author. Although she is portrayed here in habit and veil, her reputedly vivid eyes alone would have spoken to all she met as well as to this artist's imagination.

and moved his family from Toledo to Avila, hoping to find safety and perhaps tolerance. No one knows if the newly named family practiced as Jews under cover of assumed Catholicity,[4] but Teresa's upbringing was certainly Christian.

And so we meet Teresa de Ahumada y Cepeda,[5] a Spanish beauty.

As a young girl, Teresa was full of life. She was flirtatious, loved to dress up, kept her hands pretty, dressed her hair, and used perfume.[6] When Teresa was only fourteen, her mother died giving birth to her ninth child.[7] In the grieving household, her father had his hands full. Teresa had been her mother's only daughter and the two were close. In her grief and vulnerability, she and a young cousin became infatuated. Teresa later said her behavior "placed her father and brothers in danger,"[8] by which she meant it put her honor in need of their defense, a serious matter in those times. Her father managed the situation by putting his beautiful young daughter into a rigidly strict, enclosed convent school.

All went well for a while, but then Teresa became ill. Worried, her father brought her back home.[9] Poor health would burden Teresa over the long years of her life, but at that point, she couldn't have anticipated it.

During the next few years, Teresa helped her father raise the younger children. As she approached marriageable age, she was torn between the only options she could see for her life: marriage or the convent. In the midst of the busy Cepeda household, she recalled the calm and spiritual seriousness of her convent school and began to recognize her vocation. However, Our Lady of Grace, with all its severity, didn't attract her. A rather more lenient and open convent did: the Carmelite Convent of the Incarnation.[10]

Her father, ever in charge, was strongly opposed! In light of the anguish he had experienced as a young Jewish boy persecuted along with his whole family,[11] he certainly didn't want his favored daughter to enter a Catholic convent. It seems to me Teresa was very secure in her father's love, because when she was twenty she took off for the convent anyway, in her inimitable fashion.

Tradition has it that on the morning Teresa of Avila was leaving home ... a gentleman saw her climbing into the carriage and could not resist making an appreciative assessment of her ankles. "Take a good look," she is said to have called out merrily (and cryptically, for she had not told anyone but her brother she was going), "that's the last one you'll get!"[12]

Of course, she needed a dowry to enter the Incarnation and her father wasn't about to agree, much less provide her funds. Her brother, bound for the New World and presumably all its gold, pledged his wealth[13] to the superiors, and Teresa was in. The Incarnation's original Carmelite Rule had been strict, but some years before Teresa entered, it was modified. The new rule allowed nuns to keep their worldly possessions. Later Teresa instituted an egalitarian atmosphere, but when she joined, the candidates with the smallest dowries slept in dormitories and those with means slept in apartments with their own kitchens.[14] Such was her suite. We aren't sure if Teresa ever had a dog, but that also was acceptable.

Despite the financial resources of many of the nuns, the convent itself was too small and poor. According to one biographer:

> Counting servants and nuns' live-in relatives, some two hundred women were packed inside the convent walls. Scant wonder (they were) permitted ... to visit their families whenever they chose and thus eat at someone else's expense. Visitors to the convent were welcome for the same reason. They often brought sweets or a bag of fruit. Sometimes they were widowers ... or young girls pondering a vocation, but more often they were men-about-town looking for ... a pleasant conversation, perhaps even a harmless flirtation. Overall, the atmosphere seems to have been that of a sorority "at-home" or even a salon.[15]

What bothered Teresa wasn't necessarily a threat to chastity but "rather the hypnotic spell of pure triviality, the intoxicating fun of holding forth wittily."[16]

Teresa was in conflict. The extrovert in her enjoyed the superficial chat and admiring company, but her prayer life was deepening. Her confessors, perhaps not accustomed to taking nuns seriously, were no help. She struggled, asking herself, "Was this such a little thing?" She sensed it wasn't.

John of the Cross, a noted Carmelite contemporary, became Teresa's friend. Himself a mystic, he didn't think her concerns were trivial and told her, "It makes no difference whether a bird be held by a slender thread or by a rope; the bird is bound, and cannot fly until the cord that holds it is broken."[17]

Despite the atmosphere of distraction, over the first years she was at the Incarnation, Teresa made rapid progress in her prayer life. But then her inner turmoil increased.

Finally, she became ill again, and this time very seriously. Well-meaning but very aggressive healing efforts were made. These violent treatments weakened her until finally, she fell into a coma. She lay unresponsive for over four days, and the family thought she was dead. A grave was dug, while her father alone insisted, "The child is not dead!" At last, to his great relief, she awoke. She was so weak that she couldn't move and suffered great pain. After this near-death experience, Teresa wanted to return to her convent, feeble as she was, to either get better or die. Return she did, and although it took her nearly three years, in gradual stages she regained the strength to walk and finally return to a normal state of health.[18]

Her convent, however, was still filled with frivolous parlor conversations. Teresa knew she needed solitude for her intense inner life. She had experience enough of the deeper stages of mental prayer by now to understand that no one could enter them whose attention and desires were not completely unified. She explains:

It was one of the most painful lives, I think that one can imagine; for neither did I enjoy God nor did I find happiness in the world. When I was experiencing the enjoyments of the world, I felt sorrow when I recalled what I owed to God. When I was with God, my attachment to the world disturbed me. This is a war so troublesome that I don't know how I was able to suffer it even a month, much less for so many years.[19]

Then, when she was nearly forty, Teresa had a profound grace.

One minute (she) was walking past an image of the crucified Christ recently placed in a corridor of the Incarnation, and the next ... she was on her knees, sobbing, repenting of nearly twenty years' indifference, and begging God to strengthen her once and for all.[20]

She wrote in her autobiography, "I would not rise from there until He granted what I was begging Him for."[21] She refused to get up, demanding with the full force of her determined personality that God change her on the spot. God heard her: "From that moment on, the things that had been hardest for Teresa became almost effortless. The parlor exerted no pull on her now, and she eagerly went to her hours of prayer."[22]

Her life was changed. That Teresa of Avila was a true mystic and experienced ecstasies during this period is well documented in her writings and those of others. She speaks of receiving

delights and favors from God (and) moments when she was lifted up out of herself and into God's presence. She was a bride, swept off her feet now by the attentions of the lover ... She felt his presence now, accompanying her everywhere. Asked by her directors how she knew he was there, she explained, "in the dark, when someone is close by, you just know he's there ..."[23]

Italian sculptor Gian Lorenzo Bernini knew the widely told stories of Teresa's raptures in his day. In 1652, seventy years after her death, he created a sculpture portraying her ecstasy. In it, she was visited by an angel ...

very beautiful ... one of those very sublime angels that appear to be all afire ... I saw in his hands a large golden dart ... this angel plunged the dart several times into my heart and ... it reached deep within me. When he drew it out, I thought he was carrying off with him the deepest part of me; and he left me all on fire with great love of God.[24]

The Ecstasy of St. Teresa of Avila, sculpture by Bernini, 1652. Capella Cornaro, Santa Maria Della Vittoria, Rome.

The rich imagery of Teresa's vision inspired Bernini to capture the joy of the bride, the passionate love of God.

A significant influence on French and German monastics in the thirteenth century had been the sermons of St. Bernard of Clairvaux on *The Song of Songs*.[25] Did Teresa know about the bridal mysticism that developed when his sermons impacted monasteries of his day? Possibly. (We do know that Teresa wrote her own paraphrase of *The Song of Songs* that follows this chapter.) God's spirit, however, knew no boundaries of time or space where Teresa was concerned. Just as Joan of Arc didn't go looking for her voices, Teresa hadn't sought the angel of her vision. When one is open and prepared, God takes the initiative. Perhaps Bernini, ready with his chisel one hundred years later, knew about Teresa's commentary on this most passionate book of the Bible, and could well have known about bridal mysticism as well, even without the Internet!

The reform of Teresa's Carmelite convent soon followed. Enclosure of the cloister for the sake of cultivating prayer meant the end of the social parlor. In a return to the ancient rule of the order, poverty meant simplicity of dress and even wearing sandals made of rope rather than shoes.[26]

One of the most important reforms was Teresa's insistence that there be no endowments because they came from wealthy families with certain conditions. Up until then, convents had provided security and safety for unmarriageable noblewomen. The money from their endowment might lavishly decorate a memorial chapel for nobles of their family, where nuns were required to pray twenty-four hours a day for the souls of their deceased so the family knew the terms of their investment were being fulfilled.[27]

When the nuns began to provide for themselves in the simple ways at hand, Teresa knew they and their life of prayer would be authentic, and perhaps be recognized by their community for their true value.

Teresa was a woman of prodigious energy writing with brilliance to make contemplative prayer comprehensible. She kept at it with single-minded determination, even when founding monasteries all over Spain. She urged her sisters to also be constant in their work, especially when dealing with aches and pains. This woman knew herself. I can almost hear the note of humor in her offhanded observations of their womanly behavior. Teresa could smile and admit to her sisters a bit of her own attachment to comfort:

> Hardly have we begun to imagine that our heads are aching than we stay away from choir, though that would not kill us either. One day we were absent because we had a headache some time ago; another day, because our head had just been aching again; and on the next three days in case it should ache once more.[28]

Teresa wrote letters, treatises, and books about prayer with depth, profundity, and clarity throughout her lifetime. Although she lived in the sixteenth century, it was only in 1970 that she was named a Doctor of the Church.[29] Her writings and teachings on prayer were significant: *The Book of My Life* (her autobiography) written in 1562, *The Way of Perfection* in 1565, and *The Interior Castle* in 1577. Nevertheless, when her life was examined as a candidate for the title of Doctor of the Church, she was criticized at the same time for leaving her cloister. No matter that she traveled to found more than twenty monasteries across the Spanish countryside; the papal nuncio called her a "restless, disobedient gadabout."[30] A lovely statue entitled *The Vagabond* stands outside her church in Avila to this day. Teresa was simply following her call.

Undaunted, she kept up her efforts into her later years. On one trip, her donkey cart was loaded with supplies crossing a flooded river. The turbulent water was too much for the donkey. While Teresa

The Vagabond–Teresa of Avila, statue in Avila.
Photograph by the author.

watched, the cart tipped over and their baggage floated off downstream. Just then, she heard God's voice in her spirit: "This is how I treat my real friends." Not missing a beat, she replied, "Then it's no wonder ... that your Lordship has so few!"[31] I can just see her standing on the muddy bank, fists on hips, letting God know how she felt!

Teresa was always close to God despite the fact that she had no mystical experiences in her last years. Although the raptures ceased, her conversation with Him about the spill in the river and her busy life show us their intimacy. She complained to God:

How is it, my God, that you have given me this hectic busy life when I have so little time to enjoy your presence. Throughout the day people are waiting to speak with me, and even at meals I have to continue talking to people about their needs and problems. During sleep itself I am still thinking and dreaming about the multitude of concerns that surround me. I do all this not for my own sake, but for yours. To me my present pattern of life is a torment; I only hope that for you it is truly a sacrifice of love.

I know that you are constantly beside me, yet I am usually so busy that I ignore you. If you want me to remain so busy, please force me to think about and love you even in the midst of such hectic activity. If you do not want me so busy, please release me from it, showing how others can take over my responsibilities.[32]

Love talk, yes, and complaints about overwork and times of frustration. Teresa of Avila was a flesh-and-blood woman and a fully human mystic deeply kissed by God. Out of that great love came inspired writings to guide us on our way and a network of reformed monasteries to provide sanctuaries for numberless lives of prayer for more than five centuries in many countries around the world. The deep kiss of God proved most generative as Love's divine energy flowed through Teresa of Avila, mother and sister to all of us.

The Song of Songs

O that you would kiss me with the
kisses of your mouth!
For your love is better than wine,
your anointing oils are fragrant,
your name is oil poured out;
therefore the maidens love you.
Draw me after you, let us make haste.
The king has brought me into his chambers.
We will exult and rejoice in you;
we will extol your love more than wine;

rightly do they love you.
The voice of my beloved!
Behold, he comes,
leaping upon the mountains,
bounding over the hills.
My beloved is like a gazelle,
or a young stag.
Behold, there he stands
behind our wall
gazing in at the windows,
looking through the lattice.
My beloved speaks and says to me:
"Arise, my love, my fair one,
and come away;
for lo, the winter is past,
the rain is over and gone.
The flowers appear on the earth,
the time of singing has come,
and the voice of the turtledove
is heard in our land."[33]
—Teresa's paraphrase of scripture, Ch. 1 v. 2–4, Ch.2, v 8–12

Discovering Teresa of Avila

As a very young nun, I was tantalized by what little I knew about St. Teresa of Avila. She was a mystic, she had visions, and I wanted to read all about her. The only problem was that my novice mistress had other ideas. "No, no, dear sister! Not for you! Not for beginners!" Today as I reflect on that moment, a dreamlike image comes to me: I hold a lovely, embossed invitation in my hand, but then it slips away and I can't find it.

Years passed. I'd been called out of the convent, called into a time of single life, then called into marriage and motherhood. The coming together in marriage taught me a spiritual reality about union I hadn't expected. But the biggest surprise came as I sat nursing my lovely baby. Bare-breasted in the warmth of human flesh against human flesh, I fell into deep states of prayer.[34] Wonderment at God's close touch in the midst of so much sensuality somehow reminded me of ... Teresa of Avila!

In the mysterious way that our path winds to God, I had needed the lessons of marriage and motherhood to bring me to readiness for Teresa's passionate relationship with her Divine Lover. To demonstrate the truth of the adage "When the student is ready, the teacher comes," just then our diocesan institute offered the very first seminars on St. Teresa and St. John of the Cross. I signed up. Soon, under the expert tutelage of Fr. Ernie Larkin, O. Carm., I read *The Way of Perfection*, *The Interior Castle*, and Teresa's autobiography, *The Book of My Life*.

I loved Teresa's explanation of prayer as a progress through the rooms of a magnificent castle carved out of diamond. At the center were the throne room and the King.[35] At the same time, I had discovered the richness of Carl Jung's inner life and writings, and when the Phoenix Friends of Jung Institute formed, I became a member. Jung also symbolized the Self as an archetypal King at the heart of his mandalas.[36]

My study of the writings of Teresa and Jung led to my growth as a counselor and spiritual director, and portended unforeseen developments in my future. I was about to learn that my dreams and artwork could convey what my conscious mind was unable to grasp.

My unforeseen future began when a crisis hit so violently that my twenty-year marriage abruptly collapsed. I was thrust into confusion and fear. My life suddenly seemed based on sand, swept away. Stunned and disoriented, I felt powerless to keep everyday life under control.

The very morning this momentous change was about to arrive, I woke strangely unsettled:

I'd dreamed of a huge mansion surrounded by a shaded lagoon and many pools on the rolling grounds of a great estate. I'd wandered from room to room, amazed to find it filled with treasures: ornate furniture, chests overflowing with silver, richly colored tapestries and jewels, all haphazardly crowded together. I was amazed to discover the mansion was attached to my everyday house. But once I left it, I didn't know how to get into it again, I couldn't find the entryway. Sweaty with frustration, I rolled out of the tangled sheets.[37]

This was the first of a series of dreams about the mansion.

The second dream arrived the morning after another tumultuous event. After the end of my marriage, I was pulled away from my fledgling counseling practice by the need for a regular paycheck. I desperately wanted to get back to what I knew was my calling, but Fr. Ernie, now my spiritual director, told me to be patient.

I'd tried to be patient but I'd been grappling for months with a tough project at my job. I saw a remedy to the problem but lacked the authority to act without the boss's rubber stamp. Then the day arrived when the two of us were seriously at odds over a crucial decision. It wasn't the first time. If he didn't support me, I would leave and I told him so.

I fled the office in turmoil. On the long drive home, I wrestled with questions. Was this the guidance I had waited for? Was it time for me to leave?

I was in for a night of tossing and turning. Finally, toward morning, I fell asleep and drifted into a dream. It was the old dream I'd had on the day of my marriage crisis and it picked up where the first one left off.

I was home in my everyday house, still unable to get into the treasure-filled mansion, but this time ... I ascended a flight of stairs, stopping at a mirror on a door. I studied my reflection for a moment, then walked through it effortlessly, finding myself in the heart of the mansion, finally among the treasures.

I understood. By reexamining the amazing complexities

I'd lived with for a lifetime, I found the entryway and passed through to the spacious mansion and its abundant treasures. Looking at myself was the answer, not allowing myself to be confused and blocked in the darkness. Looking at myself was the way to the treasure within ...[33, 39]

The dream taught me that when I looked within, I could cross the threshold before me, trusting God for what came next. Now these decades later, as I reread Teresa, I see that despite her fears, she stepped across the thresholds in front of her both literally and figuratively. She tells us:

I had learned that it was better to rent a house and take possession first and then look for one to buy. This was so for many reasons, the principal one being that I didn't have a cent to buy one with. Once the monastery was founded, the Lord would then provide;... as for me, I was never much bothered by what happened once possession of a foundation had taken place; all my fears came before.[40]

God provided for her and He has provided richly for me! Neither of us had a cent! It was in those days that I learned to quiet my fears by repeating Teresa's prayer (this is a slight paraphrase):

Let nothing disturb you.
Let nothing affright you.
All things are changing.
God alone never changes.
She who has God has everything.[41]

I learned that my dreams could convey what my conscious mind couldn't grasp. I had long attended to them. This inner work had led me to a Jungian training program of intensive journaling designed to elicit creativity and spiritual growth. Dream visions were one thing, but I had never had a waking vision, nor particularly aspired to do so. The closest I had ever come was during an exercise at a journaling workshop. The facilitator called the meditation "twilight imaging,"[42] something I'd never heard of before. He directed us to seat ourselves comfortably and to begin to breathe deeply and slowly. His voice led me to a quiet place inside. Without suggesting any images, he lapsed into silence. The silence deepened.

Then, gradually, a "vision" gently unfolded:

I see a brown horse ... coming very close, each pore of his wet nose, his bright eyes, his shiny coat—What is not to love about this horse? I climb on his bare back, my arms around his neck, his soft mane blowing in my face as we gently rise, smoothly rise, easily rise, from the flower-filled meadow until we are flying, higher, higher, ever higher. In the mist and clouds, my lovely horse brightens until he is white. I hold tightly as we fly, as he grows a horn, a jeweled horn, as he champs his bit, a jeweled bit casting rainbow prisms everywhere. We fly up, up, up through the clouds, through the mist, through the rainbows to a castle, every turret and wall cylindrical. The doors open before us. We follow a long red carpet leading to the throne room. A king with long white hair and beard sits casually on his throne, one leg thrown over an arm of it, foot dangling, his shiny cylindrical crown cocked crookedly over one eye. He speaks: "Why have you come?" I ask him for the rest of my life. He gives me a jewel, an immense jewel. Suddenly, I am back in the meadow with the brown horse, and I have the jewel.[43]

I have painted the five scenes of this vision to capture my wonder and to honor the gift it still is in my life. The final painting portrays the jewel as I saw it, an immense diamond. Teresa's images of castle, mansion, and diamond, archetypes all, clearly carried an energy in my inner world. They flooded into my dreams and meditation for their own purpose, perhaps to bring me to greater consciousness of the One Who Loves Us.

As I read Teresa today, urging her sisters to know themselves but not to fool themselves,[44] I'm grateful to still be working on that. These days as I live alone in my widowhood of thirteen years, I consider my little home my cloister, the park where I walk each day with its overarching green canopy my beautiful cathedral, the birds trilling there my choir. In music and in silence, in solitude and in company, the voice of the Spirit speaks.

Responding to Teresa of Avila

Associations/archetypes: lover, virgin, abbess, leader, mystic, traveler, reformer, determined, author, verbal finesse, cook, wise woman/elder, angel, arrow, interior castle, Song of Songs, bride, headaches

There's quite a gap in time between Brigid of Ireland, who lived in the fifth century, and Teresa of Avila, a woman of the sixteenth century. It is striking, however, how much energy they each poured into founding monasteries all over their homelands—tireless travelers, both.

Let's look in on them sitting together by the fire, perhaps drying their rain-drenched capes and soaking their tired feet in hot water ... footsore and weary but congratulating each other on carrying the message of Jesus to more and more of their people. Brigid worked hard to provide shelter for the nuns who joined her work, and Teresa, too, depended on God's providence for one monastery after another, opening them without having the money to do so up front.

Teresa tells Brigid her story: "I would worry about how I could finance the new foundation, but once we were in, I stopped worrying. I saw time after time how God provided even though I didn't have one gold or silver coin!"

Brigid laughs. "I had to beg from the local chieftains to get a bit of land until finally a miracle happened. Then one particularly crusty old fellow was so worried God would give me his entire kingdom, he not only granted me good land, but he even built us a monastery."

Teresa, wriggles her steaming toes and smiles. "Well, despite our struggles with landlords, we had something else quite wonderful in common: our close traveling friends."

Brigid nods, "Ah, yes, Good Patrick. We crossed Ireland in all directions so many times and when we got to sleep, even had the same prophetic dreams about our work for God."

Teresa: "Yes, and I had John of the Cross watching out for me.

He really understood what God was doing in my spirit when no one else did. We both worked hard to reform our monastic way of life in Spain. Friends on the path are essential, essential! God's gift!"

Think about your work, your fatigue, your issues, your anxieties about money. How does this dialogue relate to your concerns? What friends and support has God sent you? Do you resonate with Brigid's and Teresa's feelings? Join their conversation with your stories and listen closely to what these two women so energized by God have to say to you. When you sense the exchange is complete, sit quietly for a while in the presence of the Holy One. Then you may want to journal about this meditation.

Holy Young Women

Joan of Arc

1412–31 CE

Commemorated May 30

Joan of Arc, a fifteenth-century French girl credited with saving her country from the English, lived the shortest life of the Holy Women whose stories are gathered here. Despite that, she is probably memorialized by more writers, playwrights, artists, and filmmakers than most of them put together.

Think of it. The list is a long one: Shakespeare, Voltaire, Schiller, Twain, Anouilh, Shaw[1] ... even a comic book cover from 1950. And artists: Bastien-Lepage, Auvergne, Scherrer, Ingres, Lenepveu, Cecil B. DeMille, and Haskell Coffin, who put her face on a World War I Savings Bond poster.[2]

Joan is remembered for courage in following her unshakeable belief in God's call. On a practical level, she is also in our memory because we have many documents from her trial and other sources. Even so, this young French girl, born in Domrémy in 1412 and burned at the stake in 1431,[3] captures the imagination.

By the time Joan was born in 1412, England had occupied France for seventy-five years. It was a time of social upheaval. The population had been decimated by famine, plague, war, the collapse of serfdom, and the resulting poverty.[4] France was a country of faith, but the church was in turmoil too. One of Joan's biographers documents those days: "Far from being separated from government, the Church *was* the state. Rule was by divine right; only an archbishop representing Christ on earth could anoint a king."[5]

Joan was a small child when the schism created by three popes came to an end,[6] but the reverberations were still felt in society. The French papacy's corruption caused the court and the people to turn

Preceding page: *Joan of Arc*, acrylic on canvas,
by the author.

away from ecclesiastical leadership and toward visionaries.[7] It was into this milieu that Joan was born.

At age thirteen, she started hearing voices, but she didn't tell anyone for several years. First came Archangels Michael and Gabriel. Their messages offered Joan mild encouragement: "Be good, go to church." St. Michael, of course, was known as the powerful archangel of crusaders and soldiers, those from whom the phenomenon of knighthood arose. And Archangel Gabriel, the messenger angel, was well known for inviting Mary to her momentous role.[8] Later, Joan identified the voices of St. Margaret and St. Catherine, early virgin martyrs who stood as role models for her.[9]

By the time she was fifteen, her voices spoke no longer of prayer, church-going, and virginity but of battle.[10] They directed her to contact Charles, the Dauphin, who needed to take charge of France. They promised she would find assistance in Robert de Baudricourt, a courtier with connections to Charles.[11] After many behind-the-scenes court machinations, Sir Robert did assist her.

This wooden statue of St. Catherine holds a broken wheel on which she was to be killed. When it broke, the Roman emperor had her beheaded for refusing to deny her faith. Produced by Niklaus Weckmann the Elder and Workshop, German (duchy of Swabia. Ulm) 1515. From Philadelphia Museum of Art. Photo by the author.

At this juncture, she cut her hair[12] and asked for men's clothing.[13] Without words, Joan communicated her intent to follow the voices' lead to save France, to follow her call to the role of a virgin warrior. She had vowed herself to God. Joan was convinced that her virginity would empower her with divine help to accomplish what was ahead of her.

No one could imagine this child of seventeen leading an army, but she was surprising in many ways. Joan dressed in men's clothing while waiting for armor to be made.[14, 15] When she was fitted into it, onlookers must have wondered how this slight girl would be strong enough to wear those forty pounds for days at a time.[16]

She was called the Maid of Orleans because of her great victory there in "the bloodiest military engagement of the Hundred Years War since Agincourt."[17] Although she was named Joan by her parents, Isabel and Jacque d'Arc, she later called herself La Pucelle or "Maid." The term is from the Latin *puella*, meaning a girl not yet a woman.[18] Joan wanted to emphasize with her name as well as her clothing that her virginity was inextricably connected to her powerful call and arduous undertaking.

Joan set out leading her army under a twelve-foot-long white banner. Her voices had described its design, showing Jesus holding the world with angels on either side. When the English army saw "a cloud of white butterflies unfurling" from it, they fell back in panicky disarray, as if from a startling light. To them, it was proof of Joan's frightening sorcery. Many eye witnesses said she was "luminous in battle, light not flaring off her armor so much as radiating from the girl within."[19] Followers said the light was a sign of holiness, the light she saw when her voices spoke. History attests that crowds of villagers joined her army, inspired by Joan's faith and her triumphal banner.

Later, Joan told her judges that she carried her standard into battle "so as not to kill anyone."[20] Banners as well as swords were customary accoutrements to armor in the fifteenth century, and Joan did carry a sword. However, she sought out a particular sword, although she knew it only by reputation and perhaps only through her voices. Legend held that it had been carried by Charles Martel, the first king of the Franks in the eighth-century Crusades, and had been "bathed in the blood of infidels."[21]

Joan told her judges that her voices described this renowned

Joan's banner. Harrison's illustration, figure 13.

sword to her, and even its whereabouts. Sure enough, it was found in a church in Tours, all rusted. Joan testified in her trial that "the priests rubbed it, and the rust fell off at once without effort."[22]

Forceful attempts were made to discredit all of Joan's claims, including her aversion to killing anyone. Despite the efforts of the inquisitors, only one witness testified to seeing her use a sword. Jean, Duke of Alençon, saw her "chase a girl who was with the soldiers so hard, with her sword drawn, that she broke her sword over the prostitute's back."[23]

That Joan's only known use of her historic sword was on a pros-titute tells us much about her struggles. When as a young teenager Joan told her father of her intent to join the army, he immediately concluded she meant to become a prostitute, a camp follower.[24] Later, in naming herself La Pucelle, Joan made a "preemptive strike against being seen as a camp follower because it wasn't only Jacques d'Arc who presumed prostitution was the sole purpose of a woman among soldiers."[25] As far as we know, this rift with her father was never healed and her stance on her chastity never changed.

Regarding prostitutes, not only did she drive them away from the army, but she required her soldiers to conduct themselves as

Equestrian statue of Joan by Emmanuel Frémiet,
1874. The original is in the Place des Pyramides,
Paris; this replica is in Philadephia.
Photo by the author.

chastely as their leader. She decreed that any soldier caught with a
prostitute be forced to marry her.[26]

The penalty was never imposed, however. One of her witnesses
explained, "When we were in her company we had no wish or desire

to approach or have intercourse with women," adding, "That seems to me almost a miracle."[27,28]

From the beginning, Joan's chastity was doubted and questioned. She underwent repeated physical examinations up to and during her trial. She zealously guarded it because of the absolute need to fulfill her promise to God and to be used for the immense cause of saving France.

As the time of her trial approached, her inquisitors planned to charge her with heretical blasphemy and witchcraft. Joan knew that if they could prove she wasn't a virgin, her veracity would be destroyed. While in jail and at the mercy of predatory guards, she took extreme measures. Her biographers describe that she bound herself into what was for all intents a chastity belt to prevent the possibility of rape.

> Two layers of hosen were securely fastened to the doublet, the inner layer being waist-high conjoined woolen hosen attached to the doublet by fully twenty cords, each cord tied into three eyelets apiece (two on the hosen and one on the doublet) for a total of forty attachment points on the inner layer of hosen. The second layer, which was made of rugged leather, seems to be have been attached by yet another set of cords. Once this outfit was thus fastened together by dozens of cords connecting both layers to the doublet, it would be a substantial undertaking for someone to try to pull off these garments ... the use of twenty cords on the inner layer was an excessively large and exceedingly awkward amount for this type of clothing, which normally had no more than half that number, indicating that she was deliberately taking measures to further increase its protective utility at the cost of her own convenience.[29]

The trial progressed and her virginity was once again confirmed. Finally, when Joan complained she couldn't tie these laces tightly enough to protect herself from the guards, the English realized a contemptuous rape would reflect on them. Only then were her guards "replaced by a putatively less uncivilized team."[30]

The demands and threats of the trial continued. Joan was

legally entitled to beg intervention by the pope, but the obvious power plays of the Inquisition had frightened envoys. No one would carry Joan's appeal to Pope Eugene.[31] After several trials, the judge insisted that she renounce the voices that guided her as the devil's ... she would not. Joan was condemned to death and burned as a heretic and witch.[32]

Joan of Arc died in 1431. Twenty-five years later in 1456, the trial was nullified.[33] Three prelates chosen by the pope came to Rouen, to the very spot where Joan had been dragged in chains. The prelates stood there and read the document of nullification:

> We say and pronounce that we judge this trial record and sentences that contain deceit, slander, contradiction and manifest error of law and of fact, and the execution of all that then ensured, were and are null, invalid and without effect or value. And nevertheless, as is necessary and required by reason, we quash, suppress, and annul them, removing all of their strength.[34]

Joan had saved France from the encroachment of England and had been vindicated. The wrongs done to her and her family were finally recognized.

But there ensued a cruel turn of events. Despite the nullification, Joan's trial and death set off a firestorm of witch hunts. Her death in flames was not the first, although many historians consider hers the first great witchcraft trial. A century of public burnings preceded Joan's death: deaths of midwives, healers, prostitutes, victims of rape—women without protection of father, uncle, brother, or son, judged by slander. Such violence continued after Joan's death, a "vast holocaust" of women, in the words of one historian.[35]

When compared to Joan's battles, the immensity of the outcome is clear. Joan had led just a scanty number of battles with a total loss of fewer than ten thousand men. Her trial and its verdict led to three hundred years of witch hunts, and the death of as many as one hundred thousand women.[36]

St. Joan of Arc was canonized over four hundred years later in 1920 and became a patroness of France. She stands today as a sister not only to the French but to all women victimized by cultures and systems of misogyny.

Discovering Joan of Arc

It strikes me that Joan of Arc didn't go looking for a word or a message; she just accepted the voices that spoke to her. When they first came, she was a very young adolescent, and to me, they don't seem so different from the fairy tales of my girlhood. Always filled with wonderings and intuitions, I loved the world of imagination. And it included dreams of saints and stories of angels in the Bible.

It was good news to me in those days of Catholic grade school that the nuns told us the Bible stories were inspired by the Holy Spirit. I'm not sure they said, "the Creative Spirit" in the next breath, but my mind leaped to it.

I loved to read and write and began to wonder more and more about how a writer came up with the stories I loved. I wondered about what was inside such a person. But I wasn't old enough to clearly ask my questions; I didn't have the vocabulary.

Once in college, it was a different matter. I fully expected to learn the secret of inspiration, the creative spark. I still remember my first upper-level English class. I was so excited, soaking up the professor's every word ... until I realized her focus was on plot development, historical background, setting, character, figurative language. It dawned on me, sadly, that even here I wasn't likely to get my question answered. I was disappointed! Who could explain this mystery to me?

I thought I might be getting closer when the class turned from novels to poetry. William Blake's work was lightly touched on, but even so, it registered with me that he was a visionary. Blake believed that his writing and engravings came from a source greater than himself, that he was taking dictation. The professor duly noted that he was criticized in his time by those who thought his claims unreal.

Still in the dark, my thoughts turned back to dreams, miracles, angels, and saints. What I knew about St. Francis of Assisi, the founder of the religious order I belonged to, was that he was a mystic. I thought of other mystics and realized I had yet to study their writings.

The information I gleaned was mostly historical. St. Ignatius Loyola founded the Jesuits. St. John of the Cross founded the Carmelites. St. Teresa of Avila reformed women's monasteries in her day. It was years later that I studied their writings: Ignatius's *Exercises*, John of the Cross's *Dark Night of the Soul*, Teresa of Avila's *Interior Castle*. As I read, their words carried me to what was beyond. Their lives were inspired. Like the writers of the scripture, these mystics of the monastic tradition believed they were called to teach others their innermost experience, inspired by Spirit.

Joan of Arc held a place among these saints. Once again, what I knew about her was historical, having to do with her battles and martyrdom without going into what her inner experience meant to her. Although the transcript of the trial that condemned her to burn at the stake had long been available, I had never read or heard any of her actual words.[37]

Why were Joan's words so important to me? Because they came when I most needed them, when I was at a turning point.

I had been journaling and writing poetry for years by then. Images had often seemed to come to me without effort, as if they were lined up at the door of my consciousness waiting for me to put pen to paper. And, in my creative process, I often lost track of time, forgetting where I was, absorbed ... writing for hours and only coming back when I noticed my aching back or growling stomach.[38]

So I sat one day journaling as I had done many times and am doing today, allowing inspiration to flood out onto my page. Because my God was still a God of judgment, I had a frightening experience. It was as if I sensed a denied part of myself, a part in darkness, in shadow. My fear was so great that I retreated from the powerful voice of intuition, closing off a part of my spirit's potential. It was safer to hide behind religion than open to imagination. I had known this silent place to be safe before and couldn't understand why it felt so dangerous now. I became a very, very careful journal writer and continued to seek spiritual direction, training, and psychological studies.

However, my anxiety was hard to shake. My good friend Marilyn, who was attending charismatic renewal classes on the gifts of the Spirit, noticed. When I described my upsetting inner experience, she put an arm around my shoulder. "Why don't you come to church with me tonight? I think it will do you good." I demurred. I wasn't sure.

She'd asked me several times, keeping in touch. On our next coffee date, she could see that my mixed feelings and doubt persisted. Marilyn gave me a warm smile. "Well, I'm on my way to class again. Love to have you."

I could see the concern in her eyes. "If you want to leave at any time, no problem. I'll slip out with you." Since I'd seen her last, my shaky feelings had not gone away. Just being with my friend for a while gave me a boost.

I smiled back. "Thanks, Marilyn. You're very convincing." I linked my arm through hers and whispered in her ear with a little laugh, "I give up! I give in!"

We arrived a few minutes late for the talk in the crowded church hall. As we settled into our seats, several women near us stood, one by one, giving what I learned were "testimonies" about manifestations of the Spirit. Speaking in tongues? Prophecy?

Marilyn saw my pale face. Would this storytelling take me too close to the dark place I'd discovered in my own inner world? I felt like circling carefully around these women and making a break for the door!

Just then, a religious sister in full regalia stepped to the front of the room. Despite the updating of nuns' habits after the Vatican Council, she was still old school, and in that moment, I found her garb and manner very reassuring. She began by saying she was ready to bring us to a new place of prayer. The room grew quiet. She lit a candle on the makeshift table that stood for an altar, then turned to encourage us. "Just relax. Take your time ... Now, a few deep breaths ... and you may begin to slow your breath.... Perhaps you would like to close your eyes." When she paused, the room was still.

"Come, Holy Spirit, fill the hearts of your faithful ..." Her voice was quiet but very clear as she prayed. We sat in silence. After what seemed a long time, she spoke softly. "Notice what comes into your mind now as you open to God. Listen to what is spoken inside your heart."

I sat without moving while the hushed silence expanded. Then, suddenly anxious, I opened my eyes. The sister was looking right at me. She nodded slightly as if acknowledging my apprehension, then smiled broadly. She spoke, her voice soft. "Just allow the work of the Spirit." Had she read my mind? I was left to wonder. After a few more minutes of quiet, she said, "Thank you, Holy One," and closed our brief meditation. I stretched a little, then couldn't help noticing a peacefulness in the group.

Sister continued her presentation, elaborating on ways to deepen our meditation. She encouraged us to simply release passing thoughts, should they arise. She assured us that as we spent time in prayer, we would more easily be able to discern when a thought that came up was not a distraction but a matter that deserved our notice. Yes, discernment: I wanted to know about that.

I released a breath I hadn't realized I'd been holding. Had I absorbed the calmness of her voice? Whatever had happened, I felt much more relaxed. What a relief. I was grateful.

Then, she asked us, "Do you know whose feast day this is?" I looked at Marilyn. May 30? Neither of us had a clue.

Sister chuckled. "Well, let me tell you a story about Joan of Arc."

We all knew she was a young French girl who had been burned at the stake for heresy and witchcraft in the Middle Ages. I didn't know, however, that she had been subjected to several trials after her capture by the English. Nor did I know that she had been badly mistreated in prison. Her accusers had made every effort to exhaust and wear down their young prisoner. They repeatedly demanded she recant the messages she heard, messages from God through angels and saints that told her she would put the French king on his rightful throne. By following these messages, Joan led her troops to great victories against the army of the occupying English. Her inquisitors mercilessly repeated question after question, the final trial dragging on for hours. Then the last inquisitor asked a pivotal question. He wanted to know if Joan's inner voices didn't come from her own imagination.

The sister paused for a moment before continuing her story. Her voice became very clear and resonant when she described Joan's response. Looking her judge in the eye, Joan quietly replied, "Well, of course. How else would God speak to me?"

I was electrified! Joan said that? She never doubted her imagination? Never doubted it was the channel connecting her to God, through the voices of her angels and saints?

That night Joan of Arc became a person of interest on my spiritual journey. Her words were a wake-up call, a turning point. This young virgin warrior gave me confidence. If imagination was the channel to God for Joan, I could open up. More and more, I knew my God was a God of love. If the Spirit whispered in a dream, in silent meditation, or as I sat journaling, I somehow knew I was safe. The dark experience that had frightened me began to recede. In time, it seemed more like an upsetting dream than anything else and I knew well how to imagine and pray my way to its meaning.

Hearing Joan's message at that time on my journey was providential. As I look back from the vantage point of years, I see that it strengthened me for the biggest crisis of my life. Joan's words hit home in God's timing, and what a blessing they were.

The crisis came with the force of a hurricane when my twenty-year marriage crashed. Emotionally, I was devastated. Financially, I was in a precarious spot. I had just begun a small counseling practice, seeing a few clients each week, but now I needed a paycheck. I didn't want to step back from my practice, but it didn't look like I had a choice. After what seemed an interminable period of worry and job hunting, my former boss called to tell me a slot on the management team was open. I jumped at it.

Getting into the swing of the new job meant working long hours all week. It was exhausting, but I was grateful for a bit of stability and at least some distraction from my pain. Little by little, I adjusted. Then I found I could keep my practice going on weekends, the only free time I had. Seeing clients and giving retreats, even sporadically, meant so much to me.

What I hadn't counted on was the tremendous inner urging

the retreats stirred up in me. I wanted with all my heart to spend more time on this healing work, to return to my private practice full time. I'd never intended to let it go in the first place.[39]

Two years after the divorce, leaving my day job became a topic of debate with my spiritual director. Fr. Ernie wanted practical, responsible mysticism. He urged me not to be rash. "Hang on to your salary and benefits, Shirley." I didn't like the advice, but I did share his anxiety. My teenage son needed security too. No matter how much I yearned to immerse myself in retreats and counseling, I decided to wait, to watch for circumstances to develop.

Finally, one day after a series of office crises, I wasn't sure my silent boss supported me. When I asked, he was honest enough to tell me he didn't.

Was this the circumstance I was waiting for? I spent a sleepless night asking God. In the morning, despite fear and trepidation, I submitted my resignation.

When I told Fr. Ernie, he agreed that the moment looked like divine timing. I was grateful that I could leave, that it was time.[40]

I was overjoyed to finally concentrate full time on the work I loved. I knew that people often found peace in my office. But nevertheless, in quiet moments when I least expected it, anxiety rose up and swamped me. Would I be able to pay the bills? I wasn't sure. My head knew the timing was right, but inside, a cold fear threatened to paralyze me. I told myself I needed more exercise, needed more sleep, needed more prayer time. Yes, prayer time. I remembered the peace when I'd learned to meditate in silence.

And Fr. Ernie reminded me to pray. When I asked him how long, he smiled. "Did I ever tell you about the saint who was asked that question? He was sitting with somebody like you." He could see by my face that I hadn't heard his story.

"Well, the answer was an hour each day. His visitor said, 'I'm much too busy to do that.'

"Then, the saint gave this advice: 'When you are busy, you need to pray two hours each day.'"

Needless to say, I started sitting every day. I'd just light a candle and quietly wait. Often, I sensed God's closeness in the silence. Then one day, words rose in my spirit ..." There is a divine plan of goodness for your life and work." I had never doubted the plan for my life, but these few words were like taking a deep breath of peace. They became a simple prayer, a promise from God I could tell myself in anxious moments. Then, free of worry, I could work. I trusted my call.

As far as we know, Joan never doubted her call, although many around her certainly did, and not just her inquisitors. In the heat of battle, one of her trusted captains hesitated at a crucial point. Joan chided him. "Do not doubt. The time is right when it pleases God. And one ought to act when God wishes. Act and God will act."[41]

I understood the truth of Joan's words.

Just before my marriage fell apart, I had given up a good job after a trip to Medjugorje. I wound up making a pilgrimage to Croatia after a string of coincidences that I could only decide were God's way of remaining anonymous.

When I first heard about Medjugorje, the story was that peasant children were having visions of Mary. Journalists were comparing them to those at Fatima and Lourdes. Many unexplained phenomena—call them wonders or miracles—took place while I was there. No one could have convinced me of them if I hadn't seen them myself.

This wasn't my first pilgrimage. I had known the power of this ancient practice on an earlier visit to the Holy Land. In Jerusalem, we walked the Way of Sorrows, Jesus's walk to Calvary, on the very stones that had been under his feet. Taking turns carrying a rough-hewn cross through the crowded streets, we reenacted the last hours before his death. The devotion, called the Stations of the Cross, describes Jesus's meetings with his mother and a woman who wiped his face with her veil. When Jesus fell, collapsing from loss of blood, the Roman guards drafted a bystander to help him bear the cross.

No particular order had been set as to which one of us would carry the cross at which station. My eyes filled with tears when the man I was following turned and handed it to me that day in the hot sun of Jerusalem. We were approaching the station where Simon of Cyrene, a curious bystander, had been recruited to help Jesus. I knew this was no accident. I was to help carry the cross: wasn't that my training and call? I never forgot that day walking the Via Dolorosa.

And I never forgot a powerful day in Medjugorje. It was the day

I was blessed by Fr. Jozo. He was the priest who first learned of the children's apparitions and later had visions of Mary instructing him to pray over the pilgrims flooding into the small village, touched by the stories of the children.[42] Despite the humidity in the stuffy, crowded church, a long line of pilgrims moved patiently up the aisle. I was one of them, shifting my weight from foot to foot waiting to receive his blessing.

When Fr. Jozo covered my ears with his hands, even though I didn't understand Croatian I knew well that something opened. I could hear with my heart. Then he placed his hands on my shoulders, and I understood I was to help others carry their burdens.[43]

At that moment I wasn't sure what my assignment was, but I knew I'd loved the informal counseling that always developed when I taught in Catholic schools, and the work I'd done with victims of abuse as a graduate intern. After receiving my masters in social work, I'd counseled inmates in the county jail and a variety of clients at a retreat center.

I gradually realized that despite my graduate training, I had more of a vocation than a career. I had always had a vocation. This was a new direction God had planned for me. I was convinced that even if I had to live in a one-room studio and eat peanut butter sandwiches, this work was my call. There was never a question of "if," only of "how" and "when."

When I stepped up to it, clients seemed to come out of the woodwork. It amazed me that when I acted, God acted too. I have found again and again the truth of what Joan's young faith had taught her. Her words have carried me.

Even painting Joan's portrait took me in a new direction. My other Holy Women paintings had a recognizable style. They were beauties in colorful acrylic, many embellished with glitter and collage. With Joan, I was in unfamiliar territory. It was as if I had opened a door I didn't know was just ahead of me.

It began one day while I was searching in a used furniture store for frames. One caught my eye. It was the right size and design. The frame would work, but the painting was a seascape on canvas splotched and blobbed with thick oils. I studied it and then decided I would just use a new canvas. But no ...

As I stood there musing, the image spoke to me. It was something about using what was provided, valuing an earlier foundation, building on it ... trusting what was provided. I wondered if Joan wanted me to think about approaching my art in a new way.

I'd never painted on top of another painting before. When I got home and began, I quickly realized this portrait of Joan would differ from the rest. There was no point in arguing with the paint ridges on the underlying canvas. But, when I looked with fresh eyes, I began to see that the earlier image added design and texture that the portrait wouldn't have had otherwise.

All I knew at first was to use lots of blue and orange, the colors of flame. Gradually, I could see Joan's face in the flames, a much more abstract image than my earlier women. Then, a French fleur-de-lis at her heart and a cross in her hand identified her.

I vaguely remembered her last words. She had asked a guard to hold the cross high so she could see it through the horrifying conflagration of her death.[44] I realized later how potent those symbols were for her short, dedicated life.

Once I got that far, I sat looking at the painting, remembering Joan's last days. When imprisoned in Rouen for her final trial, she had asked the village, "Art thou then to be my final abode?"[45]

Yes, I picked up my brush. Those words needed to be written in the flames. They belonged there, like the cross, the promise of her hope and salvation.

So, following Joan's lead, my art itself has changed, I began experiments with other media that would not yield to plan or control. Unique images surprised me, seeming to show up of their own volition ... images like dreams, like life. And we, the observers, make of them what we will.

I invite you to consider the twists and turns of your life as you open to these women striding before us. Women of scripture, women of history, women of the great cloud of witnesses, our forebears, ancestors, and the great communion of saints.

They are helpers at our side to teach, to inspire, to comfort, to guide and heal us in our times of turmoil. As they walked before us in their own confusion, none knew with certainty, step by step, what state they were in. Joan didn't either.

When on trial, the bishop, asked her, "Do you know if you are in God's grace?"

He hoped to trick her into admitting the capital crime of presuming God's generosity.[46] The question inspired Joan to answer quickly. "If I am not, may God put me there, and if I am, may God so keep me." These few words came to her in a flash, no doubt memorized. They were part of a prayer respected as truth by the medieval church.[47]

Joan gave the perfect answer to her inquisitor. May it become our prayer too—we don't know what we don't know. But wherever we are on our journey, it is a mercy to know God is there for our asking.

It is interesting that the only contemporary portrait we have of Joan does not include the fleur-de-lis or the cross. Instead, she holds her banner and sword. It was sketched in Paris's parliamentary record by a clerk in 1429. Illustration, Fig. 1 in Harrison, *Joan of Arc*.

At this time of life, now in my seventies, I see how much depends on simple trust. Each step of the way, I walk in a forest primeval, an unknown land of beauty and mystery. Each day, new sunrises and sunsets, unexpected shafts of light fall through the forest canopy above, illuminating my path. This forest is old growth, mature, ancient. It has withstood significant disturbance. I value its resilience when storms swirl round me and shadows fall. This unknown land has a mystic quality. It holds wonder in new vistas.

One of my recent alcohol inks seemed to arrive with
a message: its title is *Forest Primeval.*

I find joy and yes, bravery, in my heart as I walk step by step
each day for the first time in this primeval forest.

Yes, storms and shadow. Joan's call from God put her squarely
in the middle of the crises of her time. Despite her youth and
inexperience, she is a model of courage and trust. When questioned
about her very dangerous mission, Joan proclaimed she was not
afraid, saying, "I was born for this."[48] She was indeed, and so have
we each been born for our particular call.

But despite her fearlessness, Joan was also a very human young
woman. A biographer reports that at one point, she attempted to
negotiate with the English by letter. Her offer was greeted with a

barrage of taunts and insults. Adding injury to these, her messenger was taken captive. This was too much for her. According to her confessor, "Joan began to sigh and weep copious tears, invoking the King of Heaven to her aid." She would always be quick to shed tears and equally quick to dry them.[49]

As we stand challenged and frustrated by the seemingly impossible issues of our day, we also may weep. We need to remember Joan's tears. When we need to cry, that is the moment to accept our vulnerability. A strong person isn't one who doesn't cry. A strong person is one who sheds tears for a moment, and then, like Joan, picks up her sword and fights again. Strong as Joan was, she cried.

And so, she walks before us, not only as a historic figure and saint of the church, but as an archetype. She followed God's call to protect and defend her very country as a powerful warrior in times of great suffering and confusion. Let us trust God to alert us to our roles in strengthening those in need around us.

Our times, too, are tumultuous and frightening, times of war, upheaval, and threat. Like Joan, may each of us hear the still, small voice that invites us in our day to follow our individual call with courage. May we be blessed with her resiliency too, the will to begin again and again with faith and hope.

All of these Holy Women lived in times of deep unrest. Let us look to them in our day and time and know we number among them. They are our sisters, mothers, and friends, also kissed by God.

Time Transparent

It is silent there and still
In that paralyzing Presence.
Time becomes transparent, on the edge of now.
Eternity slips through uncomprehending fingers.

Is it darkness? Is it light?
Being has no dimension, has no hue.
Only the blurred outline of a whisper is there,
Not seen, not heard, but known.
Ungrasped, but wholly known,
Infinite Love gives,
There, in the silence of that Presence,
An illuminating embrace.[50]

Responding to Joan of Arc

Associations/archetypes: child, virgin, leader, warrior, visionary, Patron of France, banner, determination, questioner/challenger, martyr, St. Catherine, St. Margaret, Archangels Gabriel and Michael, flames, sword, armor, male dress, witch hunts

Joan of Arc was a true warrior. She fought because of love of God and her country and would not give up. A true warrior always comes from a place of love despite her own fears and ineptitude. Joan's response was to put her trust in God and learn how to use weapons and ride a horse in battle. Today, as in the fifteenth century, soldiers need training, discipline, and skills in planning and using their resources. Battles are won and lost because of how those in combat use what they have. The warrior needs to assess not only the enemy, but herself as well, to know what goals to set and how to use her strength.[51]

Male warriors in our myths are often called heroes; so let us call Joan a heroine. Because of the violence associated with a primitive, undeveloped warrior archetype, the term itself is somewhat negative, but the title "heroine" rests comfortably on Joan.

Let's consider the golden side of the archetype. This positive heroine/warrior wants matters settled in a win/win fashion for the good of all. In one documented incident, Joan tried to bring a turning point in the war against England by sending a letter to the other side calling for negotiation. It was spurned and her messenger was kept captive, causing Joan to weep. Her response showed us her tender heart, pained for the plight of her messenger and for the loss of her hope for peace.

So let us look at our own lives in light of this warrior/heroine archetype. Do I listen to where God's spirit is calling me? Am I determined to follow that guidance without giving up? How great is my love? Do I really believe that perfect love casts out fear? Am I willing to learn new skills in the pursuit of this call God has given me? Or is my fear of my own ineptitude too great? Can I speak up for myself honestly and respectfully? Am I comfortable negotiating to find win/win solutions with people in my life, or do I fall into thinking I have the one right way and others are wrong? Am I able to be disciplined and persistent in accomplishing the life tasks I face?

What instances in your life come to mind to help you assess your "inner heroine"? End by writing a prayer to the Spirit and to St. Joan, asking for all you need and thanking them for having already led you so far along your life path.

Thérèse of Lisieux

1873–97 CE

Commemorated October 1

T his nineteenth-century French Carmelite nun was called "the saint of the little way." Thérèse said that one does not have to do great things, but simply ordinary things with great love. And because she promised to answer prayers as if sending roses from heaven, she is also known as the Little Flower.[1]

Like others of our Holy Women—Hildegard and Kateri Tekakwitha—Thérèse Martin was an orphan. When her mother died, she was only four, the youngest of five girls. Her oldest sister, Pauline, immediately took her as a special charge. The next youngest sister, Celine, was also promptly in the care of the next oldest sister, Marie. The girls agreed to this arrangement among themselves, not by any assignment of their father or grandparents. They deeply cared for each other.[2]

The stability of this substitute mother relationship faltered for Thérèse when she was nine and Pauline, her second mother, joined the Carmelites. Then, just four years later, Marie followed Pauline to the convent.[3] In the context of this very pious family, it's not surprising that Thérèse herself felt called to religious life at age nine. There was a tradition in Europe of very young children being raised within monasteries, which we encountered in the story of Hildegard of Bingen. By Thérèse's time, however, French church authorities specified a minimum age of twenty-one for entry into

Preceding page: *Thérèse of Lisieux,* acrylic on canvas, by the author. Since Thérèse wore the traditional Carmelite garb, I honored her by painting her in full habit and veil as I imagined them, and then placed her in a bower of roses to acknowledge her promise to send roses from heaven as answers to prayer.

the Carmelite convent.

Thérèse's youth was not the only barrier to her wish. Her father had a stroke at age sixty-three and his well-being depended on their close companionship.[4] He was not unsympathetic to his daughter's desire, however. He loved her and knew her well.

Thérèse Grown Up. A pencil portrait by the author based on a photo in *The Hidden Face: A Study of Thérèse of Lisieux* by Ida Friederike Gorres.

His wife had told him about his young girl's tenacity. She observed that Thérèse was "not nearly so docile as her sister. When she says 'no,' nothing can make her change, and she can be terribly obstinate. You could keep her down in the cellar all day without getting a 'yes' out of her; she would rather sleep there."[5]

Thérèse's father knew she would be determined to join Carmel, and indeed, she was. When she was fifteen, she put her hair up, a symbol of adulthood in her time. Looking quite the young lady, she was permitted to take her petition directly to Pope Leo XIII.

The kindly and wise pontiff told her, "Well, my child, do what the superiors decide.... You will enter if it is God's will." With a determination reminiscent of the runaway Clare of Assisi, Thérèse threw herself to the floor and refused to leave the feet of the pope. The Swiss Guard had to carry her out of the room.[6]

Perhaps the pope had been strategically vague about Thérèse's request. He likely knew the prioress was willing to accept the girl. Perhaps he also guessed that when the local bishop thought things over, he would see his leeway to make an exception for her. The other Martin girls were in the same convent, after all. To Thérèse's great joy, she was allowed to enter Carmel while she was still fifteen, just after the rigors of Lent.[7]

We see that family history is important to Thérèse's story.

Two years later, when Louis Martin died, Celine also joined Carmel.[8] Pauline, Marie, Thérèse, and now Celine were together once again, their lives entwined in new fashion.

So, here she is in a very small group of nuns with her siblings. When Pauline, now Sister Agnes of Jesus, is selected by the community as prioress, she appoints Thérèse novice mistress for a group typically numbering twenty or so, all older than she was. Thérèse describes her way of carrying out her responsibilities:

> With certain souls, I feel I must make myself little, not fearing to humble myself by admitting my own struggles and defects; seeing I have the same weaknesses as they....
>
> With others, on the contrary, I have seen that to do them any good I must be very firm and never go back on a decision once it is made ...[9]

Although Thérèse loved her blood sisters who shared her monastic life, she resisted all attempts to draw her back into special family considerations,[10] or what we might call codependence today. This young French girl was inspired by another great Carmelite, Teresa of Avila, who warned against emotional entanglements among the nuns.[11]

Young as she was, Thérèse was gifted with discernment. She was especially attracted to and inspired by another young French woman, Joan of Arc. When Joan was beatified in 1894, Thérèse wrote a long prayer celebrating the event, and even a play that the nuns put on in the convent.[12] She could not have imagined that she would later, and to this day, be honored to stand beside Joan as a patron of France.

Thérèse, whose early life was so different from Joan's, likely was magnetized by her amazing and unlikely performance as a commander in response to her voices. Early on, as is common among mystics, Thérèse felt restless and wrote of wanting to be a "warrior, priest, apostle, doctor, martyr," but as her spirituality and prayer life deepened with maturity, she realized that "love comprises all vocations."[13]

Thérèse absorbed Jesus's words about love, "What you do for the least of mine, you do for me,"[14] and poured out her prayer for those in need. Her youthful dreams of being "warrior, priest, apostle, doctor, martyr" were fulfilled as grace led her to become a gentle warrior and apostle of prayer without taking one step out of her convent.

That Thérèse was a prodigious writer throughout her life would seem to be inevitable, given the overflow of her rich inner life into prayers, poems, letters, and her personal story. Two of the abbesses of her own community ordered her to write her memoir in 1895, two years before her death.[15] They had witnessed miracles worked through her intercession and also realized she was seriously ill. These women knew Thérèse's story must be told.

And so this French nun, canonized in 1925, was named the Patron Saint of Missions[16] in recognition of the power of her prayer for the needy that reached far beyond her enclosure. She knew deeply that she had all she needed within those simple walls and in her simple life. When as a girl of fourteen she had read *The Imitation of Christ,* it was if its words were for her alone: "The Kingdom of God is within you ... turn thee with thy whole heart unto the Lord and forsake this world: and thy soul shall find rest."[17]

Thérèse inspired Mother Teresa of Calcutta to take her name and carry on her amazing work, loving the poorest of the poor.[18] She also influenced Dorothy Day, an American who dedicated her life to reform and social justice for the poverty stricken.[19]

This humble nun could not have imagined such impact, nor that she would be named a Doctor of the Church in acknowledgement of her teaching, but she was. Thérèse is the youngest of only four women so honored in the history of the Catholic Church.[20]

Today, we are grateful that Thérèse stands with other Holy Women—Hildegard, Clare, and Teresa of Avila—and the women around them as a gathering of feminine authors whose sisters convinced them to share their gifts on the written page. These women understood centuries ago how powerfully we need each other as Holy Women—and how we are blessed when our stories are saved and shared. May we be inspired to carry their message of the greatness of God's love into our world.

Thoughts

God needs neither great deeds nor profound thoughts, neither intelligence, nor talents. He cherishes simplicity.

Don't drag yourself any longer to His feet–follow that first impulse that draws you into His arms. That is where your place is.

The splendor of the rose, and the whiteness of the lily do not rob the little violet of its scent nor the daisy of its simple charm. If every flower wanted to be a rose, spring would lose its loveliness.

Let us love since that is all our hearts were made for.

After my death, I will let fall a shower of roses. I will spend my heaven doing good upon earth. I will raise up a mighty host of little saints. My mission is to make God loved.[21]
—Thérèse of Lisieux

Discovering Thérèse of Lisieux

My earliest memory of a connection with one of these Holy Women kissed by God centered on my Irish grandma. When I was about six years old, we often sat in her kitchen eating her crispy sugar cookies, each with a raisin right in the center.

One day Grandma asked me, "You know how much mothers love their children, don't you?" Well, I just smiled at her because I knew I had the best mom anybody could want!

I knew Grandma also thought so.

She went on. "Did you know that Jesus's mother is our mother too?"

I wasn't completely sure, but that sounded like something I had heard from the nuns at school about the Blessed Mother. I figured that must mean Mary, so I gave a quick nod.

She smiled. "Mary is our mother too, and just like your mom, she's always ready to help us."

I had never heard that before.

Seeing a quizzical look on my face, she leaned across the table. Her voice was soft when she spoke: "Mary can ask her son to help us in all kinds of ways, especially when someone is sick and needs to get better." This was good news. I'd had some nasty earaches. "Grandma, do you think the Blessed Mother could make my earaches go away?"

She slid her chair close to mine, reaching to gently place her warm hands over my ears. She closed her eyes. I couldn't hear what she whispered, but her warm hands felt good.

In a minute, she straightened up. "There. I asked Mary to be sure you don't go getting an earache any time soon!"

We both giggled. Then she told me about Fatima and Lourdes, where children had actually seen Mary help people who were sick. I thought those might be faraway places where magical things could happen, like in fairy tales.

I usually had to be quiet at Grandma's house, because of Aunt Sis, but sometimes I got to explore a little. One day when Grandma had gone out to her garden to pick a few zinnias for the dinner table, I silently cracked open the door to Sis's room and peeked in. I'd never seen an altar except in church, but this room had one. That was when I spied the blue and white and gold statue. It was beautiful: Mother Mary holding baby Jesus. There were other statues too. They looked huge to me and I didn't know who they were. I could see Sis was asleep so I closed the door without a sound.

But now Grandma was ready to take me in for a real visit, not just a quick peek. She could tell I was looking at the big statues. Without me even asking, Grandma named them for me: St. Joseph, the Infant of Prague, St. Thérèse of Lisieux, and of course, the Blessed Mother.

Again, my young aunt was sleeping quietly in her bed. We tiptoed close to her. I didn't understand that she was bedridden and painfully dying as nerves broke away from her spine, or that only a miracle could heal her. Grandma leaned over to whisper in my ear: "Shirley, God answers the prayers of children." I looked up at her.

Her usually crinkling blue eyes were serious. She put her arm around me. "Will you pray with me?" Amazing as it was, I knew she meant it.

I'd do anything for Grandma. "What should I pray for?"

"For peace, for the end of war, for Sis to get better." Grandma smiled at me and reached over to light a little candle on the altar. I wasn't allowed to touch the box of matches beside it, but the candle sparkling in its red glass delighted me. Then I remembered that Grandma was depending on me!

Forgetting the candle, I scrunched my eyes tightly shut. I needed to pray really hard for Sis. I could feel Grandma's warmth as I knelt snuggled by her side on the hard prie-dieu, knees aching. Even with my eyes closed, I could see the light of the flickering candle flames. They looked like roses. Grandma had told me St. Thérèse of Lisieux was called the Little Flower because she promised to send answers to prayers, like roses from heaven.[22] Fragrant roses. I decided I'd ask the Blessed Mother to help Sis get better, and I liked the idea of those roses, so I asked the Little Flower too.

It wasn't much later when early one morning, Grandma's closest friend, Ella, came to the door with a pot of soup. She knew her neighbor had been too busy to cook. Once inside, she looked around and said, "Oh, Florence. Where are the roses? They smell so sweet."

Grandma flew into her arms, crying, "Oh, Ella. There are no roses. Sis just died."

I will never forget grandma's story about the day my aunt died. I have loved roses all my life because of their association with blessings from heaven.

Roses, roses, roses.

Many years later, on a pilgrimage to Medjugorje, roses came up again. Through a series of unexpected events, I found myself in the last available slot for that pilgrimage. It was to be a turning point in my life.

In the small Yugoslavian village,[23] three young people reported visions of Mary often compared to those at Fatima and Lourdes. I attended Mass every evening in the parish church among throngs of visitors. Beforehand, the visionaries knelt in the balcony to lead us in praying the rosary. During that quiet time, an unexplainable flash of light beamed from above, filling the church with brilliance. We had been told that when the light occurred, the three were focused at a point just above their eye level, in rapt attention. Not a page of a hymn book rustled as all of us sat frozen, motionless.

Some nights I saw the light; sometimes not. Others said the same thing. Our experiences varied, but we all agreed that the atmosphere in the church had a very intense charge. When the rosary ended, we celebrated Mass. Finally the entire congregation processed one by one to the altar for special blessings.

These were long evenings in the church, but I never missed one. Then it was the last evening of the pilgrimage. Absorbed, I had lingered long after the crowd had thinned. The silent, nearly darkened church was peaceful as I prayed for all those I loved as I had done on each day's visit, a long litany.

Finally, an acolyte at the high altar began to extinguish the last of many candles there. I was surprised when I looked at my watch. Realizing it was time to go, I stood for one last view of the graceful statue of the Lady of Medjugorje. She was blue and white and gold like Grandma's statue. I walked to her altar, banked with flowers. I had smelled roses. I reached out one finger to touch the nearest bud, then the next bouquet. I stood there nonplussed. The first bud was silk, the next bouquet filled with very realistic plastic flowers. I had definitely smelled roses, but there were no real roses on Mary's altar![24] Was this a miracle like the story my grandmother had told me? The fragrance of roses here, as when my aunt died? Was this unexplainable fragrance a promise my prayers were about to be answered? My heart skipped a beat as I thought about that. As it turned out, they certainly were.

Years passed. After a difficult divorce, I faced another challenge, an equally difficult decision about whether to marry a man already seriously ill with heart trouble. Roses came up again.

I'd been seeing Jerry for several months. He was a very special man who seemed just right for me. I wanted to marry and heal, but my doubts were huge and circling like birds of prey. They were on my mind day and night. He was a great guy, but I wasn't at all sure I could cope with a sick husband. I knew I wasn't a good nurse ... and I'd been angry with myself for not being Florence Nightingale. Jerry knew it; I'd told him. I didn't want to lose him or hurt him, but I just wasn't sure. The best I could do was to take a break.

It was a miserable time. Struggling with fear and loneliness, I buried myself in work. Yeah, work, the great anesthetic—I knew all about it!

One Saturday night at the end of an exhausting week in the office, sadness washed over me, spilling into tears. I shook myself. Where was all this coming from? Hadn't I been doing fine before I met Jerry? Hadn't I been okay without him? But I knew I had fallen in love with him. Was I being unrealistic hoping for a man whose health was as good as mine? Maybe I should marry Jer after all. Did I want to?

Wearily, I watched my thoughts double back over the same tired questions. Finally, I told myself, *Just go home to bed, sink into oblivion, sleep your way past this tangle of doubts.*[25]

Sunday morning was brisk but glorious, sunny under a relentlessly blue sky. I'd just returned from church, purse and car keys still clutched in my hand, when the doorbell rang. The florist's deliveryman smiled at me over two dozen fragrant tea roses.

I stood in the doorway, watching his departing back, the calmness of my morning shattered by bittersweet pain. Hugging the flowers, I fumbled to open the card scribbled in Jerry's handwriting: *"Love is like a prayer. God will not ignore it."* The words blurred through my tears.

I groped my way to the bedroom, leaving a trail of rose petals. Once there, I opened my jewelry box and brought out the beautiful diamond ring Jerry had given me. I read the little card again, *"Love is like a prayer. God will not ignore it,"*[26] tears of joy on my smiling face.

My heart told me then and there that I would marry this good man and depend on God.

Prayer and roses had worked another miracle. And when we married a few months later, how could I not carry roses?

But St. Thérèse and her roses continued to show up in my life. More roses showered down as answered prayers on the day set aside for the Little Flower's feast, October 1, 2011.

My daughter-in-law, Christie, mother of three children under ten, had called me from work a few weeks earlier. "Shirley, can you drive me home? I'm having trouble seeing and don't want to drive."

That was the beginning of many mystifying and painful symptoms and visits to a seemingly endless stream of specialists. Our entire family was anxious and concerned about this young woman struggling as her health and energy deserted her.

Finally, a leading neurologist, located in Denver and purported to be one of the best surgeons in the country, diagnosed chiari malformation, a relatively rare and perhaps genetic disorder. He recommended she come to Colorado for a dangerous brain surgery. Christie was braver than the rest of us and quickly arranged for flights for herself and my son, Kelly.

The surgery was scheduled for October 1, the day dedicated to St. Thérèse, the Little Flower. That date got me focused! Christie and her family, devout Christians, were unfamiliar with this modern Catholic saint's promise to spend her heaven doing good on earth, sending roses as answered prayers.

I had recently painted my version of Thérèse, with no particular purpose in mind except to imagine the beauty and serenity of her soul as God might see her. And, of course, I encircled her with roses.

As the day of Christie's surgery neared, I told her my grandma's story of the roses and our family history of devotion to Thérèse when in need.

"Christie, I want you to know I'm asking Thérèse to send you some roses, to make your surgery successful and safe." We both had tears in our eyes.

Later, I quietly took my son aside. I pressed some bills into his hand. "Kelly, since you will be with Christie in Denver, you need to do something for me."

October 1 dawned clear and cold, even here in Arizona, but much colder in Denver. Surgery was scheduled for morning. I realized I would spend hours clock watching before word came from Kelly.

Finally, the phone rang! "She's out of surgery and waking up, Mom. The doctor says it went well and she should make a good recovery." We both were crying when Kelly laughed: "Christie just said, 'Oh, the roses smell so good!'"

Yes, roses ... Thérèse's fragrant gifts from heaven just had to be at Christie's bedside in that hospital.

Responding to Thérèse of Lisieux

Associations/archetypes: orphan, child, virgin, mystic, lover, novice mistress/abbess, Doctor of the Church, teacher, writer, playwright, Patron of France and Missions, roses, flowers, water, fasting, determination

We might look at Thérèse of Lisieux as the orphan child or innocent archetype. Her mother died when she was only four, and though her older sister stepped in as a substitute mother, that ended when she was nine and the sister left for the convent. Then another older sister took over, but that didn't last long either, only until Thérèse was thirteen. The innocent child may unconsciously try harder to have faith, and to be lovable. The orphan may interpret her experience as an abandonment, a harsh lesson that we are each on our own in life.[27]

We know from Thérèse's life story that she focused very much on her faith and tried very hard to be good. She tells us about her struggle with scruples.[28] The good news is that over her lifetime, she came to great trust and optimism through realizing God's love for her. In the process, her anxious scruples, naïveté, and dependence were transformed. The young girl who aspired to be "warrior, priest, apostle, doctor, martyr" became the saint of the little way, thus named because she learned to trust in the value of doing little things with great love. Thérèse grew spiritually by living the healthy interdependence of community. She found her way past the abandonment of the orphan to self-reliance based in faith.

Sometimes losses and wounds in childhood lead us to the shadow orphan roles of cynic or victim. The injured innocent can hold on to grievances about childhood for many years. Am I willing to tell myself a new story about my life? Can I question any of my negative assumptions about others? Or that I may have misunderstood their motives? Am I able to forgive the people in my life, seeing that they were injured too, and may have been doing the best they could? Am I able to see goodness in others and in the world? Am I able to see both weaknesses and goodness? Am I willing to release cynicism?

When we believe there is help and we reach out for it, we grow, but we must be willing to be rescued. Such honesty requires a bit of humility. Am I willing to come out of any self-imposed isolation and victimhood I find inside? Can I own my gifts as well as noticing my weaknesses? How easily do I find closeness with others? Community life helped Thérèse experience interdependence and its comfort, as did her growing faith in God. Can I allow myself to be carried like a trusting child by a loving God? What in Thérèse's story helps me come to greater freedom?

Turn back to the introduction and read about collage in the section on How to Use This Book. Create a collage in response to what is stirring within you regarding Thérèse's message. Then spend some time in quiet reflection and journaling, asking the guidance of God's loving spirit to bring you to newness and the young child's wonder at goodness you see in your life.

Tekakwitha

1656–89 CE

Commemorated July 1

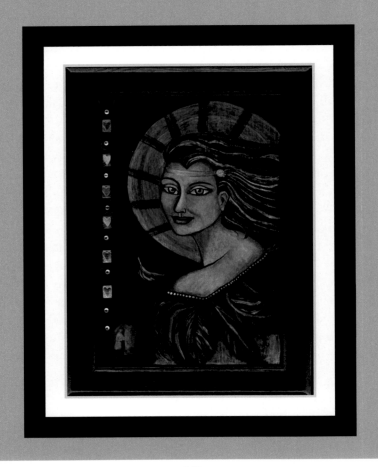

Tekakwitha was born in the seventeenth century in what is now upstate New York to a Mohawk father, Kenneronkwa, and an Algonquin Christian mother, Tagaskouita. It was a time of war over beaver trapping grounds among the tribes as eager Dutch fur traders were arriving on the Hudson River.[1]

Such was the background of the coming together of Tekakwitha's parents. Her father was a commander who had chosen his wife from among Algonquin captives. Taking captives was common practice among tribes to replace those lost through sickness or wars. As a result, native villages became diverse. Algonquins, Mohawks, and Hurons, all aggressive competitors for game, warred against each other and then lived together.[2]

Their indigenous world was filled with living spirits that influenced life's events. A Mohawk leader like Kenneronkwa would have lived that belief as he took part in his tribe's seasonal rituals and hunts. His wife, on the other hand, had been raised Catholic among French missionaries between Quebec and Montreal. Their religious rules, liturgies, and Latin language would have confounded a free Mohawk. Most worrisome, however, were the serious new diseases that had arrived with the Europeans: smallpox and yellow fever.[3]

It was smallpox that altered Tekakwitha's life. An epidemic killed many in her village, including her parents and brother. The four-year-old girl managed to survive but with a scarred face and seriously impaired vision. Tekakwitha was taken in by her father's sister. Her parents had given her a Mohawk name, Iragode—Little

Preceding page: *Tekakwitha*, acrylic and mixed media on wood, by the author.

Sunshine[4]—but later she was called Tekakwitha, meaning "she who bumps into things."[5]

In the turbulent times of the French and Indian War, many Mohawk villages were attacked, including hers. When Tekakwitha was ten, the longhouses, wigwams, and corn and squash fields of her family were burned. They escaped with their lives, but were left struggling to survive in the forest, exposed to the elements with winter fast approaching.[6]

After the disaster, little by little a new village was built and the families settled in. More hardship was ahead, however, when Mohican warriors waged a terrifying attack on the Mohawk settlement. Many were killed. Tekakwitha, now thirteen, and her friends joined one of the priests, Fr. Jean Pierron, tending the wounded, burying the dead, and carrying food and water to the defending warriors. Tekakwitha moved quietly among them, helping where she could, sometimes praying with the dying. For these young girls, the attack was a shocking encounter with the stark ravages of war. But the atrocities didn't end there. Reinforcements arrived, killing over eighty Mohicans and capturing thirteen men and three women. The tide of the war had turned and the Mohawks were furious with a desire for revenge. Fr. Pierron begged them to show their captives mercy, but to no avail. For three days, they were tortured until all were dead.[7]

These traumatic episodes so early in life aroused Tekakwitha's compassion.

Conditioned as she was by the loss of her parents and brother to smallpox and her own bout with the disease, she had endured great suffering. She understood pain. As she watched the priests working with her people for love of God, her heart was touched.

She wanted to do good too, and began to help tend the sick. This time was likely when her gift of healing began.

Soon Tekakwitha came of age in the Mohawk longhouse family where women ruled under a matriarch. Under their tutelage, she learned the traditional skills of her tribe: making clothing from animal skins, weaving mats and baskets, participating in seasonal planting, gathering, and hunting.[8]

As she reached marriageable age, Tekakwitha was expected to bring a man into the family as husband, hunter, and protector. But she had learned about Catholic women who chose to devote themselves to God and work for others rather than take a husband. Tekakwitha didn't want to marry. When her aunt made plans to bring a young man to the house to meet her, she ran away.[9]

The punishments that followed could have been taken out of the Cinderella fairy tale. Here was another orphaned victim with cruel relatives. The girl was assigned heavy chores no one else wanted, ridiculed, and sent away hungry from meals for refusing to work on Sundays. The neighbors soon joined in persecuting her. Their unkind rumors swirled around Tekakwitha: accusations of sorcery, witchcraft, and sexual promiscuity. Her mistreatment continued until a priest suggested she go to Kahnawake, a nearby village where other native converts lived, many of them women.[10]

Before that could happen, Tekakwitha completed her catechism training and professed her new faith. Now twenty years old, she was baptized, taking St. Catherine of Sienna as her patron, and became known as Kateri Tekakwitha, Kateri being a Mohawk version of Catherine. Conversion to Christianity didn't mean loss of her tribal name, as the new baptismal name was simply prefixed to it. Name change would have been familiar to the natives since an Iroquois or Algonquian might have several names over the years, each associated with a changed life stage or rite of passage. More importantly, Kateri Tekakwitha also would have believed in the power of names to carry the identity of a deceased ancestor.[11]

> It is possible that converts, in keeping with the Iroquois conception of the power of names to resuscitate the dead, made particular efforts to emulate the virtues of their saintly European namesakes. Tekakwitha, whose penitential excesses would prematurely end her life, received the baptismal name of Catherine of Siena, a mystic known, among other things, for her extreme asceticism.[12]

A number of Christian practices fit well into Iroquois society, as did these beliefs about names. For example, the tribe traditionally incorporated self-torture, fasting, and sexual abstinence into their quest for the sacred, practices not unlike the mortifications of early saints. In addition, indigenous peoples would likely have regarded priests as similar to shamans, bringing spiritual healing, wisdom, and ceremony to the community. Then, too, the Iroquois saw the Jesuit religious order providing support and fraternity, as did their tribal medicine societies.[13]

Two contemporaries of Kateri Tekakwitha, Fr. Claude Chauchetière and Fr. Pierre Cholonec, kept journals about events in the Mohawk village, including details about the young convert.[14] We have them to thank for much of the information we have about her.

Portrait of Tekakwitha by Claude Chauchetière, ca. 1690.

Ironically, the young Tekakwitha "converted" Fr. Chauchetière, in a way. He arrived among the Mohawks believing that despite conversion they were still too close to nature and their sinful environment. To him and the other missionaries, Christianity was "absolutely true, indigenous beliefs false"... and native converts of the Americas "needed the help, guidance and leadership of Christians" to set them on the right path.[15] However, as Chauchetière observed Kateri Tekawitha, he changed his mind about the difference in the two cultures, observing that he hadn't expected "a native to be so pious."[16]

A later biographer observes:

> This was when her light really began to shine. Kateri had a healing touch. Her presence was sought by ailing members of the village. She exuded a warmth in which others found

great comfort. The Jesuits were aware of her spiritual gifts and her virtue. People would come to the missionaries with their complaints; the priests would send them to Kateri.[17]

Impressed as he saw her going about doing good, Chauchetière came to believe she was a saint. His journal stressed her many virtues: charity, industry, purity, and fortitude.[18]

Kateri's other Jesuit biographer, Pierre Cholonec, emphasized her purity, calling her the "Lily of the Mohawks" to counter the stereotype of promiscuous Indian women.[19] This description also put her into the European tradition of virginity as the preferred form of female spirituality, which we have seen lived out by the other Holy Women as well.

When Kateri Tekakwitha speaks for herself, she is absolutely clear:

> I have deliberated enough. For a long time my decision on what I will do has been made. I have consecrated myself entirely to Jesus, son of Mary. I have chosen him for husband and he alone will take me for wife.[20]

Although unhesitating about her life's dedication, she seemed to have some discomfort about her physical appearance. In a portrait painted by Chauchetière, the black veil is so voluminous, it might have completely covered her. The blanket over her head certainly would have covered her pox-marked face.

Whatever her feelings about her scars, she brought a gentle spirit of healing to those she served. And then, when she died, a miraculous transformation took place, according to Fr. Cholonec: "...the pock marks from smallpox completely vanished and her face shone with radiant loveliness."[21] Perhaps her exquisite, generous spirit as seen by God shone through her face.

Not long after that incident, Kateri woke her mother's close friend Anastasia Tegonhatsiongo, clan matron of their longhouse. Anastasia saw her "at the foot of her mattress holding a wooden cross that shone like the sun."[22] Fr. Chauchetière, meanwhile, said he saw her "at her grave where ... she appeared in baroque splendor ... for two hours ... her face lifted toward heaven as if in ecstasy."[23]

Boy's miracle cure makes first Native American saint.
Associated Press, Oct. 20, 2012.

Of course, stories of visions are common in scripture, hagiography, tales of indigenous peoples, and even those of our contemporaries.[24] We are left to reflect on the thinning of the veil between the living and the dead attested to by many. People of faith speak of the "great cloud of witnesses" and "the communion of saints" and may at times sense that thin veil in experiences that go beyond our logic.

Kateri Tekakwitha was canonized in October 2012, the first Native American to be recognized as a saint. The Vatican's investigation beforehand includes documentation of a particularly striking healing miracle. In it, a five-year-old Native American boy from the state of Washington (of the Lummi tribe) was dying of flesh-eating bacteria. He had become infected through a cut on the lip. Doctors had exhausted all known treatments. Many were praying to Kateri for him. He was near death when her relic was placed on the boy's leg by a nun named Sister Kateri Mitchell. Young Jake Finkbonner survived and has since had reconstructive surgery on his face. Jake, now fifteen, believes St. Kateri Tekakwitha healed him. He has wanted to be a plastic surgeon since he was a child.

Tekakwitha's Dream

God spoke to me as he made me.

He said, "Don't be afraid of the darkness
or what your eyes cannot see.
The darkness is not dark, but light.
Trust, trust!
Out of darkness comes a great Light."

He said: "Follow it to the ends of your yearning.
When it bursts into flame,
You will see Me in the shadow.
(Had you thought to look there?)
Hold fast to Me; don't lose the way."

His voice, now soft: "Allow love, allow fear.
The Light is your spouse.
Only give me your hand."[25]

Discovering Kateri Tekakwitha

A few years back, I began painting images I associated with the feminine divine. I'd been attracted to goddesses of many cultures and approached them intuitively using color, tissue paper, wood, and old jewelry. My first adventure produced an image I decided might be Kuan Yin, the Buddhist bodhisattva of compassion. I remember chuckling a little, thinking of Michelangelo.

Didn't he say something about the face being already hidden in the marble and that he had released it with his chisel? Kuan Yin emerged on tissue paper that was glued to an old cupboard door and then dripped with blue paint. Miraculously, she was my first sale!

That's how Tekakwitha arrived too. Using an old cupboard door covered with black paint, I'd tentatively outlined an oval, wondering if it might morph into a face. My paintbrush had a mind of its own that day. Soon she was looking at me over her shoulder, long dark hair held off her face by a band across her forehead. I stepped back to survey brush strokes that might turn into her garment. They looked sort of like feathers ... I wondered, hadn't a Native American woman been canonized lately? I wasn't sure.

As I studied the composition, I looked for a long time at the area to the left of this woman's face. Something belonged there. What could I add? Putting down my paintbrush, I turned from the easel, thinking maybe I'd find something in my art junk box. It stood on the counter, a hopeless tangle of ribbon, tiny keys, sparkly jewelry, bits of glass. I poked around in some old necklaces, and suddenly I saw it!

My friend Darlene, knowing I collected little odds and ends for just such purposes, had sent me a bracelet, broken into many rectangular pieces, each inscribed with a few words. Their shapes and colors were perfect!

Resting my canvas on the worktable, I carefully placed the little handful of tiles on it. Then, one by one, I played with each tile, shifting one higher, another lower along the left side of the painting. Only when I was satisfied with the design did I get around to reading the finely scrolled words: "Guard your heart above all else, for it is the wellspring of life." The message stopped me, confounded. I asked the image now looking at me so directly, "Who are you?"

The only thing that came to mind was that a woman saint had recently been named a Doctor of the Church ... had there been a Native American woman too?

I left the woman in my art room and stepped into my office. When I started searching the Internet, Hildegard of Bingen come up, but so did Kateri Tekakwitha. And she had arrived in my art room! She was another woman of importance: the first Native American whose sanctity was recognized by the church.

I needed to know what those words from Darlene's bracelet had to do with her. I whipped off my painting apron and sat down at my computer to skim the article. Tekakwitha was a Mohawk converted by French Jesuits in the northeast of the United States near the Canadian border. She had heard about medieval women saints and modern Ursuline nuns in Canada who had vowed chastity and dedicated their lives to prayer and good works. The article described her tribal family pressuring her to marry. Then came the words I was looking for. This young Mohawk convert had said, "My decision on what I will do has been made. I have consecrated myself entirely to Jesus, son of Mary. I have chosen him for husband and he alone will take me for wife."[26]

As I read her words, I knew I needed to research the inscription on the bracelet. It sounded like scripture. My concordance quickly took me to a verse in the book of Proverbs, written by Solomon, that great wise man of the Old Testament who had also written the love poem "The Song of Songs."[27]

Kateri's heart yearned to cleave to God as the source of her life. Solomon's deep insight expressed the bridal spirituality the French Jesuit missionaries would have known and described to their new converts.

I looked again at my painting, wondering how I could honor this woman's reality in her day and time. Hoping to find an answer, I returned to my research, and here it was, presenting itself to me like a gift. I learned that her portrait had been painted a few years after her death. It was on the screen in front of me! I had my answer. I would collage her portrait into my painting as a salute to Kateri Tekakwitha's place in history.

By this time, I was pretty convinced that she must be right at my side, nudging me into exactly what I needed for this painting. I didn't have to be urged. I plunged back into the article I'd found so helpful and came upon a story about her death. A biographer reported that shortly after Tekakwitha had died,

> She woke one of her friends[28] by knocking on her bedroom wall. Then she asked if she were awake, adding, "I've come to say good-bye: I'm on my way to heaven." The friend rushed outside but saw no one; she heard a voice murmur, "Adieu, Adieu, tell the father I'm going to heaven."[29]

Then I read about the transformation of her face as she died, from pox-marked and scarred to radiant.[30] I wondered if she looked anything like the beautiful and confident face I had painted.

Had the transformed Kateri Tekakwitha turned to deliver her words of farewell over her shoulder not just to her friend, but to all of us too as she followed her heart to Jesus, the transforming love of her life?

After I finished painting this Holy Woman, it struck me again how many unknown women saints there must be, especially among indigenous people, people of color, people beyond the boundaries of the familiar and perhaps beyond the often punishing boundaries of economic or social class.

I grew up in Prairie du Chien, a town on the Mississippi River in Wisconsin where a French Jesuit missionary and explorer, Père Jacques Marquette,[31] was immortalized with a statue on the grounds of my all-girls' high school. He lived and worked in the Midwest at the same time Kateri Tekakwitha and her Jesuit mentors met in what is now upstate New York. These Jesuits could have known each other during their seminary training in France before coming to the New World. All of them

On a recent trip to Montreal, I found a stained glass window of St. Kateri Tekakwitha, testifying to the high regard with which she is held in the area first served by Ursuline nuns. The window is in Mary Queen of the World Catholic Church. Photo by the author.

chose to undertake the most difficult ministries available to Jesuits at the time: opening missions amid the dangers of the wilderness.[32]

We know about these few personalities, but there is much we don't know. Could I uncover the names of the Ursuline nuns in Quebec and Montreal from Kateri Tekakwitha's days?

Perhaps so, because of records in the religious orders, but ordinary saints? What could I learn about everyday mothers, aunts, grandmothers? Some of the women from my own family have certainly been raised to sainthood by us, their children, nieces, and grandchildren. They at least have names, more fortunate than the numbers of unnamed Holy Women in whose footsteps we have trod.

On a visit to my hometown last year, I spent an afternoon in a local historical museum. A dramatic mural of family trees caught my eye. It showed the genealogy of local residents that dated back to days of French Canadian fur trappers plying their trade there on the Mississippi river. In the 1780s, trappers and colonists came together to form what became my hometown because of the fur trade. The family trees I discovered accounted for the arrival of several families whose names were familiar to me. I'd gone to school in classrooms full of LaBonnes, DuCharmes, DeRoches, St. Jacques, Fernettes.

As I puzzled over the family trees, I noticed how many branches couldn't be completed because women's names were missing. No doubt some of them would have been Native American, and if their names were lost, their posterity might have been satisfied to keep the information to themselves. It is a loss. As we learn history to this day, nuances of social motives are often passed over lightly, if considered at all.

The opposite happened to Kateri Tekakwitha. She has not been forgotten. Some observers think Mohawks today are ambivalent about the appropriation of her legends over the centuries by nonindigenous outsiders, feeling that some of her tribal identity has been lost.[33] It is possible.

History is always written by those who "win," but let's hope Kateri Tekakwitha has won, for her people as well as for us, the outsiders.

I'm glad she was named. Too many have gone unnamed, going back further than the ancestors of my childhood schoolmates. The history of our corner of the world in the Mississippi River valley of

Wisconsin included a first nation who lived there long before the land was called America. In the Late Woodland Period (1400–750 BCE), these prehistoric people, the Effigy Moundbuilders, built more than two hundred mounds in the shape of birds, turtles, and other animals, some of them miles long. The mounds were used for burials and other ceremonies to mark celestial events or seasonal rites.[34] They were close to nature and looked to the heavens at those times sacred to all of us, times of birth and death.

Kateri Tekakwitha's people also honored turtles and birds as totems. It pleases me to remember that I first recognized her on my easel because of her feathers!

Responding to Kateri Tekakwitha

Associations/archetypes: child, virgin, orphan, lover, bride, healer, penance, poor vision, Native American Mohawk, fasting, French connection, lily, Catherine of Siena

Kateri Tekakwitha was a Mohawk woman, part of the Iroquois Confederacy in what is now southeastern Canada and northeastern New York. Of all our Holy Women, she lived closest to us geographically. She died in 1689 and we know her story, but we likely would have difficulty tracing her descendants. Records from 1995 indicate the Mohawk population in the United States was then at approximately 5,600, with about 24,000 in nearby Canada.[35] Some present-day Mohawks may be part of Kateri's family tree, but perhaps DNA testing would be the only way to find out, since with all good intention, memory even of those close to outstanding individuals fades over several generations, not to speak of centuries! Are these our first people to leave without a trace?

As I researched Kateri's story, I learned that her tribe's contact with seventeenth-century fur traders and missionaries in the east was going on simultaneously with expeditions of French voyageurs and Jesuits on the tributaries of the Great Lakes into the waters of the Midwest. The oldest town in Wisconsin, my hometown on the Mississippi, was settled by fur traders. As a girl growing up, I heard tales of intermarriage among those early voyageurs and the native women. A small historical museum there has walls full of murals tracing family trees of French surnames I recognized. However, many of the women's names were missing. No one could identify those wives and mothers and sisters. Would anyone know the names of Kateri's kin? Probably not. Many names and stories have been lost.

In these pages we have visited our Holy Women with purpose, celebrating their lives, creativity, and accomplishments for our own inspiration but also to vicariously honor many others whose stories remain untold. All lives, especially of women, who have so often been marginalized, deserve to be remembered and introduced to those still to come. I invite you to consider how you can contribute some history of women close to you, who are also our foremothers and sisters. We are mysteriously connected by stories of other lives, past or present. They deserve to be remembered for those still to come. Whose life calls to you for acknowledgement? And, how can the process begin?

A simple family tree could be your beginning.[36] Have you ever considered that even your close relatives may not know what you know now? Beginning with your parents and siblings, create a simple outline with whatever information you have: names, dates, places—births, marriages, and deaths, dates for your parents and siblings. Then go back from them on both sides of the family to grandparents and beyond, as far as you can. You will quickly discover there are many pieces of information you don't know. Leave those parts of your outline for later research. Meantime you can use what you have easily available: family letters, photographs, and other memorabilia. Assemble a scrapbook or an electronic record for ease of copying and distribution. The family tree can be anything you want it to be. If you decide to look for information you don't have, the very process may lead to a deepening of communication and shared knowledge across the generations of your family.

If you feel called to this remembering as an ongoing reflection and project, set aside time regularly and begin each session with prayer to the Spirit for guidance. You will know if a parent or grandparent's story has particularly impacted or inspired you and if it is an episode that you could write for your family. Even if some of the details are known, there may well be meanings that are yours alone to tell. Such events may have had significant spiritual impact on you or even explain some family question left to conjecture or misunderstanding. Or you may be the one who has a very rich memory of a touching exchange, family event, holiday celebration, significant birthday, wedding, or graduation. Consider the possibility of writing the story, perhaps as a gift for those closest to you. Who knows? Your experiment might be the beginning not only of your family tree but also of your spiritual autobiography. What a family gift that would be!

Conclusion:
Holy Women, Create!

Did I say earlier in these pages that every pilgrimage arises out of a story? Now, as I write the last words of this book, I realize that the reverse is also true. The pilgrimage of this writing has more deeply unfolded for me not only these Holy Women's stories, but also—to my surprise—the ongoing story of my own life.

Pilgrimage springs from a mysterious yearning in the depth of the heart and promises a joyful satisfaction. So I "pilgrimmed" on—deep in the creative process, willing but not knowing where it would take me—drawn forward by these diverse women kissed by God who insisted they wanted to get out into the world. If I had a destination in mind, it is beyond my imagining now. But I see that this path led me, step by step, to that Creative Spirit who urged me to sing more of the song that wanted to be sung through my little life.

As you have read these pages, you have joined me. We have been on this pilgrimage together as you witnessed the flowering creativity of our sisters and mothers in so many ways. Will you respond? Will you join hands with the Holy Women who are reaching out to you? Will you too open to the Creative Spirit and sing that precious song that only you can sing, that wants to sing through you, to fill you and your part of the world with healing and joy?

I invite you, Holy Women of today, to create!

Readings by and About
Holy Women Kissed by God

The Giveaway

Saint Bridget was
A problem child.
Although a lass
Demure and mild,
And one who strove
To please her dad,
St. Bridget drove
The family mad.
For here's the fault in Bridget lay:
She would give everything away
To any soul
Whose luck was out.
She'd give her bowl
Of stirabout;
She'd give her shawl,
Divide her purse
With one or all.
And what was worse,
When she ran out of things to give

She'd borrow from a relative.
Her father's gold,
Her grandson's dinner,
She'd hand to cold
And hungry sinner;
Give wine, give meat,
No matter whose;
Take from her feet
The very shoes,
And when her shoes had gone to others,
Fetch forth her sister's and her mother's.
She could not quit.
She had to share;
Gave bit by bit
The silverware,
The barnyard geese,
The parlor rug,
Her little niece's
Christening mug,
Even her bed to those in want,
And then the mattress of her aunt.
An easy touch
For poor and lowly,
She gave so much
And grew so holy
That when she died
Of years and fame,
The countryside
Put on her name,
And still the Isles of Erin fidget
with generous girls named Bride or Bridget.

Well, one must love her.
Nonetheless,
In thinking of her
Givingness

There's no denial
She must have been
A sort of trial
Unto her kin.
The moral, too, seems rather quaint.
WHO had the patience of a saint,
From evidence presented here?
Saint Bridget? Or her near and dear?
—Phyllis McGinley, *The Love Letters of Phyllis McGinley*
(Viking, 1957)

Prayer
St. Teresa of Avila

Let nothing disturb you,
Let nothing affright you.
All things are changing.
God alone never changes.
Who has God lacks nothing.
God alone suffices.
—*Complete Works of Teresa of Avila*

On Growing Older
St. Teresa of Avila

Lord, thou knowest better than I myself that I am growing older and will someday be old.

Keep me from the fatal habit of thinking I must say something on every subject and on every occasion. Release me from craving to straighten out everybody's affairs. Make me thoughtful but not needy, helpful but not bossy.

With my vast store of wisdom, it seems a pity not to use it all, but thou knowest, Lord, that I want a few friends at the end. Keep my mind free from the recital of endless details—give me wings to get to the point. Seal my lips on my aches and pains; they are increasing and the love of rehearsing them is becoming sweeter as the years go by.

I dare not ask for improved memory, but for a growing humility and a lessening cocksureness when my memory seems to clash with the memories of others. Teach me the glorious lesson that occasionally I may be mistaken. Keep me reasonably sweet, for a sour old person is one of the crowning works of the devil. Give me the ability to see good things in unexpected places and talents in unexpected people. And give me, O Lord, the grace to tell them so. Amen.

—*Complete Works of Teresa of Avila*

Prayers
St. Thérèse of Lisieux

My little way is the way of spiritual childhood, the way of trust and absolute self surrender. Jesus has shown me the only way that leads to the fire of divine love: it is that of a little child who, full of trust, falls asleep in its father's arms.

A word or a smile is often enough to put fresh life into a despondent soul.

Advice to the sisters: The world is thy ship and not thy home.
—*The Story of a Soul*, John Beevers, translator (Doubleday, 1989); *Thoughts of Saint Thérèse*, an Irish Carmelite, translator (Tan Books and Publishers, 1915)

The Holy Mother

What I want you to know is: I am one. All you learn is related to me. There are many manifestations of my love and life and beauty and wisdom. In your living and your dying, you are bringing me to birth. Know that by leaving the former house of prayer, you approach me in the darkness of the garden where all that grows and blooms is beautiful and connected to me and my life. You will lose nothing of the foundation I have already provided for you, but now your path leads in new and labyrinthine ways on which you meet me at every turn.

What I want you to know is: Your body is sacred, a manifestation of me, made in my image full of goodness, beauty, and life. Your energy flows from my creative energy and is part of all the energy moving in the universe. Gently let go of whatever you see that blocks that divine flow, and encourage all you meet to surrender to my divine love and leading in the same way.

What I want you to know is: You are being led. You know the darkness of the garden is full of fragrance. It is a safe and enclosed place, like the womb from which you came and will return, buried deep with the secrets of the Earth, your mother. Bless the darkness and invite it. Enter eagerly with joy, trusting that as the light fades, mystery is revealed without word or thought, in beauty and wonder.

Release what needs releasing to enter the deepest place of beauty and love—the rose of Engedi, the rose of Sharon. Labyrinthine ways are a continual flow, and you will learn at every turn until you enter the rose. Remain in the center of the deepest rose, enclosed and embraced until you are called forth to bring the richness of my gifts to all in your life. Know that you are part of each one on your path.
—Shirley Cunningham, *Chasing God*

A Holy Woman's Lament
(a Rap Song)

One point I hope you took as you listen to this speech,
Mary Magdalene's story is one we need to preach.
For some ungodly reason, she got a bad name
When, in fact, she was a leader—it's just not the same!
And Mary's not the only one to get a bad rap.
Lots of sisters had accusation dumped in their lap.
Just think of Suzanna and those dirty old men.
Now why should sex keep coming up again and again?
The sisters been blamed back to first mother Eve.
Too tempting, too sexy, they'd have us believe.
The saints could be virgins, perhaps anorexic—

(We know that whores who repent could be good picks!)
The good Virgin Mary is made out as great,
But for us married sisters, it's hard to relate.
So what has been lost in the stories of women?
What has been lost with this focus on sinnin'?
For sure, the connection to the body and sex.
Lots of women were burned for fear of their hex!
Today what a different world we would live in
If sex were seen truly as God's gift in women.
One thing's for sure 'bout the Sweet Magdalene.
She truly met Jesus in that Easter Garden scene.
He sent her to the 'postles, despite her bad rap—
To wake them and shake them up, out of their nap!
Like all holy women, she wanted some fun,
To hang out with Jesus, as the brothers have done.
Could be Peter felt jealous of Magdalene Sweet,
And later clamped down on women who lead.
The thing is, for Jesus, this story has sadness—
He wants brothers and sisters together—that's gladness!
The feminine part of God's image is lost.
Shekinah, Sophia, God's wisdom—big cost!
It behooves us as brothers and sisters tonight
To think hard on this story and set out to do right.
To hold women as equal as Jesus has done.
And give them full power, beyond whore or nun.
So Mary, we celebrate this day with you.
The darkness surrounds us—lead us to the new.
Like you, we've been touched. We have gifts from our God.
To be used for God's people, on this holy sod!
Give us your blessing, full of feminine power,
Fill our hearts with your love of Jesus...full flower.
Help us to claim that female part of God that we need,
Let it grow to a mighty tree from this tiny seed.

And that's a rap! Go in Peace! Yeah!
—Shirley Cunningham

How to Be a Queen

Put on my crown. Look around for my ermine robe.
Gather my council.
Tell them how to proceed in running the affairs of the land.
Fill my pockets with golden coins.
Distribute them to the poor nearby.
Send forth an edict forbidding television.
Gather my subjects and proclaim a holiday—
From complaints! which is to be filled with:
Celebratory fiddling, jigs and reels,
Colorful dancing costumes, drum rolls and piping flutes.
Let the stars know they are to shine each night,
except when the Goddess of the Night
brings her luminous moon out from behind the clouds.
Dispatch my navy to all foreign ports
Carrying the riches needed by each nation's children:
Health, learning, and love.
This is how to be a Queen.
—Shirley Cunningham, www.artfromheartnsoul.net, blog post:
"Thinking about Queens and Love"

La Magdalena

Easter morning in the Garden,
He returns to her
From divine realms.
The Alpha and Omega. She understands.
The graceful falconer
Has called the Christ,
Her falcon,
To her, to us ...
thus speaks the medieval mystic.
May we also
Be tethered to these two.
—Shirley Cunningham, www.artfromheartnsoul.net,
blog post: "La Magdalena"

Readings Contributed by Retreatants 2015–16

Brigid's Imbolc: Psalm of Spring

In the deep hours of winter keeping vigil at the hearth
darkness is softened by flame
Sinking down in stillness she weaves straw for the wind
for promise and possibility
Time is coming for the awakening dawn
the impulse of a new season
Breath streams at the threshold of this thin place
the essence of a deeper knowing
Out of mist and into the clearing
rainfall has blessed the fields with
water for the well of Imbolc
Frozen earth softens for seeds to break open
weaving the way upward their yawning stretch

Sending down roots that reach toward the invisible stream
Strength of spirit
Courage of fire
The eastern sky lifts the veil of Samhain
For Spring emerging out of the silence
the tender hark of a forgotten melody woven on the wind
instills the song of the universe singing within all who listen
—Renie Reilly

Prayer Given Me by the Samaritan Woman

Woman searching
Yearning for home,
A name to call her own
Herself.

Walk with me,
Shuffle and skip
Cry
Dance
Pray.

Your tears
Living water pouring
Bubbling out from the pot
Bursting with wisdom
Settling into solace.

May my tears mingle with your tears
Become one with Christ
So I may stand tall
Head held high
Holy
Kissed by God.
—Reverend Carolyn Herold

A Blessing of Woman

May the music of Miriam
Bring you joy
May the exclusion of the Samaritan Woman
Remind you to welcome all
May the sacred oils of Mary Magdalene
Anoint you
May the humility of Mary
Serve as an example
May the generosity of Brigid
Guide you to embrace a life of giving
May the visions of Hildegard
open your eyes to the wonders of nature
May the friendship of Clare and Agnes
strengthen you to keep alive
your long-distance relationships
May the suffering of Teresa of Avila
show you a path to God during times of distress
May the confidence of Joan of Arc
give you the courage to step forward
May the surrender of Thérèse of Lisieux
lead you to the open arms of Jesus
May the life of Kateri Tekakwitha
Bring you closer to the spirit of nature
May the stories of these Holy Women
of yesterday and today bless you
with the promise of a
Kiss from God.
—Barbara Gowan

To Miriam

You who walked the parting sea in peace,
Protector of Moses,
May we walk in peace through the waters
That part our lives.
When illusions of contrast
And separation manifest,
May we know the deep truth of oneness
And may that knowing center us,
Bring us peace,
Support us in flowing and moving
with our inner spirit.
—Jeanne Colasanti

Prayer to the Holy Women

Miriam, help me sing my song of freedom.
Mother Mary, remind me that all things are possible in God.
Mary Magdalene, help me to know Jesus's intimate love.
Samaritan Woman, pray that Jesus gazes upon me.
Brigid, remind me that a happy heart is true.
Hildegard, may I hear your voice ask "Are you blooming?
Are you growing?"
Clare of Assisi, remind me that a gentle spirit can be
powerful and courageous.
Terese of Avila, prompt me to gently draw inward.
Joan of Arc, may I remember that I was born for this
and not be afraid.
Thérèse of Lisieux remind me to enter His arms with love.
Tekakwitha, may I sense your presence in the woodlands.
—Heather Wiest

May We Go Forward

Go forward, women,
Go forward, self,
Go forward, saints.
Carry the light burden,
Carry the joyful burden,
Carry each other.
—M. L.

O Holy Women of God

You have touched my life:
with wisdom and your whispers.

Miriam: "Forgive the prophets, do not judge, but smile."
The Samaritan Woman: Take time day and night for Jesus' gaze."
Mary Magdalene: "Remember to be humble."
Mother Mary: "Love your sons but let go gracefully."
Brigid: "Serve those poor in material and spirit."
Hildegard: "Don't be bossy, surrender."
Clare: "Keep loving Francis; he has plans for you!"
Teresa of Avila: "Search within for light and rest."
Joan of Arc: "Be brave and believe."
Thérèse of Lisieux: "Do the ordinary with great love."
Tekakwitha: "Take care of the earth."
—Jane Dietzman

The Holy Women Speak

We holy women embrace you—
Never despair for you are
Beloved,
Called,
Cherished,
and Wanted.

Go and let your light shine:
Virgin,
Mother,
Crone.

You are ours.
—Gail Hartman

What Kateri Teaches Me

When I first heard of Kateri Tekakwitha, I felt drawn to her immediately. Maybe it was because she was Native American and knew the ancient ways of living off the land. As a farm wife for thirty years, I loved the land and observed the growth of our corn crop from seedling, to mature plant, to fully formed ears ripe for harvest. Living here in the Midwest, the Bread Basket of the World, I learned about food production and developed an intense interest in harvesting wild plants that grew in our farm yard, along fence rows or in ditches. I was a budding forager! Then, while on a Kissed by God: Holy Women Create retreat, I prayed a simple prayer to Kateri asking her to teach me about eating wild plants. She heard me and I'll share what I have learned with you!

Purslane, a pesky plant that crops up among my garden vegetables, turns out to be good for us. I wasn't looking for information about it, but perhaps it was the spirit of Kateri that led me to read an online posting about it. You can eat the whole plant, leaves, stems and all, raw. Wash it, chop it, mix it with other greens, and you have a great salad. Freezes well, too, for later use in soups and stews.

Garlic mustard is another invasive here in our part of Iowa. The county tries to keep it under control so it won't overtake other vegetation in our oak savannah, but it is edible. Makes an excellent pesto—I learned all this from a local naturalist's workshop recently.

Palmer Amaranth also is an edible invasive. Native Americans ate it raw, baked, or boiled. They also dried and stored their leaves and seeds, or ground them to use as meal. Once dried, Palmer Amaranth can easily be stored.

Golden Seal is a perennial herb well known to the Native Americans, who used it to remedy respiratory, digestive, and urinary tract infections. A friend grows this natural antibiotic and immune enhancer on her farm and offered me some. I said yes!

"Thank you, Kateri, for leading me to what our indigenous family in this part of our land valued for food and health. Help me to learn more from you. Amen."
—Mary Jane Keppler Cole

Reflection on Jesus and the Woman at the Well

I imagine myself in the woman's position for a moment. I look at the foreign face of this person who stands at the place that quenches my thirst and the thirst of those whom I love, and wonder why he's in my way. Why is he talking to me? Is he going to try to take something from me? Am I safe? I am nervous and I am prepared to run if he tries to touch me.

Instead of reaching toward me in power or gawking at my feminine figure, he looks at my face. Recognition alights in his eyes. If he's like the others, he will regard me as nothing, a piece of flesh, an unholy other. I wait, preparing to make my hasty retreat, wondering if my bucket can help me fend him off if he tries to attack me. He doesn't move. He continues to look at my face, as if I am the living well and he is refreshing his parched lips and mouth with the story of my life. He takes time, setting aside his ego to make space for my story—and then he tells it to me—as he has perceived it.

It is strange, because no grown man has ever made the effort to learn my story. It is always the man's story that matters, that needs to be told. I am a woman, and therefore I am a thread in a man's tapestry—many tapestries, in my case. Why is this stranger bothering with me? What does he want?

Again, the threat of harm puts fear in my heart, but still, he takes nothing from me—not even my bucket for claiming a drink. He offers me a gift instead—no favors required.

As I become the woman in this story, I am able to ask the myriad questions that lead to greater understanding about Jesus—the Christ. I perceive that this Christ is the one who offers rather than takes; this Christ is one who silences his heart in order to hear the stories buried in the heart of a complete stranger.

Is this what the follower of Christ is called to, then? To take risks, to cross boundaries, to silence egos? To listen so I might learn from this other who has almost nothing in common with me, religion and social rank included?

Let us ask ourselves!

—Rev. M. Kate Allen, posted on Sophia Network, March 7, 2014

Appendix
Mary–A Sufi's Mystical View

One visionary of our own time comes out of the Islamic tradition of Sufism. A contemporary mystic, Frithjof Schuon (1907–98), had visions of Mary that inspired him to write about her and attempt to paint his impressions of her. Schuon's strong creative impulse immediately reminds us of Hildegard of Bingen, another mystical writer and artist whose story is found in an earlier section of this book. Schuon was profoundly impacted by his visions and led to share them with the world:

> Since that experience I could hardly paint anything other than the Holy Virgin. I painted her not as she is portrayed in Christian religious art, but as I had inwardly experienced her, that is as virginal Mother or as motherly Virgin, and beyond all the theological forms as the embodiment of the Divine Mercy and at the same time of Religio Perennis,[i] somehow uniting in her person Christianity, Islam and Hinduism, in conformity with my own nature ... in my pictures

---

i   Wisdom that always remains true to itself.

of Mary there is something of the golden earth-barakah.[ii]

In Schuon's extensive writing, Mary is named the Divine Femininity that he experienced as a protective patroness, the Queen of Heaven and the Queen of all Saints. See the author's painting *Queen of Poland*, page 18.

ii   Barakah: the continuity of spiritual presence and revelation that begins with God and can be found flowing through physical objects, places and people chosen by God.

Responding to the Holy Women: Exercises

These exercises can focus on any one or several of the Holy Women together. They are suitable for individual or group reflection and can be used specifically on their feast days. They can also be selected one at a time for a personal retreat over a period of weeks, such as Advent or Lent. It is completely possible to take elements from various exercises and combine them in new ways. Follow your inspiration! Many blessings!

Exercise 1: Journaling

Consider Miriam—her name means "bitter."
Consider the Samaritan woman—beyond her tribe, she is unnamed in scripture.
Consider Clare—her name means "clear light."
Consider Joan of Arc—she called herself "Pucelle," maid/virgin of Orleans.
Consider Tekakwitha—she was called "one who bumps into things" and "Lily of the Mohawks."

Does your name have any inherent meaning? Are you your name? When someone calls your name, are they calling you or some idea of you, for example, "Teacher"? If you are not your name, what do you call yourself? Journal about your many names. Do any new realizations or surprises arise from this reflection? What does it mean to you to remember that God says, "I call you each by name"?

Exercise 2: Overhearing the Holy Women/ Journaling

Imagine eavesdropping on several of the Holy Women having an energetic dialogue with each other. What is on their minds? Does their exchange relate to some of your issues? Allow them to notice you and invite you into the exchange. What do they have to say about your concerns?

Capture the complete dialogue in your journal and share it with a close friend or spiritual director. (If you want an idea to start you off, you may read "Holy Women of Scripture Meet," beginning on page 63.)

Exercise 3: A Holy Woman Visits Today/ Journaling

Choose the Holy Woman who wants to visit you today. Reread her story. Were you charmed, resistant, validated, challenged, surprised by it? Joan of Arc listened to her inner voice. Have you ever listened to the voice of your imagination and found it led you to an important experience? How do you sense when you are being led? Is it a logical process—or do you wish it were? After you consider Joan or any of your Holy Women's stories and relate them to your own, journal about it.

Exercise 4: Walking Where She Walked/ Journaling

Have you ever visited the country or area where your Holy Woman lived? If so, what brought you there? Why were you familiar with it?

Imagine being there now with her. Where are the two of you? In a building? In a garden? Is she a child, a grown woman living her call, or an elder? What is she doing? Is something of her way of life part of your life too? As you observe her in her time and place, does her life have any similarity to yours? What does she convey to you? Any surprises? How do you feel walking where she walked before you? Spend some time with your thoughts, and then journal about this visit. Don't forget to thank your Holy Woman for being with you.

Exercise 5: Write to a Woman in Your Life

In these exercises, after you have had conversations with several of the Holy Women, review them. Do they inspire you to have a few words with a woman in your life? A friend? A sister? A daughter? A daughter-in-law? A granddaughter? Your mother? If so, what has she inspired you to express? The words may be a turning point of reconciliation or of loss, or a recognition of a special time: a birthday, Christmas, graduation, or wedding. Consider what she is prompting you to say. Your words may be a special gift deserving to be printed on fine paper, a gift only you can give to someone important in your life.

Exercise 6: A Letter from Your Holy Woman/ Journaling

Sit in quiet meditation, perhaps with some music playing that relates to one of your Holy Women. For example, with Brigid, it might be the melodies of the Irish harp. When you are ready, without choosing your words, write a personal message from your Holy Woman to you. Begin by letting her call you by name: "My dear _____ ..." Continue to write for as long as her words flow in your imagination. If there seems to be a pause, wait a bit. More words may come. When you feel complete, read what you have written and add whatever else comes to mind. Finish by sitting in silence for a few moments to express your gratitude to the Spirit for this gift.

Exercise 7: A Visit from Mary/Journaling

Our Holy Women had a deep love of Jesus. They had that in common with Mary, his mother, and likely it was the main thing that brought them close to her. Choose one of the women and imagine Mary paying her a visit, perhaps in a modest room with a fire glowing in the hearth nearby. They are seated across from each other at a small table with steaming cups of a fragrant drink in front of them while cold winds whistle outside. What do they talk about? Ask each of them what their friendship means to them. Perhaps the advice they offered each other was of most value. Ask them about the best advice anyone ever gave them. And perhaps they will tell you the best advice they feel they ever gave. Reflect on advice you have given and received. Do you see similarities to what they are discussing? Your Holy Women invite you to join their conversation. Do so, and when you sense it is complete, thank them both and spend some time in quiet meditation and journaling.

Exercise 8: Exploring the Queen Archetype/ Speech Writing/Journaling

A number of the Holy Women were abbesses or other leaders. A woman with such gifts likely carried the archetypal energy of a ruler, a queen. The goal of any ruler would be to establish and maintain a peaceful realm. A good queen would take this responsibility very seriously and be intent on growing in her ability to do all in her power for her people. She would need to see clearly and lead energetically and with confidence, considering the good of all. Now imagine that you are the queen of your very own domain. You are in charge. You may need to convince your subjects or the rulers of bordering kingdoms of the wisdom of your judgment on some matters.

Imagine yourself writing the speech you will make to persuade them. Imagine using your power to create a better world in your own life and in the community of nations across the world. Does this reflection prompt you to action on an important issue in today's world, whether local, national, or international? Is it time?

(See "How to Be a Queen" as an idea-starter. See Readings by Holy Women, page 199.)

Exercise 9: Exploring the Visionary Archetype/ Journaling

Visionaries among the Holy Women shared their mystical experiences with respected spiritual guides. They realized their divine inspirations needed to be authentic and sought the good judgment and confirmation of true listeners, trustworthy witnesses. Their decision-making process was guided by prayer, prudence, and trust in collaboration. When it comes to decision making, what is your approach to everyday concerns? How do you discern God's call? Sometimes one carrying visionary energy tends to focus on the future with anxiety or vacillation.

How do you deal with your uncomfortable awareness of challenging future scenarios? Do you struggle to balance anxiety about unanticipated outcomes with hopeful aspects of the present moment? Meditate on the prayer of St. Teresa of Avila and then journal about this reflection:

Let nothing disturb you.
Let nothing affright you.
All things are passing.
God alone never changes.
She who has God has everything.

Exercise 10: Exploring the Fool Archetype/ Collage

Consider the archetype of the fool. As you have read the stories of these Holy Women, you may have seen attributes that seem to be those of the holy fool. The fool goes to extremes to make a point others may fear to bring up. In royal courts, the fool is free and safe to do this in words and actions because even rulers under criticism know truth is being told. The shadow side of the everyday fool, however, may show off without any goal of betterment for himself or others. And one may well wonder if part of the value of the fool is simply to provide merriment. If you feel you don't know this archetype well, pause here and browse some magazines for images of various fools, merrymakers, sad clowns, scary clowns, happy clowns.

Collage them and let them speak to you, and then return to this exercise. Invite one of your Holy Women to tell you about her holy fool energy and yours. She may help you recognize the light and shadow in yourself, or she may invite you to experiment with the fool's spontaneity. If you choose to open these questions with more than one Holy Woman, you may be surprised by the variety of their observations about you!

Exercise 11: Exploring the Healer Archetype

Many of the Holy Women carry the healer archetype. We know the positive energy of the healer as compassionate, nurturing and restorative. However, there is a shadow side to the healer also: the tendency to hover too much, to feel overly responsible for the problems of others, to doubt that a loved one is able to care for herself or himself. The healer needs to develop an attitude of trust in those she sees as needy and develop awareness of her own need of self-care. What do you recognize about your healer energy? Write a prayer to your Holy Woman asking for her help as you follow your call to be a compassionate healing presence for those on your path.

Exercise 12: Portrayals of Holy Women/ Photography/Collage/Journaling

Churches, hospitals, schools, and shrines are named after the Holy Women. If some are nearby, plan a visit. Take photos of the artwork you find there, whether it's paintings, sculptures, statues, or stained glass. Do the portrayals fit comfortably with your impression of the one represented? If not, go on the Internet to see what you find when you enter her name in Wikipedia—or Google Images—or visit any website dedicated to her. Select the images that appeal to you and print them for a collage. Add captions with colored marker and any other elements your creativity may suggest. Spend some time reflecting on your collage and then journal your impressions, inspirations, and a prayer. Be sure to date it, including the year.

Exercise 13: A Shrine/Art/Collage/Assembly

Suppose you have been assigned responsibility to design a shrine for one of the Holy Women and told you could use any materials—the sky's the limit. Perhaps remember details about shrines you may have visited. What would your shrine be like? Describe it in words or a sketch or collage—or in all three ways. Arrange a prayer corner for your finished product in your home, adding a candle, photos, or small decorative objects such as buttons, shells, broken jewelry, or dried flowers. Spend some time there reflecting on how these symbols speak to you about the Holy Woman you had in mind.

Exercise 14: A Holy Woman's Story Happens to You/Collage

Choose a story you liked about your Holy Woman. Imagine what the story might be like if it happened to you in modern times. Let the ideas flow freely as if you are reporting a dream. Allow surprises and humor to arise as you put words into her mouth and yours. The details do not need to be strictly logical but when you consider them, look for a message that may be an invitation or instruction for you. You could tell this story in a collage if you feel attracted to the process. It might surprise you to find that very apt images are right there in a few magazines you have handy ... or the images may come across your path in the next few days. Later, write a few lines about how these little coincidences—sometimes called synchronicities— have come to your notice. Could be God is just being anonymous!

Exercise 15: Visit from a Holy Woman/ Dream Work

Make up a dream in which one of your Holy Women shows up. You needn't have an actual dream. Your imagination can bring you the same things as a dream since it comes from the same place in your psyche. As ideas come to you, write them in your journal. Capture as many details and images as you can: time, place, names, numbers, colors, sounds, and natural elements like the sea. Then consider what these details might suggest symbolically for your Holy Woman. For example, the well and its water have several meanings as the Samaritan woman's story unfolds. Would your association be like hers or different? Another association with her might be "outsider." Have you ever felt yourself an outsider? Your made-up dream of the Holy Woman could have very different details. For example in your dream, you could invite her water jar to speak: "I am one who gets filled to overflowing, but sometimes can be completely empty ..."

When you are finished, give your dream a title, whatever pops into your mind—no working on it! Then ask yourself what the theme of the dream seems to be. Write it down in just a few words. Next, ask yourself what the main feeling of the dream is and jot that down. Finally, ask yourself, "What question is life asking of me in this dream?" Without judging it or struggling to be logical, write what immediately comes to your mind. When you feel complete, sit quietly and ask your Holy Woman to present your dream to Jesus.

Exercise 16: A Rambling Poem

Write a non-poem about your Holy Woman, being sure to double space between the lines. A non-poem has no rules about structure, counting syllables, rhyme schemes, or anything else. Just ramble; let her lead you on. When you are finished, cut the lines of the poem apart so you have a separate statement on each strip of paper. Fold the strips in half so you can't see the text. Now without planning, draw one strip at a time whatever way it comes, without reading it. Lay them out, one following the other. See if you like the way this poem has put itself together. You are free to add and take away any words or lines until you have the poem just as you like it. Copy your final version, then date it and put it away. Look at it again in a few days. Perhaps in the meantime, you will have a dream rich with images or words related to your Holy Woman that want to be in your poem. It's all material you can use if you wish to "polish" the poem.

Exercise 17: A Rambling Drawing/Collage/ Journaling

You can take this rambling approach to drawing too. Start by writing your Holy Woman's name on an 8 x 10 sheet of paper or larger. Use any colored markers you choose. Once the name is there, scribble on the page with whatever color you like: no plan, no pattern—just have fun. Then turn your page upside down, reversing it from one side to the other. Add more little images connected with your Holy Woman. For example, a feather for Tekakwitha, a rose for Thérèse, a golden arrow for Teresa. If you prefer, clip whatever appeals to you from magazines to fill in spaces with various shapes and colors. You can also cut up whatever images you have collected into various sizes and shapes and lay them out on a larger sheet of colored paper in patterns that please you. Remember: you don't have to cover every spot of background; it can show through, adding to the general effect. Afterward, choose the images that call to you and write about them, starting with the words "I am one who ..." Journal about your ramble, being sure to date it, and then spend some time reflecting on your creation.

Exercise 18: Stepping Stones on the Labyrinth/ Journaling

This exercise is like walking through your life without leaving the room. To prepare, get your journal, a pen, and two colored markers. You will also need the sample labyrinth at the end of this exercise, which you may use or duplicate. When you have your materials, find a quiet spot to comfortably sit and write. Before beginning, take time to breathe deeply, centering yourself in silence. Then invite the Creative Spirit to be with you.

In this journal exercise, you are invited on an inner journey that will lead you to some specific events in your unique life that are easily accessible during this time of reflection. When you think of your life path now, certain experiences may seem to be stepping stones from one period to another. List them, beginning with your "I was born." Don't worry about chronology for now. The next event that springs to mind might be from many years later, such as the death of a loved one. That's fine. Simply identify each inner or outer experience that occurs to you in a word or two. When your list of a dozen or so is complete, review it to see how the events go chronologically. Number them as best you can. If you aren't sure, just guess which would go fourth or fifth, for example. Approximations are fine! This list represents what is in your consciousness now, so it will not be comprehensive. (On another occasion, you could possibly recall very different events.)

The next step is to consider one of your Holy Women. Call to mind significant events you know or suppose were likely to have happened in her life. Make a similar list for her of no more than a dozen, and then number them in chronological order.

You may be familiar with the ancient meditative practice of walking a labyrinth, but we can also use this ancient walk symbolically. If you have never wound your way through a labyrinth, the journey is made up of three parts: walking in, arriving at the center, and walking out. Those three phases can suggest the stages of the spiritual life.[i] For this exercise, consider the first part symbolic of your early life, the third part your later life, and the center symbolic of an experience of special closeness to God, regardless of when it occurred.

Choose the colored marker you will use to write a word or a number—you can choose which— for the stepping stones of your own life on the labyrinth. Decide where you will place them. Some may be placed near the beginning, some may seem to belong on a long stretch in one direction, some at an abrupt twist or turn, some close to the center or toward the end. Once they are all placed, use the other colored marker to follow the same procedure for your Holy Woman's stepping stones. Give some thought to where they feel they want to go! Don't try to "plan" too much, but enjoy the

---

i   For further information about the labyrinth, Lauren Artress's book *Walking a Sacred Path* provides a rich introduction. Riverhead Books, 1995.

surprise of where they land at various junctures on the labyrinth.

What does your journey reveal to you? What does your Holy Woman's journey reveal? Are there points of comparison? Journal about your observations and any similarities and differences. What do you feel as you reflect on this journey? What has this process been like for you?

When your reflection seems complete, write a few words of prayer thanking the Spirit for any gift you received in this meditation, and even for any questions that may have arisen. The questions themselves may be inviting you to a new place on your path.

The labyrinth at Chartres Cathedral, France. Note the entrance at the bottom. (Feel free to copy and enlarge.)

Illustration Credits

Prophet Miriam, page 8; *Brigid of Kildare*, page 72; and *Hildegard of Bingen*, page 95. Marcy Hall.

Our Lady of Perpetual Help, a Byzantine icon, page 21. Wikimedia Commons.

Pietà by Michelangelo, page 36. Wikimedia Commons.

St. Bride by John Duncan, page 79. National Gallery of Scotland, Edinburgh.

Hildegard's Awakening: A Self-Portrait, page 92. *Illuminations of Hildegard of Bingen*, Matthew Fox.

The Creator's Glory, Creation's Glory, page 93. *Illuminations of Hildegard of Bingen*, Matthew Fox.

Women Doctors of the Church, page 96. Master craftsman Paul Coulaz, St. Thérèse of Lisieux Church, Montauk, New York.

St. Clare with Monstrance, page 110. Photo by Br. Michael-Francis, O.S.B., St. John Cantius Church, Chicago.

The Ecstasy of St. Teresa of Avila, page 125. Wikimedia Commons.

Joan's banner, page 143. *Joan of Arc: A Life Transfigured by Kathryn Harrison.*

Sketch of Joan from 1429, page 156. *Joan of Arc: A Life Transfigured* by Kathryn Harrison.

Portrait of Tekakwitha by Claude Chauchetière, page 179. Wikimedia Commons.

Associated Press photograph, October 20, 2012, page 181.

Chartres Labyrinth drawing on page 221 by Jo Edkins.

Notes

Introduction

1. Acts 2:17, paraphrased.

2. Frederick L. Downing, *Elie Wiesel: A Religious Biography* (Macon, GA: Mercer University Press, 2008), 121.

3. Lyn Brakeman, *Spiritual Lemons: Biblical Women, Irreverent Laughter, and Righteous Rage* (Philadelphia: First Augsburg Books, 2005), 11.

4. I do not find the exact wording of this sentence in Francis Gross's discussion of Teresa of Avila's inner and outer journey. He does use other words but I think the statement above is suggested. Francis L. Gross, Jr. with Toni Perior Gross, *The Making of a Mystic: Seasons in the Life of Teresa of Avila* (Albany, NY: State University of New York Press, 1993), 186–88.

5. Shirley Cunningham, *Chasing God* (Scottsdale, AZ: Amoranita Publishing, 2002), 291–92.

6. Robert Johnson, *Inner Work* (San Francisco: HarperSanFrancisco, 1986), 59–62.

7. Gospel stories also can be understood as arising from the archetypal realm. For further reading, consult sources in the bibliography by Walter Wink, Edward F. Edinger, and Christine Valters Paintner as well as Carl Jung.

8. Bridal spirituality was also a theme in early apocryphal and Gnostic sources.

9. Carol Flinders, *Enduring Grace* (New York: HarperCollins, 1993), 2.

10. Ibid., 3.

11. Contemporary clergywoman and author Lyn Brakeman humorously reminds us, "God is not a boy's name" in her book, *Spiritual Lemons.*
12. David Richo, *Mary Within Us* (Berkeley, CA: Human Development Books, 2007), 115.

Miriam

1.   Numbers 12.
2.   Exodus 2.
3.   Exodus 15.
4.   Tamar Meir, "Miriam: Midrash and Aggadah." *Jewish Women: A Comprehensive Historical Encyclopedia.* 20 March 2009. Jewish Women's Archive. https://jwa.org/encyclopedia/article/miriam-midrash-and-aggadah (accessed 2/14/2017).
5.   Exodus Rabbah 1:17 quoted by Nissan Mindel, Kehot Publication Society on Chabat.org.
6.   Exodus 1:19.
7.   Tamar Meir, "Miriam: Midrash and Aggadah."
8.   Ibid.
9.   Christine Valters Paintner, *Illuminating the Way* (Notre Dame, IN: Sorin Books, 2016), 131-2.
10. It is possible that Miriam lived to a very ripe old age, since she was older than her brothers Moses and Aaron. We know from Exodus 7:7 that they were in their early eighties when the Israelites began demanding their freedom in Egypt. Miriam could have been eighty-seven, but remembering use of numbers in the early books of the Bible, the extreme age may be intended to indicate wisdom rather than actual age in years. Nevertheless, we can admire Miriam as a leadership model for mature and elderly women. Wilda C. Gafney, *Daughters of Miriam: Women Prophets in Ancient Israel* (Minneapolis: Fortress Press, 2008), 80.
11. Ross Shepherd Kraemer and Mary Rose D'Angelo, eds., *Women and Christian Origins* (New York: Oxford University Press, 1999), 316-19.
12. Ibid., 317.
13. This is the position of Giorgio Otranto, "Notes on the Female Priesthood in Antiquity," translated in Rossi, "Priesthood, Precedent, and Prejudice." Martimort, *Deaconesses*, 196-200, associates them with widows who receive diaconal blessing: Gryson, *Ministry of Women*, 105, simply asks whether they were deaconesses and finds the evidence insufficient to decide. This is footnote 73 in Kraemer and D'Angelo, eds., *Women and Christian Origins*, 320.
14. Miriam Therese Winter, *WomanWisdom* (New York: Crossroad Publishing Co., 1997), 75-6.

15. Meir, "Miriam: Midrash and Aggadah."
16. Exodus 2:1–10.
17. Exodus 2:15–21.
18. The Book of Numbers.
19. Exodus 14, 15.
20. Shirley Cunningham, "Miriam Remembers," 2016, previously unpublished.

Mary

1. Matthew 1:16, 18, 20, 2:11, 13:55; Mark 6:3, 3:31, 3:32; Luke 1:27, 30, 34, 38, 39, 41, 46, 56, 2:5, 16, 19, 34; John 2:1–12, 19:25–26; Acts 1:14.
2. Book of Revelation, 12:1.
3. John, 2:4.
4. John, 2:5.
5. Acts, 2:4.
6. Marina Warner, *Alone of All Her Sex* (New York: Vintage, 1976), 280.
7. Frithjof Schuon, "Wisdom of the Virgin," *Dimensions of Islam*, P. N. Townsend, tr. (Bloomington, Ind: World Wisdom Books, 1970). See appendix, page 209 in this book re Frithoj Schuon for more.
8. Emma Wegner, "Hagia Sophia, 532–37" in Heilbrunn Timeline of Art History (New York: Metropolitan Museum of Art, 2000). https://www.metmuseum.org/toah/nd/haso.htm (October 2004). The Hagia Sophia was originally a Christian cathedral. It became a mosque in the fifteenth century and is now a museum. Pilgrimage was a significant devotion for many devotees from ancient times, and still is. Today a pilgrimage from Ephesus to Istanbul is a day trip. Even without benefit of modern transport, a motivated Muslim of the fifteenth century with a bit of extra time could have made the trip too. A prime example of Islamic sacred journey today is the centuries-old trip to Mecca in the footprints of Mohammed.
9. Phyllis G. Jestice, *Holy People of the World: A Cross-Cultural Encyclopedia*, Vol. 123, 2004 (Santa Barbara, CA: ABC-CLIO), 558, Sayyidana Maryam.
10. Cyril Glasse, "Mary," *Concise Encyclopedia of Islam* (London: Stacey International, 3rd ed., 2008).
11. Ibid.
12. Warner, *Alone of All Her Sex*, 28. The Book of James 19:2: A cloud of light overshadows the cave "until the young child appeared: and it went and took the breast of its mother Mary." The idea of a miraculously painless birth fits with the notion of Mary as ever

virgin and sinless. She had no pain because she was considered to be a sinless new Eve, in contrast to that first woman who was sent from the Garden condemned to bear her children in pain.

13. Koran, 19:24-25.

14. Amira El-Azhary Sonbol, ed., *Beyond the Exotic: Women's Histories in Islamic Societies* (Syracuse: Syracuse University Press, 2005), 402.

15. Matthew 1:18-25.

16. Canaan, T, "Mohammedan Saints and Sanctuaries in Palestine," *Journal of the Palestine Oriental Soc.*, iv/1-2, 1924, 1-84.

17. Richo, *Mary Within Us*, 86.

18. Lawrence Cunningham and John J. Reich, *Culture and Values: a Survey of the Humanities* (Belmont, CA: Thomson/Wadsworth, 2006).

19. This was a common title of her perpetual virginity from the fourth century and became a dogmatic title at the Lateran Council of 647. Donald W. Wuerl and Kris D. Stubna, *The Teaching of Christ, A Catholic Catechism for Adults*, Our Sunday Visitor Publishing, 2004.

20. Richo, *Mary Within Us*, 83.

21. Mark 6:3.

22. Luke 1:35.

23. *Pietà*, Michelangelo Buonarroti. Italian sculpture, 1499.

24. Richo, *Mary Within Us*, 121-22.

25. Ibid., 38.

26. Cunningham, *Chasing God*, 219.

27. Richo, *Mary Within Us*, 7.

28. Ibid., 17.

29. Cuningham, *Chasing God*, 215.

30. Richo, *Mary Within Us*, 51.

Magdalene

1. Susan Haskins, *Mary Magdalen: Myth and Metaphor* (New York: Riverhead Books, 1993), 93-94.

2. Elizabeth A. Elliott, "Magdalene gets her Feast," *National Catholic Reporter*, June 10, 2016.

3. Haskins, *Mary Magdalen*, 62.

4. Miriam Therese Winter, *WomanWord: A Feminist Lectionary and Psalter* (New York: Crossroads, 1992), 157.

5. Haskins, *Mary Magdalen*, 61-62, citing Canticle of Canticles 3:1-3 and Luke 24:22.

6. Ibid., 63-64, citing Canticle 8:6-7.

7. Elliott reports in the *National Catholic Reporter* that Pope Francis in the context of his proclaimed Year of Mercy 2016 has elevated Magdalene's memorial observance to a major feast in the Catholic liturgical calendar equal to that of the apostles. He cites this decision based on her great love for Christ and his great love for her, part of the story of Luke 7: 36–50.

8. Some early theologians call her fall a "happy fault," and there is a liturgical hymn using that term.

9. Haskins, *Mary Magdalen*, 62.

10. Luke 7:47.

11. Krista Tippett, *Speaking of Faith* (New York: Penguin, 2007), 66–67, quoting Luke Timothy Johnson.

12. Ean Begg, *The Cult of the Black Virgin* (Boston: Arkana, 1985), 220–21.

13. Ibid.

14. China Galland, *Longing for Darkness: Tara and the Black Madonna* (New York: Penguin, 1990), 176.

15. Haskins, *Mary Magdalen*, 218.

16. Ibid., "The *Grandes Heures* of Vézelay," 95–130.

17. Ibid., 126.

18. "Starting at St. Maximin-de-la-St. Baume." Camino de Santiago Forum. https://www.caminodesantiago.me/community/threads/starting-at-st-maximin-de-la-st-baume.15901/ (accessed 2/9/2017).

19. I was surprised to find an amazing text on display in St. Trophime's Church in nearby Arles when I visited in 2013. It detailed the significance of these arrivals in Provence with specific reference to Marseille and Saintes-Maries-de-la-Mer. The display reported that the future Pope John XXIII, Monsignor Roncalli, had visited in 1948 to celebrate the five hundredth anniversary of the discovery of the tombs of Mary Jacobe and Mary Salome. It also noted that "Sainte Sara, patronne des Gitans est venerée dans le sanctuaire" (St. Sara, patron saint of the Gypsies is venerated in the sanctuary).

20. Warner, *Alone of All Her Sex*, 229, footnote 4 cites R. M. Grant, *After the New Testament* (Philadelphia: Fortress, 1967), 188; for the Gnostics' treatment of Mary Magdalene see Robert Murray, *Symbols of Church and Kingdom: A Study in Early Syriac Tradition* (London: Bloomsbury T & T Clark, 1975), 332–3.

21. Cynthia Bourgeault, *The Meaning of Mary Magdalene* (Boston: Shambhala, 2010), 56.

22. Ibid., 154, 156.

23. Ibid., 156.

24. Ibid., xi.

25. We can imagine she was close to Jesus's age when he was crucified: thirty-three. We are told she may have lived as a hermit in the cave for thirty years. When we add in a few extra years she spent preaching, Magdalene could have lived to seventy or older.

26. Warner, *Alone of All Her Sex*, 235.

27. Ibid.

28. Shirley Cunningham, previously unpublished.

29. Luke 8:1–3.

30. Luke 8:1–4.

31. John 19:25.

32. John 20:1–18.

33. Winter, *WomanWord*, 157.

34. Ibid.

35. Haskins, *Mary Magdalen.*

36. Ibid., 386.

37. Lynn Picknett and Clive Prince, *The Templar Revelation* (London: Transworld Publishers Ltd, Touchstone Books, 1997).

38. Revelation 3:20.

39. Paraphase of Luke 7:47.

The Samaritan Woman

1. Kraemer and D'Angelo, eds. *Women and Christian Origins*, 40.

2. John 4: 23–24.

3. Kraemer and D'Angelo, eds., *Women and Christian Origins*, 39.

4. Ibid., 40. Men with Jesus were seldom identified by marital status either. This could either mean that most of the followers of Jesus were unmarried or that the evangelists just weren't interested in the issue.

5. Mark 12:18–27.

6. B. A. Robinson, Women's Roles in the Bible, "The Status of Women in the Christian Gospels" (Religioustolerance.org, Ontario Consultants on Religious Tolerance, Copyright 1998–2012, last update July 7, 2015). Sections on Divorce and Levirate Marriage.

7. Ibid., section on Levirate Marriage.

8. Kraemer and D'Angelo, eds., *Women and Christian Origins*, 48, footnote 24.

9. Ibid., 42.

10. Ibid., 43–44.

11. Before I learned about the Samaritan Woman's baptism as described in these other traditions, I wrote a dramatic reading imagining a

conversation with the other Holy Women of Scripture in this book, Miriam, Mother Mary, and Mary Magdalene. In it, she reminds them that Jesus did baptize her and she subsequently celebrated Passover with them. See "Holy Women of Scripture Meet," page 63.

12. Orthodox Church of America, oca.org. Martyr Photina (Svetlana), the Samaritan Woman and Her Sons, copyright 1996–2016. https://oca.org/100846-martyr-photina-svetlana-the-samaritan-woman-and-her-sons.

13. Topping, Eva Catafygiotu, *Saints and Sisterhood: The Lives of Forty-eight Holy Women* (Minneapolis: Life and Light Publishing Co., 1990).

14. Orthodox Church of America, Martyr Photina (Svetlana), the Samaritan Woman and Her Sons.

15. Cunningham, *Chasing God*, 174–180.

16. Psalm 34:18.

17. John 4:10.

18. John 4:14.

19. John 4:18.

20. John 4:19, 25, 39.

Brigid

1. Paintner, *Illuminating the Way*, 83.

2. Dara Molloy, Writings, http://www.daramolloy.com/DaraMolloy/Writings/AnCrannDair.html, 2001 (accessed 2/2/2017).

3. Conrad Jay Bladey, *Brigid of the Gael* (New York: Hutman Productions, 2009), Ch. 3, "A Life—Cultural Setting," Locations 593 and 604 of 8099.

4. "St. Brigid of Ireland," Catholic Online, http://www.catholic.org/saints/saint.php?saint_id=453.

5. Bladey, "Life of Brigid from Book of Lismore," Location 1477 of 8099.

6. Bladey, Ch. 4, "The Lives," Locations 1607 and 2313 of 8099.

7. Bladey, Ch. 4, "The Lives," Locations 1607 and 1617 of 8099.

8. John O'Donohue, *Anam Cara* (New York: Harper-Collins, 1997), 13–17.

9. Bladey, "The Martyrology of Oengus the Culdee," Stokes Whitley, ed. (London: Henry Bradshaw Society, 1905), 65.

10. Bladey, Appendix 6, "Scottish Catholic Traditions," Location 7872 of 8099.

11. Thomas Cahill, *How the Irish Saved Civilization* (New York: Doubleday, 1995), 174–75.

12. Bladey, Ch. 6, "Schemata," Locations 4813 and 4824 of 8099.

13. Bladey, Ch. 6, "The Lives," Location 5024 of 8099.

14. Patrick Kennedy, *Legendary Fictions of the Irish Celts* (Charleston, SC: BiblioBazaar, 2008, original copyright 1891), 356.

15. Bladey, Ch. 6, "Schemata," Location 4989 of 8099.

16. Bladey, Ch. 3, "A Life," Location 585 of 8099.

17. Bladey, Ch. 7, Hymns and Charms and Poems, "A Vision of St. Bride," Locations 6318–6424 of 8099.

18. Bladey, Ch. 4 "Life of St. Brigid of Lismore," Locations 1945 and 7761 of 8099.

19. Bladey, Ch. 4, Location 2884 of 8099.

20. Bladey, Ch. 6, "Schemata," Location 4995 of 8099. The reader will note that St. Clare of Assisi is also named as the first to write a rule for women. The Roman church in the fifth century had not yet developed a process of formally recognizing the early structures for dedicated women emerging in Ireland, although Brigid had created a rule. Later in the thirteenth century, St. Clare's rule was the first for women formally recognized by Rome.

21. Bladey, Ch. 2, "St Brigid," Location 458 of 8099.

22. Shirley Cunningham, prevously unpublished.

23. Jan Richardson, *In the Sanctuary of Women* (Nashville: Upper Room Books, 2010), 66.

24. Bladey, Ch. 4, "The Lives," Location 2130 of 8099.

25. "Highland Clearances," Crann Tara. https://cranntara.scot/clear.htm (accessed 2/2/2017).

26. Richardson, 67.

27. Bladey, Ch. 4, "The Lives," Locations 2782, 2884, and 2893 of 8099.

Hildegard of Bingen

1. Matthew Fox, *Hildegard of Bingen* (Vancouver, BC: Namaste Publishing, 2012), 9.

2. Renate Craine, *Hildegard: Prophet of the Cosmic Christ* (New York: Crossroad), 1997, 23.

3. Ibid., 24.

4. Ibid., 25.

5. Ibid.

6. Jan Richardson, *In the Sanctuary of Women* (Nashville: Upper Room Books, 2010), 166, footnote on 211. Mother Columba Hart and Jane Bishop, tr. *Hildegard of Bingen: Scivias*, introduction by Barbara J. Newman, preface by Caroline Bynum (New York: Paulist Press, 1990), 59.

7. Richardson, *In the Sanctuary of Women*, 166.

8. Craine, *Hildegard*, 34.

9. Matthew Fox, *Illuminations of Hildegard of Bingen* (Rochester, VT: Bear & Company, 1985), 10, footnote 15: See J. Schomer, *Die Illustrationen der hl. Hildegard von Bingen als künstlerische Neuschopfung* (Diss.), Bonn: 1937; Ch. Meier, *Text und Bild im überlieferten Werk Hildegarde von Bingen* (Wiesbaden), 1978.

10. Craine, *Hildegard*, 27.

11. Fox, *Illuminations*, 44.

12. Ibid., *Hildegard of Bingen*, 29–30.

13. Gabriele Uhlein, *Meditations with Hildegard of Bingen* (Santa Fe, NM: Bear & Company, 1983), 31.

14. Craine, *Hildegard*, 24.

15. Fox, *Illuminations*, 40–41.

16. Craine, *Hildegard*, 26.

17. Fox, *Illuminations*, 126.

18. Ibid., 74.

19. Fox, *Hildegard of Bingen*, 84, citing in footnote 11: Barbara Newman, *Sister of Wisdom: St. Hildegard's Theology of the Feminine* (Berkeley, CA: University of California Press, 1997), 160.

20. Craine, *Hildegard*, 38–39.

21. Ibid., 39.

22. Hildegard of Bingen, *Symphonia*, Barbara Newman, ed. (Ithaca, NY: Cornell University Press, 1988), 158 and 284–85.

23. Dan Graves, MSL, "Hildegard: Sybil of the Rhine," http://www.christianity.com/church/church-history/timeline/901-1200/hildegard-sybil-of-the-rhine-11629806.html (accessed 2/24/2017).

24. Doctor of the Church is a title accorded by the church to certain saints. It indicates that their writings and preachings are useful to Christians in any age. These men and women are recognized for the depth of understanding of their theological teachings.

25. Paintner, *Illuminating the Way*, 174–75.

26. Matthew Fox, *Original Blessing* (Santa Fe, NM: Bear & Co., 1983), 308.

27. Craine, *Hildegard*, 24.

28. Fox, *Original Blessing*, 308.

29. Cathy Caridi, J. C. L., in Canonical Issues Involving Non-Catholics, Marriage and tagged Canon Law, Catholic Marriage, Non-Catholics, http://canonlawmadeeasy.com, posted 8/9/2007 (accessed 2/2/2017).

30. JPL Small Body Database, NASA Propulsion Laboratory. (accessed 5/2/2016).

31. The Flower Expert, http://www.theflowerexpert.com/ (TFE v.1.2, last modified 11/17/2016 (accessed 2/2/2017).

Clare

1. "Saint Francis of Assisi," geni.com. https://www.geni.com/people/Saint-Francis-of-Assisi/6000000020340400849 (accessed 2/9/2017).

2. Paschal Robinson, "St. Clare of Assisi." *The Catholic Encyclopedia,* vol. 4. New York: Robert Appleton Company, 1908. http://www.newadvent.org/cathen/04004a.htm (acessed 5/11/2016).

3. Paolo O. Pirlo, SHMI, "St. Clare." In *My First Book of Saints* (Parañaque City, Phillipines: Sons of Holy Mary Immaculate—Quality Catholic Publications, 1997), 178–79.

4. Flinders, *Enduring Grace*, 18–21.

5. Robinson, "St. Clare of Assisi."

6. Flinders, *Enduring Grace,* 19.

7. Ibid., 17.

8. Ibid., 17. I had not read these words before when I first learned of Francis and Clare. The poem at the end of this section was my own heartfelt salute to Francis, and I see now that it could have been Clare's as well.

9. While praying before an ancient crucifix at St. Damiano, Francis heard the voice of Jesus telling him, "Repair my church." Although he knew well the failings of the church of his times, he nevertheless took the message literally and proceeded to repair several churches. Gilbert Keith Chesterton, *St. Francis of Assisi* (Garden City, NY: Image Books, 1924), 54–6.

10. Flinders, *Enduring Grace,* 20.

11. Ibid., 20.

12. Ibid., 20–21.

13. Ibid., 26.

14. Encyclopedia Britannica Online, "Saint Francis of Assisi." https://www.britannica.com/biography Saint-Francis-of-Assisi (accessed 9/21/2016).

15. Flinders, *Enduring Grace,* 23.

16. Ibid. Poor Clares continue to live by faith today, depending on the generosity of the faithful. In our times, we are less familiar with them as they still live enclosed lives. Today, however, we have seen the great work of recently sainted Mother Teresa of Calcutta. Like Clare, and perhaps inspired by her, from the beginning she founded

her austere order on prayer and dependence on God's providence.

17. Flinders, *Enduring Grace*, 35.

18. Diarmuid O'Murchu in his history of women's communities observes that Brigid was certainly an early leader and seemingly came up with "the concept of a double monastery with male and female groups living adjacently." However, he goes on to explain that Clare was the first woman whose rule received papal approval: The Form of Life of Clare of Assisi, a formality that clarifies her position here. *Religious Life in the 21st Century: The Prospect of Refounding* (Maryknoll, NY: Orbis Books, 2016 Kindle edition). Chapter 6, The Parable of Paradigmatic Foundresses.

19. Regis J. Armstrong, O.F.M., Cap, tr. and ed., *Clare of Assisi: The Early Documents* (New York: Paulist Press, 1988), Document 40. In Flinders, *Enduring Grace*, 32.

20. Armstrong, *Clare of Assisi: Early Documents*, Document 62. In Flinders, *Enduring Grace*, 35.

21. Flinders, *Enduring Grace*, 36.

22. Ibid.

23. Ibid., 38.

24. I learned about Franciscan poverty shortly after I became a novice. A few weeks before Christmas, our mistress said we could suggest possible gifts to family and friends who wanted to give them. I was delighted on Christmas morning when a lovely decorated box was passed to me. Opening the layers of tissue, I found a pair of soft black leather gloves that fit me perfectly. I watched as others opened equally delightful gifts. When the bell for chapel rang, our superior asked that we put our packages on the central table. A bit confused, we all quickly deposited them as we lined up to go to choir. Seeing our faces, she smiled and said, "Dear Sisters, remember—we are Franciscans. Whichever one of you needs gloves will receive them, maybe not the ones you received today, but whatever is available when your need arises." With that, I took one last look at my gloves and turned to quietly proceed to chapel with my classmates. A few days later, I received a pair of knitted mittens.

25. Armstrong, *Clare of Assisi: Early Documents*, Document 169. In Flinders, *Enduring Grace*, 42.

26. Ibid.

27. Armstrong, *Clare of Assisi: Early Documents*, Document 157. In Flinders, *Enduring Grace*, 40.

28. Flinders, *Enduring Grace*, 40.

29. Ibid.

30. Shirley Cunningham, "Francis," in *Touchstone, Viterbo Literary Magazine*, vol. 16, no. 1. LaCrosse, WI: Viterbo College, 8.
31. Cunningham, *Chasing God*, 10–12.
32. Soeur Sourire, "Entre les Étoiles," paraphrase from the original French, "Dominique" (Philips Records, 1963), in Cunningham, *Chasing God*, 39.
33. Cunningham, *Chasing God*, 39.
34. Flinders, *Enduring Grace*, 23.
35. Ibid., 16.
36. Ibid.
37. Armstrong, *Clare of Assisi: Early Documents*, Document 47. In Flinders, *Enduring Grace*, 16–17.
38. Ibid.

Teresa of Avila

1. Flinders, *Enduring Grace*, 159–60.
2. Ibid., 156–57.
3. Ibid.
4. Ibid., 160.
5. Ibid. Beatriz de Ahumada was Teresa's mother. The Spanish practice of christening at that time included her name in the name of her child.
6. Flinders, *Enduring Grace*, 162.
7. Ibid., 161.
8. Ibid., 162.
9. Ibid., 163.
10. Ibid.
11. Ibid., 168. The anxiety of any converso would have been extreme in the days of the Spanish Inquisition. I toured Spain in 2010. On that trip, I remember seeing the entire outside church wall in one Spanish city dating back to the sixteenth century, still hung with dozens of shackles, a testimony to the accusation, arrest, torture, and murder of reverted conversos.
12. Ibid., 155.
13. Ibid., 163.
14. Ibid.
15. Ibid., 164.
16. Ibid.
17. Ibid. Flinders cites on p. 164 by footnote 3: St. John of the Cross, *The Ascent of Mount Carmel*, 1.1.11.

18. Ibid., 165–66.

19. Ibid., 167, citing Teresa's autobiography, *The Book of Her Life*, 8:2.

20. Ibid., 169.

21. Gross and Gross, *The Making of a Mystic*, 36. Footnote 11 references Teresa's autobiography, *The Book of Her Life*, ch. 9, v.1–3. "Tradition has it that this was an Ecce Homo [devotional image] ... some writers have described it as a representation of Christ bound to the Column." From *The Autobiography of St. Teresa of Avila*, E. Allison Peers, ed. and tr. (Garden City, NY: Doubleday, 1960), 114–15, n. 1.

22. Flinders, *Enduring Grace*, 170.

23. Ibid.

24. Gross and Gross, *The Making of a Mystic*, 60. Footnote 40 references Teresa, *The Book of Her Life*, ch 29, 13.

25. Full text of "St. Bernard of Clairvaux's Commentary on the Song of Songs" found at archive. org.

26. The followers of Teresa are called the "Discalced" or shoeless Carmelites.

27. Flinders, *Enduring Grace*, 172.

28. St. Teresa of Avila, *The Way of Perfection* (Garden City, NY: Image Books, 1960), 92.

29. Tejvan Pettinger, *Biography of St. Teresa of Avila* (Oxford, UK) www. biographyonline.net, updated Jan. 12, 2013.

30. *Biography of St. Teresa of Avila.* http://www.biographyonline.net/ spiritual/st_teresa_avila.html (accessed 2/09/2017).

31. Flinders, *Enduring Grace*, 174.

32. *Complete Works.* Exact page number unavailable. An unknown person may have written this prayer, paraphrasing some of Teresa's statements.

33. Gross and Gross, *The Making of a Mystic*, 204–5. These authors say, "It seems apropos to quote a bit of this famous love poem for the reader to see, from another source, the heart of Teresa of Avila."

34. Cunningham, *Chasing God*, 298.

35. John Welch, O Carm., *Spiritual Pilgrims: Carl Jung and Teresa of Avila* (New York: Paulist Press, 1982), 33–34, quotes *The Interior Castle* I, chapter 1, no. 1.

36. Ibid., 74.

37. Cunningham, *Chasing God*, 172.

38. Ibid., 190.

39. A final dream in the series promised a new chapter in my life. It occurred shortly after I met Jerry, who became my second husband: I

was in my mansion setting some of the rooms in order. It felt good to unpack the trunks, lay down the carpets, hang the richly embroidered drapery, position the furniture, hang the pictures. Then, standing back to survey my work, I thought, Good, a beautiful room.

But I hesitated. Something was missing. What was it? I stood there a minute, noticing some empty furniture cartons in a corner. Once those boxes were gone, I'd have the perfect spot for ... hmm. What? A love seat, that was it! And not just any love seat. It had to be purple satin. Well, so there was one more chore: shopping. I was tired; it had been a long day. Hoping it wouldn't take long to find that love seat, I started shoving the cartons aside. Then I stopped in my tracks. There, partially obscured, was a perfectly beautiful purple love seat! I'd had it all along and didn't know it!

That dream was a promise of new life and love.

40. St. Teresa of Jesus. *The Letters of Saint Teresa of Jesus*, E. Allison Peers, tr. (London: Sheed and Ward, 1941), 492–3.

41. St. Teresa of Avila. *The Collected Works of St. Teresa of Avila*, Vol. 3, E. Allison Peers, trans. (Garden City: Image Books, 1964), "Poetry," n. 9.

42. Progoff, Ira. *At a Journal Workshop* (New York: Dialogue House, 1975), 78.

43. Cunningham, www.artfromheartnsoul.net, blog for Dec. 31, 2010.

44. Flinders, *Enduring Grace*, 183.

Joan of Arc

1. Kathryn Harrison, *Joan of Arc: a Life Transfigured* (New York: Random House, 2014) 16.

2. Ibid., illustrations: Fig. 6, Fig. 8, Fig. 16, Fig. 20, Fig. 21, Fig. 22, Fig. 34, Fig. 36.

3. Ibid., 328.

4. Ibid., 21.

5. Ibid., 14.

6. Ibid., 281.

7. Ibid., 85.

8. Ibid., 35.

9. Ibid., 220.

10. Ibid., 51.

11. Ibid., 54.

12. Ibid., 68.

13. Ibid., 66.

14. Ibid., 26.

15. Ibid., 189. That cross-dressing was held in ill repute before Joan's time is attested to by its connection to tournaments where women dressed in male clothing mounted on chargers and "abused their bodies in wantonness." Henry Knighton, an Augustinian canon writing then, specified that "cross-dressing was a catalyst for plague." This amazing historical assertion testifies to the taboo and likely scapegoating of those who might have done it.

16. Ibid., 27.

17. Ibid., 155. Harrison quoting Kelly DeVries, *Joan of Arc: a Military Leader* (Stroud, UK: Sutton, 1999), 87.

18. Ibid., 47.

19. Ibid., 5.

20. Ibid., 118.

21. Ibid., 117.

22. Ibid., 115.

23. Ibid., 117.

24. Ibid., 46–47.

25. Ibid., 125.

26. Ibid., 117. This page carries Harrison's footnote, which cites Régine Pernoud, *The Retrial of Joan of Arc: The Evidence for Her Vindication*, J. M. Cohen, tr. (San Francisco: Ignatius, 2007), 160.

27. Ibid., 128.

28. Joan didn't permit swearing or gambling among the troops either. It is a testament to the regard these men held for her that a girl of seventeen could successfully deny them these behaviors.

29. Ibid., 251–52.

30. Ibid., 252.

31. Ibid., 281.

32. Ibid., 5.

33. Ibid., 315.

34. Ibid.

35. Ibid., 256.

36. Ibid. This page carries Harrison's footnote, which cites Frances Gies, *Joan of Arc: The Legend and the Reality* (New York: Harper and Row, 1981), 159.

37. Joan's words were important even though she did not herself write them. Like most of the common people of her time, she was illiterate. Joan didn't even know how to sign her name until a document of war required it. Then just the signature took her six months to master. But in fairness, we must acknowledge that she had little time

to practice penmanship. She was busy fighting a war! Harrison, *Joan of Arc*, 126.

38. I fell into a quiet timelessness. It was familiar, the same inner space I had discovered kneeling in the convent chapel. It felt just the same. I struggled for words to describe it and wrote the poem you will find at the end of this section.

39. Cunningham, *Chasing God*, 189.

40. Ibid., 190.

41. Harrison, *Joan of Arc*, 172.

42. Cunningham, *Chasing God*, 159.

43. Ibid., 160.

44. Harrison, *Joan of Arc*, 300.

45. Actual quote: "Rouen! Rouen! Must I die here? I fear you will have to suffer for my death." Allen Williamson, tr., *Famous Sayings of St. Joan of Arc*, St. Joan's Center, Albuquerque, NM, http://www.stjoan-center.com/quotable/.

46. Harrison, *Joan of Arc*, 264.

47. Ibid., referencing Craig Taylor, *Joan of Arc: La Pucelle* (Manchester, UK: Manchester University Press, 2006), 148.

48. Pernoud, *The Retrial of Joan of Arc*, 100. In Harrison, *Joan of Arc*, 62 footnote.

49. Pernoud, *The Retrial of Joan of Arc*, 167. In Harrison, *Joan of Arc*, 150–51.

50. Shirley Cunningham, *Touchstone, Viterbo College Literary Magazine*, Vol. 16, No. 1, La Crosse, WI.

51. Carol Pearson, *Awakening the Heroes Within* (New York: HarperCollins, 1991), 95.

Thérèse of Lisieux

1. John Clarke, O.C.D., trans. *St. Thérèse: Her Last Conversations* (Washington DC: Institute of Carmelite Studies, 1996), 62.

2. Flinders, *Enduring Grace*, 196.

3. Patricia O'Connor, *Thérèse of Lisieux: A Biography* (Huntington, IN: Our Sunday Visitor, 1984), 19.

4. Flinders, *Enduring Grace*, 201–2.

5. Ibid., 196, citing Ida Friederike Görres, *The Hidden Face: A Study of St. Thérèse of Lisieux* (New York: Pantheon, 1959), 44–45.

6. Jestice, *Holy People of the World*, 200.

7. Flinders, *Enduring Grace*, 203.

8. Ibid., 204.

9. Ibid., 207, citing *Story of a Soul: The Autobiography of St. Thérèse of Lisieux*, John Clarke, O.C.D., tr. (Washington DC: Institute of Carmelite Studies, 1972), 240.

10. Ibid., 219.

11. Ibid.

12. Görres, *The Hidden Face*, 407.

13. Flinders, *Enduring Grace*, 209.

14. Matthew 25:40.

15. Flinders, *Enduring Grace*, 208–9.

16. Catholic.org, "St. Thérèse of Lisieux," http://www.catholic.org/saints/saint.php?saint_id=105.

17. Thomas à Kempis, *The Imitation of Christ* (Mineola, NY: Dover Press, 2003).

18. Flinders, *Enduring Grace*, 214.

19. Ibid.

20. Thomas R. Nevin, *Thérèse of Lisieux: God's Gentle Warrior* (New York: Oxford University Press, 2006), 26.

21. "Thoughts" appears in John Beevers, tr., *The Autobiography of Saint Thérèse of Lisieux: The Story of a Soul* (New York: Doubleday, 1989) and *Thoughts of Saint Thérèse*, an Irish Carmelite, tr. (Rockford, IL: Tan Books and Publishers, 1915).

22. Cunningham, *Chasing God*, 132–33.

23. I was there before the various provinces split out of the loosely connected union that was postwar Yugoslavia. Medjugorje later became part of Bosnia-Herzegovina.

24. Cunningham, *Chasing God*, 150.

25. Ibid., 209.

26. Ibid.

27. Carol Pearson, *Awakening the Heroes Within* (New York: HarperCollins, 1991), 82.

28. *Story of a Soul*, 84–85.

Tekakwitha

1. Alice Camille and Paul Boudreau, *Fearless: Stories of the American Saints* (Cincinnati, OH: Franciscan Media, 2014), 37.

2. Ibid.

3. Camille and Boudreau, *Fearless*, 38.

4. Ibid., 36.

5. Ibid., 38.

6. Daniel Sargent, *Catherine Tekakwitha* (New York: Longmans, Green and Co., 1936), 164.

7. Francis X. Weiser, S.J., *Kateri Tekakwitha* (Caughnawaga, Canada: Kateri Center, 1972), 50–52.

8. Allan Greer, *Mohawk Saint: Catherine Tekakwitha and the Jesuits* (New York: Oxford University Press, 2005), 110.

9. Camille and Boudreau, *Fearless*, 40.

10. Ibid., 41.

11. Leslie Choquette, review of Allan Greer, *Mohawk Saint* (*H-France Review*, Institut Français, Assumption College, Vol. 5, Oct. 2005, No. 109), 450.

12. Ibid.

13. Choquette footnotes Greer's book in her review and this information is in his book, 112–19.

14. Camille and Boudreau, *Fearless*, 43.

15. Greer, *Mohawk Saint*, 5.

16. C. J. Jaenen (1979), [1969] "Chauchetière, Claude" in David Hayne, *Dictionary of Canadian Biography*, Vol II, 1701–40, University of Toronto Press (online ed.).

17. Camille and Boudreau, *Fearless*, 43.

18. Choquette, review of Greer, 452.

19. Ibid.

20. K. I. Koppedrayer, "The Making of the First Iroquois Virgin: Early Jesuit Biographies of the Blessed Kateri Tekakwitha," *Ethnohistory* 40.2 (1993), 277–306.

21. "The Last Hour of the Life of Catherine Tekakwitha, Holy Wednesday April 17, 1680," from the narrations of Frs. Claude Chauchetière, SJ, and Pierre Cholenec, SJ, published in "Kateri, Lily of the Mohawks," No. 221, Autumn 2004. http://www.katerishrine.com/ (accessed 2/23/2017).

22. Greer, *Mohawk Saint*, 18.

23. Ibid., 19.

24. In *Final Gifts*, two hospice nurses have gathered stories of eyewitnesses telling of unexplainable events surrounding the dying. Maggie Callanan and Patricia Kelley, *Final Gifts* (New York: Bantam Books, 1993).

25. Shirley Cunningham, previously unpublished.

26. Koppedrayer, "The Making of the First Iroquois Virgin."

27. Proverbs, Ch. 4, v. 23. The Song of Songs was the subject of sermons by St. Bernard of Clairvaux which compared the love between God and the soul with married love. These sermons led to notions of

bridal mysticism among monastics at a time when spirituality was often put in somewhat military metaphors, especially for men's orders like the Jesuits.

28. Marie-Thérèse Tegaiaguenta, in Greer, *Mohawk Saint*, 23.
29. Greer, *Mohawk Saint*, 23–24.
30. Ibid., 21.
31. Charles Herbermann, ed.,"Jacques Marquette," *Catholic Encyclopedia* (New York: Robert Appleton Company, 1913).
32. Camille and Boudreau, *Fearless*, 42.
33. Choquette, review of Greer, 452.
34. Article on Effigy Moundbuilders—https://www.nps.gov/history/archeology/sites/npSites/effigyMounds.htm (accessed 2/16/2017).
35. Doug George-Kanentiio, Iroquois Populations 1995. radical.org, retrieved May 27, 2016.
36. Many resources are available: www.myheritage.com includes downloadable trees; www.familytreemagazine.com; Allison Dolan and Diane Haddad, *Family Tree Memory Keeper is* a useful book with many charts, available on Amazon.com.

Appendix: Mary—A Sufi's Mystical View

1. Bismillahir Rahmanir Rahim, "Mother Mary in Sufism and Maryamiyya Sufi Tariqa" in Technology of the Heart, http://www.techofheart.co/2011/05/maryamiyya-tariqa-mother-mary-sufism.html (accessed 2/13/2017).

Bibliography

à Kempis, Thomas. *The Imitation of Christ.* Mineola, NY: Dover, 2003.

Armstrong, Regis J. *Clare of Assisi: The Early Documents.* New York: Paulist Press, 1988.

Associated Press, "Boy's Miracle Cure Makes First Native American Saint." *Arizona Republic*, Oct. 20, 2012. Retrieved 10/20/2012.

Beevers, John, tr. *The Autobiography of Saint Thérèse of Lisieux: The Story of a Soul.* New York: Doubleday, 1989.

Begg, Ean. *The Cult of the Black Virgin.* Boston: Arkana, 1985.

Bennett, Judith, and Warren Hollister. *Medieval Europe: A Short History.* New York: McGraw-Hill, 2001.

Biography of St. Teresa of Avila. Biography Online. http://www.biographyonline.net/spiritual/st_teresa_avila.html (accessed 2/9/2017).

Bladey, Conrad Jay. *Brigid of the Gael.* New York: Hutman ebook, 2009.

Bourgeault, Cynthia. *The Meaning of Mary Magdalene.* Boston: Shambhala, 2010.

Brakeman, Lyn. *Spiritual Lemons: Biblical Women, Irreverent Laughter, and Righteous Rage.* Philadelphia: First Augsburg Books, 2005.

Cahill, Thomas. *How the Irish Saved Civilization.* New York: Doubleday, 1995.

Callanan, Maggie, and Patricia Kelley. *Final Gifts.* New York: Bantam, 1993.

Camille, Alice, and Paul Boudreaux. *Fearless: Stories of the American Saints.* Cincinnati, OH: Franciscan Media, 2014.

Caridi, Cathy, J.C.L. Canonical Issues Involving Non-Catholics, Marriage and tagged Canon Law, Catholic Marriage, Non-Catholics. http://

canonlawmadeeasy.com/2007/08/09/cath_noncath_marriage/, posted 8/9/2007 (accessed 2/2/2017).

Canaan, T. "Mohammedan Saints and Sanctuaries in Palestine," *Journal of the Palestine Oriental Society,* Vol. 4, 1924.

Catholic Online, "St. Brigid of Ireland," http://www.catholic.org/saints/saint.php?saint_id=453 (accessed 2/2/2017).

Chesterton, Gilbert Keith. *St. Francis of Assisi.* Garden City, NY: Image Books, 1924.

Choquette, Leslie. Review of Allan Greer, *Mohawk Saint.* Society for French Historical Studies, *H-France Review,* Vol. 5, No. 109, Oct. 2005. http://www.h-france.net/vol5reviews/vol5htmlreviews/choquette.html (accessed 2/9/2017).

Craine, Renate. *Hildegard: Prophet of the Cosmic Christ.* New York: Crossroad, 1997.

Cunningham, Lawrence, and John J. Reich. *Culture and Values: a Survey of the Humanities.* Belmont, CA: Thomson/Wadsworth, 2006.

Cunningham, Shirley. artfromheartnsoul.net blog, 12/31/2010.

——. *Chasing God.* Scottsdale, AZ: Amoranita Publishing, 2002.

——. "Time Transparent" and "Francis." LaCrosse, WI: *Touchstone,* Viterbo College Literary Magazine,Vol. 16, No. 1.

Downing, Frederick L. *Elie Wiesel: A Religious Biography.* Macon, GA: Mercer University Press, 2008.

Durka, Gloria, *Praying with Hildegard of Bingen.* Winona, MN: Saint Mary's Press, 1991.

Edinger, Edward F. *The Christian Archetype: A Jungian Commentary on the Life of Christ.* Toronto: Inner City Books, 1987.

"898 Hildegard (1918 EA)." JPL Small Body Database. http://ssd.jpl.nasa.gov/sbdb.cgi#top (accessed 5/2/2016).

Elliott, Elizabeth A. "Magdalene gets her feast," *National Catholic Reporter.* June 10, 2016. "Equal-to-Apostles."

Encyclopedia Britannica Online, "Saint Francis of Assisi." https://www.britannica.com/biography/Saint-Francis-of-Assisi, 2011 (accessed 9/21/2016).

Flinders, Carol Lee. *Enduring Grace.* New York: HarperCollins, 1993.

Flower Expert, The. http://www.theflowerexpert.com/(TFE v. 1.2, last modified 11/17/2016) (accessed 2/2/2017).

Fox, Matthew. *Hildegard of Bingen.* Vancouver, BC: Namaste Publishing, 2012.

——. *Illuminations of Hildegard of Bingen.* Rochester, VT: Bear & Company, 1985.

——. *Original Blessing.* Santa Fe, NM: Bear & Company, 1983.

Gafney, Wilda C. *Daughters of Miriam: Women Prophets in Ancient Israel.* Minneapolis: Fortress Press, 2008.

Galland, China. *Longing for Darkness: Tara and the Black Madonna.* New York: Penguin, 1990.

Glasse, Cyril. "Mary," *Concise Encyclopedia of Islam,* 3rd ed. London: Stacey International, 2008.

Görres, Ida Friederike. *The Hidden Face.* New York: Pantheon, 1959.

Graves, Dan, MSL. "Hildegard: Sybil of the Rhine." http://www.christianity.com/church/church-history/timeline/901-1200/hildegard-sybil-of-the-rhine-11629806.html (accessed 2/24/2017).

Greer, Allan. *Mohawk Saint: Catherine Tekakwitha and the Jesuits.* New York: Oxford University Press, 2005.

Gross, Francis, with Toni Perior Gross. *The Making of a Mystic: Seasons in the Life of Teresa of Avila.* Albany, NY: State University of New York Press, 1993.

Harrison, Kathryn. *Joan of Arc: A Life Transfigured.* New York: Doubleday, 2014.

Haskins, Susan. *Mary Magdalen: Myth and Metaphor.* New York: Riverhead, 1993.

Herbermann, Charles, ed., "Jacques Marquette." *Catholic Encyclopedia.* New York: Robert Appleton Company, 1913.

"Highland Clearances." Crann Tara. https://cranntara.scot/clear.htm (accessed 2/2/2017).

Hildegard of Bingen. *Symphonia.* Barbara Newman, ed. Ithaca, NY: Cornell University Press, 1988.

Hillerbrand, Hans Joachim. *Encyclopedia of Protestantism,* Vol. 3. New York: Routledge, 2003.

Jaenen, C. J. "Chauchetière, Claude" in Hayne, David, ed., *Dictionary of Canadian Biography,* Vol. 2, 1701–40. University of Toronto Press online edition.

Jestice, Phyllis G. *Holy People of the World.* vol. 123. Santa Barbara, CA: ABC-CLIO, 2004.

Johnson, Robert. *Inner Work.* San Francisco: HarperSanFrancisco, 1986.

Jung, Carl G. *Psychology and Religion: West and East.* Vol. 11 of *The Collected Works of C. G. Jung,* Gerhard Adler and R. F. C. Hull, ed. Princeton, NJ: Princeton University Press, 1969.

Kateri Tekakwitha Shrine. http://www.katerishrine.com/kateri.html

Kennedy, Patrick. *Legendary Fictions of the Irish Celts.* Charleston, SC: BiblioBazaar, 2008.

Koppedrayer, K. I. "The Making of the First Iroquois Virgin: Early Jesuit

Biographies of the Blessed Kateri Tekakwitha," *Ethnohistory* 40.2 (1993).

Kraemer, Ross Shephard, and Mary Rose D'Angelo, eds.. *Women and Christian Origins.* New York: Oxford University Press, 1999.

Meir, Tamar. "Miriam: Midrash and Aggadah." *Jewish Women: A Comprehensive Historical Encyclopedia.* March 20, 2009. Jewish Women's Archive. https://jwa.org/encyclopedia/article/Miriam_midrash_and_aggadah (accessed 2/17/2017).

Mindel, Nissan. Exodus Rabbah 1:17. quoted by Kehot Publication Society. http://www.chabad.org/library/article_cdo/aid/112396/jewish/Miriam.htm (accessed 2/9/2017).

Molloy, Dara. The Sacred Oak—An Crann Dair. November 2001. http://www.daramolloy.com/DaraMolloy/Writings/AnCrannDair.html (accessed 2/19/17).

Nevin, Thomas R. *Thérèse of Lisieux: God's Gentle Warrior.* New York: Oxford University Press, 2006.

New American Bible. New York: Catholic Book Publishing Co., 1986.

Newman, Barbara. *Sisters of Wisdom: St. Hildegard's Theology of the Feminine.* Berkeley, CA: University of California Press, 1997.

O'Connor, Patricia. *Thérèse of Lisieux: A Biography.* Huntington, IN: Our Sunday Visitor, 1984.

O'Donohue, John. *Anam Cara.* New York: HarperCollins, 1997.

O'Murchu, Diarmuid. *Religious Life in the 21st Century: The Prospect of Refounding.* Maryknoll, NY: Orbis Books, 2016. Kindle edition.

Orthodox Church of America. *Martyr Photina (Svetlana), the Samaritan Woman and Her Sons.* https://oca.org/saints/lives/2016/03/10/100846-martyr-photina-svetlana-the-samaritan-woman-and-her-sons (accessed 2/9/2017).

Paintner, Christine Valters. *Illuminating the Way.* Notre Dame, IN: Sorin Books, 2016.

Pettinger, Tejvan. *Biography of St. Teresa of Avila.* http://www.biographyonline.net/spiritual/st_teresa_avila.html (accessed 2/09/2017).

Pickett, Lynn, and Clive Prince. *The Templar Revelation.* New York: Touchstone, 1997.

Pirlo, Paolo O. *My First Book of Saints.* Paranaque City, Philippines: Quality Catholic Publications, 1997.

Progoff, Ira. *At a Journal Workshop.* New York: Dialogue House, 1975.

Rahim, Bismillahir Rahmanir. "Mother Mary in Sufism and Maryami-yya Sufi Tariqa." *Technology of the Heart.* http://www.techofheart.co/2011/05/maryamiyya-tariqa-mother-mary-sufism.html (accessed 2/09/2017).

Richardson, Jan. *In the Sanctuary of Women.* Nashville: Upper Room Books, 2010.

Richo, David. *Mary Within Us: A Jungian Contemplation of Her Titles and Powers.* Berkeley, CA: Human Development Books, 2007.

Robinson, B. A. Women's Roles in the Bible: "The Status of Women in Christian Gospels." Religious Tolerance.org, Ontario Consultants on Religious Tolerance. Sections on Divorce and Levirate Marriage. http://www.religioustolerance.org/cfe_bibl.htm (accessed 2/9/2017).

Robinson, Paschal. "St. Clare of Assisi." *The Catholic Encyclopedia,* vol. 4. New York: Robert Appleton Company, 1908. http://www.newadvent.org/cathen/04004a.htm (acessed 5/11/2016).

"Saint Francis of Assisi." Geni.com. https://www.geni.com/people/Saint-Francis-of-Assisi/6000000020340400849 (accessed 2/9/2017).

Saint Thérèse of Lisieux. *Thoughts of Saint Thérèse.* An Irish Carmelite, tr. Rockford, IL: Tan Books, 1915.

Saint Teresa of Avila. *The Collected Works of St. Teresa of Avila.* Peers, Allison E., tr. Garden City, NY: Image Books, 1964.

Saint Teresa of Avila. *The Way of Perfection.* Garden City, NY: Image Books, 1946.

Saint Teresa of Jesus. *Letters of Saint Teresa of Jesus.* Peers, Allison E., tr. London: Sheed and Ward, 1941.

Saint Thérèse of Lisieux, *St. Thérèse of Lisieux: Her Last Conversations.* Clarke, John, tr. Washington, DC: Institute of Carmelite Studies, 1996.

Sargent, Daniel. *Catherine Tekakwitha.* New York: Longmans, Green and Co., 1936.

Schipperges, Heinrich. *Hildegard of Bingen: Healing and the Nature of the Cosmos.* Princeton, NJ: Markus Wiener, 1997.

Schuon, Frithjof. "Wisdom of the Virgin," in *Dimensions of Islam.* P. N. Townsend, tr. Bloomington, IN: World Wisdom Books, 1970.

Sonbol, Amira El-Azhary, ed. *Beyond the Exotic: Women's Histories in Islamic Societies.* Syracuse, NY: Syracuse University Press, 2005.

Sourire, Souer. "Dominique." New York: Phillips Records, 1963.

"Starting at St. Maximin-de-la-St. Baume." Camino de Santiago Forum. https://www.caminodesantiago.me/community/threads/starting-at-st-maximin-de-la-st-baume.15901/ (accessed 2/9/2017).

Tippett, Krista. *Speaking of Faith.* New York: Penguin, 2007.

Topping, Eva Catafygiotu. *Saints and Sisterhood: The Lives of Forty-Eight Holy Women.* Minneapolis: Light and Life Publishing, 1990.

Uhlein, Gabriele. *Meditations with Hildegard of Bingen.* Santa Fe, NM: Bear & Company, 1983.

Warner, Marina. *Alone of All Her Sex*. New York: Vintage, 1976.

Wegner, Emma. "Hagia Sophia, 532–37." Heilbrunn Timeline of Art History. New York: Metropolitan Museum of Art, 2000. http://www.metmuseum.org/toah/hd/haso/hd_haso.htm (accessed 2/24/2017).

Weiser, Francis X. *Kateri Tekakwitha*. Caughnawaga, QC, Canada: Kateri Center, 1972.

Welch, John. *Spiritual Pilgrims: Carl Jung and Teresa of Avila*. New York: Paulist Press, 1982.

Williamson, Allen, tr.. *Famous Sayings of St. Joan of Arc*. Albuquerque, NM: St. Joan's Center. http://www.stjoan-center.com/quotable/ (accessed 2/24/2017).

Wink, Walter. "Easter: What Happened to Jesus?" *The Network of Spiritual Progressives*. http://spiritualprogressives.org/newsite?p=685 (accessed 2/09/2017).

Winter, Miriam Therese. *WomanWisdom*. New York: Crossroad, 1997.

Winter, Miriam Therese. *WomanWord*. New York: Crossroad, 1992.

Wuerl, Donald W., and Kris D. Stubna D. *The Teachings of Christ: A Catholic Catechism for Adults*. Huntington, IN: Our Sunday Visitor Publishing, 2004.

About the Author

Shirley Cunningham, MA, MSW, is a spiritual director, counselor, retreat facilitator, artist, and the author of *Chasing God: One Woman's Magnificent Journey to Spirit*. A long-time student of spirituality, creativity, psychology, journaling, dreams, intuition, art, and imagery, she has taught on the college and university level as well as offering workshops and retreats in a variety of settings. The retreat based on *Kissed by God–Holy Women Create!* is also available. She lives in Arizona and is a proud grandmother! See www.artfromheartnsoul.net.